A More Beautiful Question

Praise for *A More Beautiful Question*

"The genesis of many great startups is the simple question, 'Wouldn't it be cool if?' Warren Berger helps you understand the power of questions to change the world. Real men ask questions, they don't spout out answers." —**Guy Kawasaki, former chief evangelist at Apple and author of** *APE: Author, Publisher, Entrepreneur*

"Mastering the art of asking questions is essential to creativity and innovation. *A More Beautiful Question* should be standard reading for all aspiring design thinkers as well an inspiration to those searching for a life of curiosity and meaning." —**Tim Brown, chief executive at IDEO and author of** *Change by Design*

"In an age of instant information, it's easier than ever to find answers, but also easy to forget how important it is to ask the right kinds of questions. In this deeply thought-provoking book, Warren Berger shows how learning the art of good questioning is the path to a far more fruitful and creative way of engaging with the world, at work, and in life as a whole." —**Oliver Burkeman, columnist at** *The Guardian* **and author of** *The Antidote: Happiness for People Who Can't Stand Positive Thinking*

"*A More Beautiful Question* provides a framework to help leaders ask the most important questions—which is one of the most fundamental characteristics of a great leader—while sharing inspiring stories to show the incredible power of this concept." —**Jim Stengel, former global marketing officer at Procter & Gamble and author of** *Grow: How Ideals Power Growth and Profit at the World's Greatest Companies*

"Why has a book like this never been written before? Here is a persuasive case for the simple and yet extraordinary power of a question. Fascinating, engaging stories give life to a strong argument about how much can be accomplished, in every domain of our lives, 'just' by asking questions. Innovators, entrepreneurs, citizens, parents, teachers, idealists, and realists—all of us have much to gain by reading *A More Beautiful Question*." —**Dan Rothstein and Luz Santana, co-directors of the Right Question Institute and co-authors of** *Make Just One Change: Teach Students to Ask Their Own Questions*

A More Beautiful Question

THE POWER OF INQUIRY
TO SPARK BREAKTHROUGH IDEAS

WARREN BERGER

BLOOMSBURY

NEW YORK • LONDON • NEW DELHI • SYDNEY

Published by Bloomsbury USA, New York

All papers used by Bloomsbury USA are natural, recyclable products made from wood grown in well-managed forests. The manufacturing processes conform to the environmental regulations of the country of origin.

LIBRARY OF CONGRESS CATALOGING-IN-PUBLICATION DATA
Berger, Warren.
A more beautiful question : the power of inquiry to spark breakthrough ideas / Warren Berger.
pages cm
Includes bibliographical references and index.
ISBN 978-1-62040-145-3 (hardback)
1. Creative ability in business. 2. Entrepreneurship. 3. Inquiry-based learning.
I. Title.
HD53.B448 2014
658.4'03—dc23
2013036021

First U.S. edition 2014

3 5 7 9 10 8 6 4 2

Designed by Rachel Reiss
Typeset by Hewer Text UK Ltd, Edinburgh
Printed and bound in the U.S.A. by Thomson-Shore Inc., Dexter, Michigan

Always the beautiful answer
Who asks a more beautiful question.
                —E.E. Cummings

Contents

Why Questioning?

As a journalist, I've been asking questions my whole professional life. But until a few years ago, I hadn't thought much about the art or the science of questioning. And I never considered the critical role questioning plays in enabling people to innovate, solve problems, and move ahead in their careers and lives.

That changed during my work on a series of articles, and eventually a book, on how designers, inventors, and engineers come up with ideas and solve problems. My research brought me in contact with some of the world's leading innovators and creative minds. As I looked at how they approached challenges, there was no magic formula, no single explanation, for their success. But in searching for common denominators among these brilliant change-makers, one thing I kept finding was that many of them were exceptionally good at asking questions.

For some of them, their greatest successes—their breakthrough inventions, hot start-up companies, the radical solutions they'd found to stubborn problems—could be traced to a question (or a series of questions) they'd formulated and then answered.

I thought this was intriguing, but it only had a small part in the book I was working on, so I tucked the idea away. Subsequently, I began to notice—as is often the case when something has come onto your radar—that questioning seemed to be everywhere I looked. In the business world, for instance, as I interviewed corporate executives for my writing in *Harvard Business Review* and *Fast Company*, I found a great deal of interest in questioning. Many businesspeople seemed to be aware, on some level, of a link between questioning and innovation. They understood that great products, companies, even industries, often begin with a question. It's well-known that Google, as described by its chairman, is a company that "runs on questions," and that business stars such as the late Steve Jobs of Apple and Amazon's Jeff Bezos made their mark by questioning everything.

Yet, as I began to explore this subject within the business sector, I found few companies that actually encouraged questioning in any substantive way. There were no departments or training programs focused on questioning; no policies, guidelines, best practices. On the contrary, many companies—whether consciously or not—have established cultures that tend to discourage inquiry in the form of someone's asking, for example, *Why are we doing this particular thing in this particular way?*

MUCH THE SAME could be said about schools. Here again, as I talked to educators, I found a genuine interest in the subject—many teachers acknowledge it's critically important that students be able to formulate and ask good questions. Some of them also realize that this skill is apt to be even more important in the future, as complexity increases and change accelerates. Yet, for some reason, questioning isn't taught in most schools—nor is it rewarded (only memorized answers are).

In talking to social entrepreneurs working on big, thorny global problems of poverty, hunger, and water supply, I found that only a few rare innovators were focused on the importance of asking the right questions about these issues. For the most part, the old, entrenched practices and approaches tend to hold sway. The nonprofit sector, like much of industry, is inclined to keep doing what it has done—hence, well-meaning people are often trying to solve a problem by answering the wrong question.

In a way, this is true of all of us, in our everyday lives. The impulse is to keep plowing ahead, doing what we've done, and rarely stepping back to question whether we're on the right path. On the big questions of finding meaning, fulfillment, and happiness, we're deluged with answers—in the form of off-the-shelf advice, tips, strategies from experts and gurus. It shouldn't be any wonder if those generic solutions don't quite fit: To get to *our* answers, we must formulate and work through the questions ourselves. Yet who has the time or patience for it?

On some level, we must know—as the business executive knows, as the schoolteacher knows—that questions are important and that we should be paying more attention to them, especially the meaningful ones. The great thinkers have been telling us this since the time of Socrates. The poets have waxed on the subject: E. E. Cummings, from whom I borrowed this book's title, wrote, *Always the beautiful answer / who asks a more beautiful question.* Artists from Picasso to Chuck Close have spoken of questioning's inspirational power. (This great quote from Close was featured recently on the site BrainPickings: "Ask yourself an interesting enough question and your attempt to find a tailor-made solution to that question will push you to a place where, pretty soon, you'll find yourself all by your lonesome—which I think is a more interesting place to be.")

Scientists, meanwhile, have been great proponents of questioning, with Einstein among the most vocal champions. He was asking smart questions from age four (when he wondered why the compass pointed north), and throughout his life Einstein saw curiosity as something "holy." Though he wondered about a great many things, Einstein was deliberate in choosing which questions to tackle: In one of his more well-traveled quotes—which he may or may not have actually said—he reckoned that if he had an hour to solve a problem and his life depended on it, he'd spend the first fifty-five minutes making sure he was answering the right question.

WITH SO MUCH evidence in its favor and with everyone from Einstein to Jobs in its corner, why, then, is questioning underappreciated in business, undertaught in schools, and underutilized in our everyday lives?

Part of it may be that we see questioning as something so fundamental and instinctive that we don't need to think about it. "We come out of the womb questioning," noted the small-schools-movement pioneer Deborah Meier. And it's true—any preschooler can ask questions easily and profusely. A recent study found the average four-year-old British girl asks her poor mum 390 questions a day; the boys that age aren't far behind. So then, it might be said that questioning is like breathing: It's a given, an essential and accepted part of life, and something that anyone, even a child, can do.

Yet chances are, for the rest of her life, that four-year-old girl will never again ask questions as instinctively, as imaginatively, or as freely as she does at that shining moment. Unless she is exceptional, that age is her questioning peak.

This curious fact, in and of itself, gives rise to all sorts of questions.

Why does that four-year-old girl begin to question less at age five or six?

What are the ramifications of that, for her and for the world around her?

And if, as Einstein tells us, questioning is important, why aren't we trying to stem or reverse that decline by finding ways to keep questioning alive?

On the other hand, that four-year-old may turn out to be an exception; she may be one of the rare people who *doesn't* stop questioning, like Bezos and Jobs, or like one of the "master questioners" featured in this book. And if that's the case, well, that raises questions, too.

Why do some keep questioning, while others stop? (Was it something in the genes, in the schools, in the parenting?)

And if we look at the questioners versus the nonquestioners, who
seems to be coming out ahead?

THE BUSINESS WORLD has a kind of love/hate relationship with
questioning. The business-innovation guru Clayton Christensen—
himself a master questioner—observes that questioning is seen as
"inefficient" by many business leaders, who are so anxious to *act*,
to *do*, that they often feel they don't have time to question just
what it is they're doing.

And those not in leadership roles frequently perceive (often
correctly) that questioning can be hazardous to one's career:
that to raise a hand in the conference room and ask "Why?" is
to risk being seen as uninformed, or possibly insubordinate, or
maybe both.

Yet—as recently documented in a fascinating research study of
thousands of top business executives—the most creative, successful business leaders have tended to be expert questioners. They're
known to question the conventional wisdom of their industry,
the fundamental practices of their company, even the validity of
their own assumptions. This has not slowed their rise in business—rather, it has "turbocharged" it, to quote Hal Gregersen, a
business consultant and INSEAD professor who, along with
Christensen and another business professor, Jeff Dyer, coauthored the research showing questioning to be a key success
factor among innovative executives.

Indeed, the ability to ask the right questions has enabled business leaders to adapt in a rapidly changing marketplace, Gregersen
notes. Inquiring minds can identify new opportunities and fresh
possibilities before competitors become aware of them. All of
which means that, whereas in the past one needed to appear to
have "all the answers" in order to rise in companies, today, at least
in some enlightened segments of the business world, the corner
office is there for the askers.

Considering all of this, one almost can't help but ask the
following:

If we know (or at least strongly suspect) that questioning is a starting point for innovation, then why doesn't business embrace it?

Why don't companies train people to question and create systems and environments that would encourage them to keep doing so? And if companies were to do this, how might they go about it?

Regarding those first two questions, one possible answer—and it may also apply to similar questions about why nonprofit organizations don't question more, and why schools don't teach or encourage questioning—is that questions challenge authority and disrupt established structures, processes, and systems, forcing people to have to at least *think* about doing something differently. To encourage or even allow questioning is to cede power—not something that is done lightly in hierarchical companies or in government organizations, or even in classrooms, where a teacher must be willing to give up control to allow for more questioning.

ANYTHING THAT FORCES people to have to think is not an easy sell, which highlights the challenge of questioning in our everyday lives—and why we don't do it as much as we might or should. Clearly, it is easier (and more "efficient," as a nonquestioning business executive might say) to go about our daily affairs without questioning everything. It's natural and quite sensible to behave this way. The neurologist John Kounios observes that the brain finds ways to "reduce our mental workload," and one way is to accept without question (or even to just ignore) much of what is going on around us at any time. We operate on autopilot—which can help us to save mental energy, allow us to multitask, and enable us to get through the daily grind.

But when we want to shake things up and instigate change, it's necessary to break free of familiar thought patterns and easy assumptions. We have to veer off the beaten neural path. And we do this, in large part, by questioning.

With the constant change we face today, we may be forced to spend less time on autopilot, more time in questioning mode—attempting to adapt, looking to re-create careers, redefining old ideas about living, working, and retiring, reexamining priorities, seeking new ways to be creative, or to solve various problems in our own lives or the lives of others. "We've transitioned into always transitioning," according to the author and futurist John Seely Brown. In such times, the ability to ask big, meaningful, beautiful questions—and, just as important, to know what to *do* with those questions once they've been raised—can be the first steps in moving beyond old habits and behaviors as we embrace the new.

How CAN WE develop and improve this ability to question? Can we rekindle that questioning spark we had at age four? During my conversations and visits with more than a hundred business innovators, scientists, artists, engineers, filmmakers, educators, designers, and social entrepreneurs, they shared methods of asking questions and solving problems. Some shared stories of how questioning guided their careers or their businesses. Others recounted how a particular question helped change their life. Many offered insights, techniques, and tips on the art of inquiry.

Based on their experience—while also borrowing ideas and influences from existing theories of creativity, design thinking, and problem solving—I devised a three-part Why–What If–How model for forming and tackling big, beautiful questions. It's not a formula, per se—there is no formula for questioning. It's more of a framework designed to help guide one through various stages of inquiry—because ambitious, catalytic questioning tends to follow a logical progression, one that often starts with stepping back and seeing things differently and ends with taking action on a particular question.

A journey of inquiry that (hopefully) culminates in change can be a long road, with pitfalls and detours and often nary an answer in sight. That's why it can be helpful to approach inquiry systematically, as a step-by-step progression. The best innovators are able to live with not having the answer right away because they're focused on just trying to get to the next question.

THIS BOOK IS structured around questions, with one leading to another. Forty-four questions divide up sections within the chapters, and lots more questions are embedded within each section. The thirty "question sidebars" scattered throughout the book tell stories of breakthrough ideas, innovations, or new ways of thinking that began with a powerful (and sometimes offbeat) question. A "Question Index" is at the back of the book—because if facts are entitled to an index, then why not questions?

As to what, exactly, constitutes a "beautiful question": When I first launched the idea behind this book as the blog A More Beautiful Question, I laid out the following entirely subjective definition:

> A beautiful question is an ambitious yet actionable question that can begin to shift the way we perceive or think about something—and that might serve as a catalyst to bring about change.

That definition makes clear that this book is *not* about grand philosophical or spiritual questions—*Why are we here? How does one define "good"? Is there life after death?*—all of those great questions that spark endless, impassioned debate. I am not particularly qualified to discuss such questions, nor do they fit within the category of what I would call actionable questions.

The focus here is on questions that can be acted upon, questions that can lead to tangible results and change. The esteemed physicist Edward Witten told me that in his work he is always searching for "a question that is hard (and interesting) enough that it is worth answering and easy enough that one can actually answer it."

We don't often ask such questions; they're not the kind of queries typically typed into the Google search box. While it could be said that ours is a Golden Age of Questioning—with all the online resources now available for getting instant answers, it's reasonable to assume people are asking more questions than ever before—that distinction would be based purely on volume, not necessarily on the quality or thoughtfulness of the questions being asked. Indeed, on Google, some of the most popular queries are which celebrity is or isn't gay. In many cases, our Google queries are so unimaginative and predictable that Google can guess what we're asking before we're three words into typing it.

This book is more concerned with questions that Google cannot easily anticipate or properly answer for you—questions that require a different kind of search. *What is the fresh idea that will help my business stand out? What if I come at my work or my art in a whole different way? How might I tackle a long-standing problem that has affected my community, my family?* These are individualized, challenging, and potentially game-changing questions.

In my inquiry into the value of inquiry, I've become convinced that questioning is more important today than it was yesterday—and will be even more important tomorrow—in helping us figure out what matters, where opportunity lies, and how to get there. We're all hungry for better answers. But first, we need to learn how to ask the right questions.

CHAPTER 1

The Power of Inquiry

If they can put a man on the moon, why can't they make a decent foot?

What can a question do?

What business are we in now—and is there still a job for me?

Are questions becoming more valuable than answers?

Is "knowing" obsolete?

Why does everything begin with Why?

How do you move from asking to action?

If they can put a man on the moon, why can't they make a decent foot?

Back in 1976, long before there was a Google to field all of our queries, a young man named Van Phillips started asking the question above, first in his head and then aloud. Phillips felt his future depended upon finding a good answer, and no one seemed to have one for him.

He was twenty-one years old and had been living the charmed life of an athletic, handsome, and bright young college student.

But one day in the summer of that year, Phillips's fortunes changed. He was water-skiing on a lake in Arizona when a small fire broke out on the boat pulling him. In the ensuing confusion, the boat's driver didn't see that a second motorboat, coming around a blind curve in the lake, was headed straight at Phillips.

Phillips awoke from anesthesia the next morning in a hospital. He recalls, "I did the proverbial 'I don't want to look, but let's see'" and checked under his blanket to find "an empty place where my left foot should have been." The limb had been severed, just below the knee, by the other boat's propeller.

At the hospital, Phillips was fitted with "a pink foot attached to an aluminum tube." The "foot" wasn't much more than a block of wood with foam rubber added; such was the state of prosthetic limbs at the time. Phillips left the hospital with instructions: Get used to your "new best friend," walk on it twice a day, and "toughen up that stump." One of the first times he tried to walk on the foot, Phillips recalls, he tripped "on a pebble the size of a pea." He knew, right then, this was not going to work for him. He recalls visiting his girlfriend's parents' house around that time, and being taken aside by her father, who said, "Van—you're just going to have to learn to accept this." When he heard that, Phillips recalls, "I bit my tongue. I knew he was right, in a way—I did have to accept that I was an amputee. But I would *not* accept the fact that I had to wear this foot."

At that moment, Phillips exhibited one of the telltale signs of an innovative questioner: a refusal to accept the existing reality. He'd shown other signs before that in childhood—as a kid, he once went through his house and removed all the doorknobs (mischievous *What If I take this apart?* childhood stories are common among questioners). But now, as an adult, he was experiencing a critical Why moment, as in *Why should I settle for this lousy foot?*

This did not seem an unreasonable question to Phillips, particularly since he was very aware—as was everyone else at the time—that amazing things were happening in the world of technology, particularly in the U.S. space program. Hence, he naturally wondered why some of the vast means and know-how that enabled a man to walk on the moon couldn't somehow be applied to his down-to-earth problem.

What he hadn't thought of at that time—it would become clear to him later, as he got to know more about the field of prosthetics—was that some problems do not have governments or large corporations rushing to solve them. The prosthetics industry had been "in a time warp for decades," Phillips recalls. No one was investing in it because the customer base, amputees, was no one's idea of an attractive business market. "But this worked to my advantage in a way," Phillips told me, years later. Since progress had been stalled for so long, it left plenty of room to question outdated approaches and status quo practices—and to inject much-needed fresh thinking.

Still, Phillips quickly found, as a naïve questioner sometimes does, that his Why and What If inquiries weren't particularly welcome in the realm of What Is. Frequently in various professional domains—in hospitals or doctors' offices, in business conference rooms, even in classrooms—basic, fundamental questions can make people impatient and even uncomfortable. Phillips's questions about why there weren't better prosthetic limbs, and whether that could be changed, could be taken as a challenge to the expertise of those who knew far more than he did on the subject—the doctors, the prosthetics engineers, and others who understood "what was possible" at the time.

As an outsider in that domain, Phillips was actually in the best position to ask questions. One of the many interesting and appealing things about questioning is that it often has an inverse relationship to expertise—such that, within their own subject areas, experts are apt to be poor questioners. Frank Lloyd Wright put it well when he remarked that an expert is someone who has "stopped thinking because he 'knows.'" If you "know," there's no reason to ask; yet if you *don't* ask, then you are relying on "expert" knowledge that is certainly limited, may be outdated, and could be altogether wrong.

Phillips was not going to convince the experts that he knew better (and in fact, he didn't "know" better—he only suspected).

Somewhere along the line, he took another critical step for a questioner tackling a challenge: He took ownership of that question, *Why can't they make a better foot?* To do this, he had to make a change of pronouns: Specifically, he had to replace *they* with *I*.

THIS IS AN important concept, as explained by the small, independent inventor and inveterate questioner Mark Noonan, who once, after suffering his umpteenth backache from shoveling snow, wondered, *Why don't they come up with a better shovel?* Noonan solved the problem himself, inventing a shovel with a long handle, a lever, and a wheel—when you use it, you no longer have to bend your back. Noonan observes that if you never actually *do* anything about a problem yourself, then you're not really questioning—you're complaining. And that situation you're complaining about may never change because, as Regina Dugan, a former Defense Advanced Research Projects Agency (DARPA) director, has observed about problems in general, "We think someone else—someone smarter than us, someone more capable, with more resources—will solve that problem. But there isn't anyone else."

When Van Phillips realized that he was going to have to answer his own question, he also understood, almost immediately, that to inquire about prosthetics in a meaningful way he would have to wade into that world. He had been a broadcast major in college, but now changed directions and enrolled in one of the top prosthetics study programs in the United States, at Northwestern University, from whence he found work in a prosthetics lab in Utah. He began to understand how and why prosthetic limbs were designed the way they were.

He would spend nearly a decade grappling with his original question, then forming new ones, and eventually acting upon those. Phillips's journey of inquiry led him to some unusual places: He extracted lessons from the animal kingdom and borrowed influences from his local swimming pool as well as from the battlefields of ancient China.

In his pursuit of a better foot, he faltered many times—literally, he fell to the ground again and again. This would happen as he was trying to answer his latest question (*I wonder if this prototype will hold up better than the last one?*) by taking it for a test run. He would receive his disappointing answer each time the new version of the foot broke under him. He would curse and swear, and then, inevitably, he would begin to ask new questions—attempting to understand and learn from each of his failures.

Then one day, the foot under him didn't break. And Phillips knew, at that moment, that he was about to change the world.

What can a question do?

The Pulitzer Prize–winning historian David Hackett Fischer observed that questions "are the engines of intellect—cerebral machines that convert curiosity into controlled inquiry." Fischer's "engine" is just one of many metaphors that have been used to try to describe the surprising power that questions have. Questions are sometimes seen as spades that help to unearth buried truths; or flashlights that, in the words of Dan Rothstein of the Right Question Institute (RQI), "shine a light on where you need to go."

The late Frances Peavey, a quirky, colorful social activist whose work revolved around what she called "strategic questioning" aimed at bridging cultural differences between people, once observed that a good question is like "a lever used to pry open the stuck lid on a paint can."

Maybe we talk about what a question is *like* because it's hard to wrap our minds around what it actually is. Many tend to think of it as a form of speech—but that would mean if you didn't utter a question, it wouldn't exist, and that's not the case. A question can reside in the mind for a long time—maybe forever—without being spoken to anyone.

We do know that the ability to question, whether verbally or through other means, is one of the things that separates us from lower primates. Paul Harris, an education professor at Harvard University who has studied questioning in children, observes, "Unlike other primates, we humans are designed so that the young

look to the old for cultural information." He sees this as an important "evolutionary divide"—that from an early age, even before
speech, humans will use some form of questioning to try to gain
information. A child may pick up a kiwi fruit and indicate, through
a look or gesture directed at a nearby adult, a desire to know more.
Chimpanzees don't do this; they may "ask" for a treat through
signaling, but it's a simple request for food, as opposed to an infor-
mation-seeking question.

So then, one of the primary drivers of questioning is an
awareness of what we don't know—which is a form of higher
awareness that separates not only man from monkey but also
the smart and curious person from the dullard who doesn't
know or care. Good questioners tend to be aware of, and quite
comfortable with, their own ignorance (Richard Saul Wurman,
the founder of the TED Conferences, has been known to brag,
"I know more about my ignorance than you know about yours").
But they constantly probe that vast ignorance using the question flashlight—or, if you prefer, they attack it with the question
spade.

The author Stuart Firestein, in his fine book *Ignorance: How It
Drives Science*, argues that one of the keys to scientific discovery
is the willingness of scientists to embrace ignorance—and to use
questions as a means of navigating through it to new discoveries.
"One good question can give rise to several layers of answers, can
inspire decades-long searches for solutions, can generate whole
new fields of inquiry, and can prompt changes in entrenched
thinking," Firestein writes. "Answers, on the other hand, often
end the process."

This expansive effect of questions has been studied by Dan
Rothstein, who along with his colleague Luz Santana established
the Right Question Institute, a small and fascinating nonprofit
group formed in order to try to advance the teaching of questioning skills. Rothstein believes that questions do *something*—he is
not sure precisely what—that has an "unlocking" effect in people's
minds. "It's an experience we've all had at one point or another,"
Rothstein maintains. "Just asking or hearing a question phrased a

certain way produces an almost palpable feeling of discovery and new understanding. Questions produce the lightbulb effect."

Rothstein has seen this phenomenon at work in classrooms where students (whether adults or children) are instructed to think and brainstorm using only questions. As they do this, Rothstein says, the floodgates of imagination seem to open up. The participants tend to become more engaged, more interested, in the subject at hand; the ideas begin to flow, in the form of questions. *Harvard Business Review* writer Polly LaBarre echoes this in describing the effect that lively and imaginative questioning can have in business settings: Such questions can be "fundamentally subversive, disruptive, and playful" and seem to "switch people into the mode required to create anything new."

How DO QUESTIONS do this? The neurologist and author Ken Heilman, a leading expert on creative activity in the brain, acknowledges that scant research has been focused on what's happening in the brain when we ask questions. Neurologists these days can tell us what's going on in the cerebral cortex when we daydream, watch a commercial, or work on a crossword puzzle, but, strangely, no one has much to say about the mental processes involved in forming and asking a question. However, Heilman points out, there *has* been significant neurological study of divergent thinking—the mental process of trying to come up with alternative ideas. Heilman notes, "Since divergent thinking is about saying, 'Hey, what if I think differently about this?' it's actually a form of asking questions."

How might we prepare during peacetime to offer help in times of war?

The exigencies of war have brought forth many a beautiful question. In 1859, a young Swiss Calvinist named Henry Dunant traveling in Italy came upon the aftermath of a bloody battle between the Austrian and French armies. On the battlefield some forty thousand men lay dead or wounded, and Dunant hastily organized the locals in binding wounds and feeding the injured. Upon his return home, Dunant wrote: *"Would there not be some means, during a period of peace and calm, of forming relief societies whose object would be to have the wounded cared for in time of war by enthusiastic, devoted volunteers, fully qualified for the task?"* And thus the Red Cross national relief societies were born. The subsequent idea of pooling the skills and resources of various Red Cross Societies to provide humanitarian assistance in peacetime, and not just during war, also was championed by Dunant.

What we know about divergent thinking is that it mostly happens in the more creative right hemisphere of the brain; that it taps into imagination and often triggers random association of ideas (which is a primary source of creativity); and that it can be intellectually stimulating and rewarding. So to the extent that questioning triggers divergent thinking, it's not surprising that it can have the kind of mind-opening effect that Rothstein has observed in classrooms using RQI's question-based teaching.

Rothstein points out, however, that questions not only open up thinking—they also can direct and focus it. In his exercises, students may begin with wide-open, divergent "what-if" speculation, but they gradually use their own questions to do "convergent" (focused) thinking as they get at the core of a difficult problem and reach consensus on how to proceed. They even use questions for "meta cognitive thinking," as they analyze and reflect upon their own questions. "People think of questioning as simple," Rothstein says, but when done right, "it's a very sophisticated, high-level form of thinking."

It is also egalitarian: "You don't have to hold a position of authority to ask a powerful question," noted LaBarre. In some ways, it can be more difficult or risky for those in authority to question. In Hal Gregersen's study of business leaders who question, he found that they exhibited an unusual "blend of humility and confidence"—they were humble enough to acknowledge a lack of knowledge, and confident enough to admit this in front of others. The latter is no small thing given that, as author Sir Ken Robinson has observed, "In our culture, not to know is to be at fault, socially."

Being willing to question is one thing; questioning well and effectively is another. Not all questions have the positive effects described above. Open questions—in particular, the kind of Why, What If, and How questions that can't be answered with simple facts—generally tend to encourage creative thinking more than closed yes-or-no questions (though closed questions have their place, too, as we'll see).

What may be even more important is the tone of questions.

Confronted with a challenge or problem, one could respond with the question *Oh my God, what are we going to do?* Faced with the same situation, one might ask, *What if this change represents an opportunity for us? How might we make the most of the situation?*

Questions of the second type, with a more positive tone, will tend to yield better answers, according to David Cooperrider, a Case Western professor who has developed a popular theory of "appreciative inquiry." Cooperrider says that "organizations gravitate toward the questions they ask." If the questions from leaders and managers focus more on *Why are we falling behind competitors?* and *Who is to blame?*, then the organization is more likely to end up with a culture of turf-guarding and finger-pointing. Conversely, if the questions asked tend to be more expansive and optimistic, then *that* will be reflected in the culture. This is true of more than companies, he maintains. Whether we're talking about countries, communities, families, or individuals, "we all live in the world our questions create."

What business are we in now— and is there still a job for me?

One of the most important things questioning does is to enable people to think and act in the face of uncertainty. As Steve Quatrano of the Right Question Institute puts it, forming questions helps us "to organize our thinking around what we *don't* know." This may explain why questioning is so important in innovation hotbeds such as Silicon Valley, where entrepreneurs must figure out, seemingly daily, how to create new products and businesses from thin air, while navigating highly competitive, volatile market conditions.

Sebastian Thrun, the engineer/inventor behind Google's experimental self-driving X car and the founder of the online university Udacity, acknowledges the two-way relationship between technological change and questioning. The changes are fueled by the questions being asked—but those changes, in turn, fuel more questions. That's because with each new advance, Thrun said, one must pause to ask, *Now that we know what we now know, what's possible* now?

In some sense, innovation means trying to find and formulate new questions that can, over time, be answered. Those questions, once identified, often become the basis for starting a new venture. Indeed, the rise of a number of today's top tech firms—Foursquare, Airbnb, Pandora Internet Radio—can be traced to a *Why doesn't somebody* or *What if we were to* question, in some cases inspired by the founder's personal experience.

One such example, which has become a modern classic business story, is the origin of the Netflix video-rental service. The man who would go on to start the company, Reed Hastings, was reacting to one of those frustrating everyday experiences we've all had. Hastings had been lax in returning some movies rented from a Blockbuster video store, and by the time he got around to it, the late charges were exorbitant. A frustrated Hastings wondered, *Why should I have to pay these fees?* (He has admitted that another question on his mind at the time was *How am I going explain this charge to my wife?*)

Surely, others have been similarly outraged by late fees. But Hastings decided to do something about it, which led to a subsequent question: *What if a video-rental business were run like a health club?* He then set about figuring out how to design a video-rental model that had a monthly membership, like a health club, with no late fees. (Years later, Hastings would question whether Netflix could and should expand its model: *Why are we only renting the films and shows? What if we* made *them, too?*)

Through the years, companies from Polaroid (*Why do we have to wait for the picture?*) to Pixar (*Can animation be cuddly?*) have started with questions. However, when it comes to questioning, companies are like people: They start out doing it, then gradually do it less and less. A hierarchy forms, a methodology is established, and rules are set; after that, what is there to question?

But business leaders sometimes find themselves thrust back into questioning mode during dire or dynamic times, when those rules and methods they've come to rely on no longer work. Such is the case in today's business market, where the speed of, and need for, innovation has been ratcheted up—forcing some companies to ask bigger and more fundamental questions than they've asked in years about everything from the company's identity, to its mission, to a reexamination of who the customer is and what the core competencies should be. Much of it boils down to a fundamental question that a lot of companies find themselves asking right now:

With all that's changing in the world and in our customers' lives, what business are we really *in?*

As COMPANIES ARE forced to ask tough questions in the face of change, so, too, are the people working for those companies, or, increasingly, working for themselves or just trying to find work, period. The same forces roiling businesses—rapid technological upheaval, leading to changes in how jobs are performed and what skills are required—are creating what the *New York Times* recently characterized as a perfect storm in which no one, whether blue-collar or white-collar and whatever level of expertise, can afford to stand pat. "The need to constantly adapt is the new reality for many workers" was the theme of the piece headlined "The Age of Adaptation." The story had a term for what is now required of many workers—*serial mastery.*

To keep up, today's worker must constantly learn new skills by, for example, taking training courses. But as the *Times* article points out, these workers "are often left to figure out for themselves what new skills will make them more valuable, or just keep them from obsolescence."

Stories like this have been appearing with greater frequency— the *Times* columnist Thomas Friedman has written extensively about a new global economy that is ruthlessly demanding more skills and more inventiveness from the workforce. A quick scan of the stories' online comment sections reveals how people feel about all of this: worried and bewildered, but also, in some cases, angry and bitter. *I went to school, got a degree, picked up a skill, gained expertise in my field—I* established *myself over the years. Why should I have to start over?*

Unfortunately, that's a Why question that, however justified and reasonable it may seem, doesn't lead anywhere. The rules Friedman is talking about have already changed; fair or not, like it or not. The challenge now is to figure out what these new conditions mean for each of us—what openings they create, and how best to exploit those openings and possibilities. A training program may be appropriate, but before taking any action, fundamental questioning is essential. How can you know whether retraining is worthwhile, or which kinds of training, without first spending time on questions such as:

- How is my field/industry changing?
- What trends are having the most impact on my field, and how is that likely to play out over the next few years?
- Which of my existing skills are most useful and adaptable in this new environment—and what new ones do I need to add?
- Should I diversify more—or focus on specializing in one area?
- Should I be thinking more in terms of finding a job—or creating one?

Changing tracks in a career is a form of innovation, on a personal level—and requires the same kind of rigorous inquiry that a business should undertake in pursuing a new direction or strategy. What's required is not just a onetime adaptation; more likely, we'll all have to be adept at *continually* changing tracks as we move forward.

Joichi Ito, the director of the esteemed MIT Media Lab, offers an interesting theory about the need for lifelong adaptation. When the world moved at a slower pace and things weren't quite so complex, we spent the early part of life in learning mode. Then, once you became an adult, "you figured out what your job was and you repeated the same thing over and over again for the rest of your life." Today, Ito explains, because of constant change and increased complexity, that rinse-and-repeat approach in adult life no longer works as well. In a time when so much of what we know is subject to revision or obsolescence, the comfortable expert must go back to being a restless learner.

Are questions becoming more valuable than answers?

As expertise loses its "shelf life," it also loses some of its value. If we think of "questions" and "answers" as stocks on the market, then we could say that, in this current environment, questions are rising in value while answers are declining. "Right now, knowledge is a commodity," says the Harvard education expert Tony Wagner. "Known answers are everywhere, and easily accessible." Because we're drowning in all of this data, "the value of explicit information is dropping," according to Wagner's colleague at Harvard, the innovation professor Paul Bottino. The real value, Bottino added, is in "what you can do with that knowledge, in pursuit of a query."

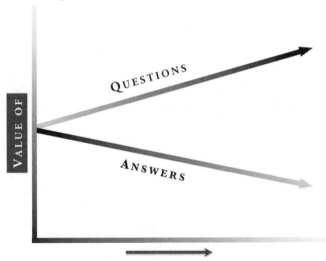

*As the world becomes more **complex and dynamic***

The glut of knowledge has another interesting effect, as noted by author Stuart Firestein: It makes us *more* ignorant. That is to say, as our collective knowledge grows—as there is more and more to know, more than we can possibly keep up with—the amount that the individual knows, in relation to the growing body of knowledge, is smaller.

The good news, Firestein notes, is that there is more ignorance for us to explore. There are more "collectively known" things that we, as individuals, can learn about and a vast expanse of unknown things we could, potentially, discover. Overall, there's more darkness into which we can shine that "question flashlight."

Another way to think of it is that as we increasingly find ourselves surrounded by the new, the unfamiliar, and the unknown, we're experiencing something not unlike early childhood. Everywhere we turn, there's something to wonder and inquire about. MIT's Joi Ito says that as we try to come to terms with a new reality that requires us to be lifelong learners (instead of just early-life learners), we must try to maintain or rekindle the curiosity, sense of wonder, inclination to try new things, and ability to adapt and absorb that served us so well in childhood. We must become, in a word, *neotenous* (*neoteny* being a biological term that describes the retention of childlike attributes in adulthood). To do so, we must rediscover the tool that kids use so well in those early years: the question. Ito puts it quite simply: "You don't learn unless you question."

QUESTIONS TRUMP ANSWERS: Some people have been saying this for a while, among them John Seely Brown. The former chief scientist at Xerox Corporation, Brown headed up its famous Palo Alto Research Center (PARC) for years. More recently, as cofounder of an innovation think tank known as the Deloitte Center for the Edge, Brown advises some of the world's leading companies on how to keep pace in a turbulent environment. He has also written about how our approach to education must be completely rethought, in light of what he calls the "exponential change" that is upon us.

Things are changing so fast, Brown told me, "I have to reframe how I even think about using all of this technology. I find myself asking all kinds of fundamental questions. And as I do that, I eventually realize that the lenses I'm looking through to see the world around me are wrong—and that I have to construct a whole new frame of reference."

The problem is not just rapid change—it's also the sheer volume of information rushing at us from all directions and many sources. Without a filtering device, we can't separate what's relevant or reliable from what's not. When we're overloaded with information, "context becomes critical," Brown says. "What matters now is your ability to triangulate, to look at something from multiple sources, and construct your own warrants for what you choose to believe." That can involve "asking all kinds of peripheral questions," Brown notes, such as *What is the agenda behind this information? How current is it? How does it connect with other information I'm finding?*

What if we could paint over our mistakes?

When electric typewriters became popular in the 1950s, the ribbons made it harder to erase typing errors—a problem noticed by Bette Nesmith Graham. Graham worked two jobs: bank secretary (and heavy typist) by day, commercial artist at night. One night while doing artwork, she wondered, *What if I could paint over my mistakes when typing, the way I do when painting?* She filled a small bottle with a paint and water formula and brought it to the office. Her "miracle mixture" made it easy to cover over typing errors, and soon Graham was supplying hundreds of other secretaries with her correction fluid. The year before she died in 1980, Graham sold Liquid Paper for close to $50 million, giving half of that to her son, the former Monkees band member Mike Nesmith—who used it to fund innovations of his own at the pioneering multimedia recording company Pacific Arts.

The author Seth Godin is touching on a similar idea when he writes, "Our new civic and professional life is all about doubt. About questioning the status quo, questioning marketing or political claims, and most of all questioning what's next." To navigate in today's info-swamp, we must have, according to Bard College president Leon Botstein, "the ability to evaluate risk, recognize demagoguery, the ability to question not only other people's views, but one's own assumptions." The more we're deluged with information, with "facts" (which may or may not be), views, appeals, offers, and choices, then the more we must be able to sift and sort and decode and make sense of it all through rigorous inquiry.

CAN TECHNOLOGY HELP us ask better questions? For the most part, it is better suited to responding to questions—not so good at asking them. Picasso was onto this truth fifty years ago when he commented, "Computers are useless—they only give you answers."

On the other hand, technology can serve up amazing, innovative, life-changing answers—if we know how to ask for them. The potential is mind-boggling, as IBM's Watson system demonstrates. Its winning appearance in 2011 on the TV quiz show *Jeopardy!* proved it could answer questions better than any human. Today, IBM is feeding the system a steady diet of, among other things, medical information—so that it can answer just about any question a doctor might throw at it (*If patient exhibits symptoms A, B, and C, what might this indicate?*). But the doctor still has to figure out what to ask—and then must be able to question Watson's response, which might be technically accurate but not commonsensical.

When I visited Watson and its programmers recently at IBM's main research facility—where the machine, consisting of a stack of servers, resides alone in a basement, humming quietly and waiting for questions to crunch on—I inquired (directing my queries to the nearby humans, not the machine) whether Watson might ever turn the tables on us and start asking *us* wickedly complex questions. While that's not its purpose, its programmers point out something interesting and quite promising: As Watson comes in increasing contact with doctors and medical students currently using the system, the machine is slowly training them to ask more and better questions in order to pull the information they need out of the system. As it trains them to be better questioners, Watson will almost certainly help them to be better doctors.

Is "knowing" obsolete?

Today, only a small group of medical professionals are using the Watson system to answer their questions. But eventually, all doctors—and all the rest of us, as well—will have access to some form of cloud-based super-search-engine that can quickly answer almost any factual question with a level of precision and expertise that's way beyond what we have now. Which reinforces that the value of questions is going to keep rising as that of answers keeps falling.

Clearly, technology will have the answers covered—so we will no longer need to fill our heads with those answers as much as we once did, bringing to mind a classic Einstein story. A reporter doing an interview concludes by asking Einstein for his phone number, and Einstein reaches for a nearby phone book. While Einstein is looking up his own number in the book, the reporter asks why such a smart man can't remember it. Einstein explains that there's no reason to fill his mind with information that can so easily be looked up.

> **Why did my candy bar melt? (And will my popcorn pop?)**
>
> During the World War II years, Percy Spencer, a self-taught engineer leading the power tube division at defense contractor Raytheon, focused his efforts on the magnetron—the core tube that made radars so powerful they enabled U.S. bombers to spot periscopes on German submarines. Standing next to a magnetron one day, Spencer noticed that a candy bar in his pocket had melted. He then wondered, *Could the energy from the radio waves be used to actually cook food?* He placed some popcorn kernels near the tube and soon was munching on the world's first microwave popcorn. In 1947, Raytheon put the first Radarange microwave ovens on the market—but it took another twenty years before the appliances were small enough to fit on a countertop.

In the current era of Google and Watson, with databases doing much of the "knowing" for us, many critics today question the wisdom of an education system that still revolves around teaching students to memorize facts. One such education critic, the author Sugata Mitra, made just this point at a TED Conference by tossing out the provocative question *Is "knowing" obsolete?* Of course, not all knowledge is mere factual information; the TED question, as worded, is overly broad. But if we zero in on a narrow kind of knowledge—stored facts or "answers"—then that kind of "know-ing" might be better left to machines with more memory.

But if we can't compete with technology when it comes to storing answers, questioning—that uniquely human capacity—is our ace in the hole. Until Watson acquires the equivalent of human curiosity, creativity, divergent thinking skills, imagina-tion, and judgment, it will not be able to formulate the kind of original, counterintuitive, and unpredictable questions an inno-vative thinker—or even just your average four-year-old—can come up with.

Moreover, only through effective inquiry can we fully explore, probe, access, and, hopefully, figure out what to do with all those answers the technology has in store for us. This goes beyond just being able to query a search engine or a database; immense resources and capabilities are available today to those who are able to access and traverse the network that now exists online.

By tapping into social networks, online sources of information, and digital communities, it is increasingly feasible, MIT's Ito points out, for an individual to tackle a large challenge or question, or to launch an initiative or movement. One can do so relatively quickly by "pulling resources—answers, expert advice, partners, sources of funding, influence—from the network as you need it." However, "the main way you pull support from the network is by querying it. And you need to understand how to frame the ques-tions to get the best response."

In light of this, there's never been a better time to be a ques-tioner—because it is so much easier now to begin a journey of inquiry, with so many places you can turn for information, help, ideas, feedback, or even to find possible collaborators who might be interested in the same question.

As John Seely Brown notes, a questioner can thrive in these times of exponential change. "If you don't have that disposition to question," Brown says, "you're going to fear change. But if you're comfortable questioning, experimenting, connecting things—then change is something that becomes an adventure. And if you can see it as an adventure, then you're off and running."

Why does everything begin with Why?

As Van Phillips began to proceed further on his own journey, he was, to use Brown's words, "questioning, experimenting, connecting things." He revised his initial Why question—*If they can put a man on the moon, why can't I (not they) make a decent foot?*—and began to immerse himself deeply in the world of prosthetics.

The more Phillips learned, the more questions he had: about the materials being used (*Why wood, when there were so many better alternatives?*); about the shape (*Why did a prosthetic foot have to be shaped like a bulky human foot? Did that even make sense?*); about the primary purpose of a replacement foot (*Why was there so much emphasis on trying to match the look of a human foot? Wasn't performance more important?*).

This all comprises the first stage of innovative questioning—first confronting, formulating, and framing the initial question that articulates the challenge at hand, and trying to gain some understanding of context. I think of this as the Why stage, though not every question asked at this juncture has to begin with the word *why*. Still, this is the point at which one is apt to inquire:

- Why does a particular situation exist?
- Why does it present a problem or create a need or opportunity, and for whom?
- Why has no one addressed this need or solved this problem before?
- Why do you personally (or your company, or organization) want to invest more time thinking about, and formulating questions around, this problem?

The situation Van Phillips confronted was unusual in some ways. He didn't have to go looking for his Why problem; it came to him. He didn't have to wonder about whom it affected or whether it was worth his time. But when the problem was thrust upon him, he asked a proactive Why question (instead of just passively wondering, *Why did this have to happen to me?*). Then he kept asking more Why questions as he explored the nature and the dimensions of the problem.

Innovative questioners, when faced with situations that are less than ideal, inquire as to why, trying to figure out what's lacking. Oftentimes, these questions arise out of mundane, everyday situations, such as that "late fees" problem encountered by Reed Hastings before he founded Netflix. Similarly, Pandora Internet Radio founder Tim Westergren, a former band musician, observing all the talented-yet-struggling musicians he knew, wondered why it was so difficult for them to connect with the audience they deserved. Airbnb cofounder Joe Gebbia, along with roommate Brian Chesky, wanted to know why people coming to his town at certain times of the year had so much trouble getting hotel accommodations.

The *New York Times* technology reporter David Pogue has written about how so many things that are now part of our everyday lives—such as ATM machines, computer documents, and shampoo bottles—all started the same way: We get these breakthroughs, Pogue writes, "when someone looks at the way things have always been done and asks why?"

And the phenomenon isn't limited to business innovation and invention stories; asking Why can be the first step to bringing about change in almost any context. Gretchen Rubin showed how a simple Why question could be applied to one's everyday life—and be the spark that leads to dramatic change. One rainy day, looking out the window of a New York City bus, Rubin pondered, *Why am I not happy with my life as it is?* This question got her thinking about the nature of happiness, then researching that, then applying what she learned to her own life—and, importantly, to the lives of others. Thus was born her immensely successful multimedia venture known as *The Happiness Project*.

We can and should ask Why about career, family relationships, local community issues—anywhere we might encounter a situation that is ripe for change and improvement. *Why is my career not advancing in the way I'd hoped? Or if it is advancing, and I'm still not happy, why is that? Why is my product or service failing to connect with customers who ought to love it? Why is my father-in-law so difficult to get along with?*

Sometimes questioners go out looking for their Why—searching for a question they can work on and answer. The term *problem-finding* is used to describe this pursuit, and while it may seem odd to go looking for problems, according to the business consultant Min Basadur—who teaches problem-finding skills to executives at top companies—it's one of the most important things to do for an established business, large or small. As Basadur notes, if you are able to "find" a problem before others do, and then successfully answer the questions surrounding that problem, you can create a new venture, a new career, a new industry. Here again, as Basadur attests, it applies to life, as well—if you seek out problems in your life before they're obvious, before they've reached a crisis stage, you can catch and address them while they still offer the best opportunities for improvement and reinvention.

Why aren't the players urinating more?

Many companies and even entire industries can be traced back to a question—but they're usually not as odd as this one. In 1965, Dwayne Douglas, a football coach at the University of Florida, wondered, *Why aren't the players urinating more after the games?* The coach was baffled because he knew his players were drinking water on the sidelines; what he didn't realize was that they were sweating away more fluids than could be replaced with water. Douglas shared his question with J. Robert Cade, a professor of renal (kidney) medicine at the university—who set about formulating a drink that could replace the electrolytes lost through sweat. Cade's mixture was first tested on the freshman football team—who proceeded to defeat the upperclassmen in a practice session. The drink became known as Gatorade (named after the team mascot) and helped launch a sports drink industry now worth almost $20 billion.

JUST ASKING WHY without taking any action may be a source of stimulating thought or conversation, but it is not likely to produce change. (Basic formula: *Q (questioning)* + *A (action)* = *I (innovation)*. On the other hand, *Q – A = P (philosophy)*. In observing how questioners tackle problems, I noticed a pattern in many of the stories:

- Person encounters a situation that is less than ideal; asks Why.
- Person begins to come up with ideas for possible improvements/solutions—with such ideas usually surfacing in the form of What If possibilities.
- Person takes one of those possibilities and tries to implement it or make it real; this mostly involves figuring out How.

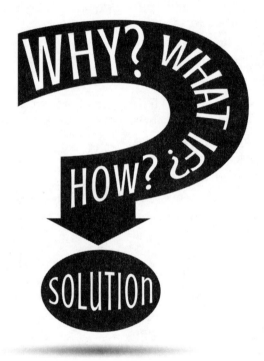

The Why/What If/How sequence represents a basic and logical progression, drawing, in part, on several existing models that break down the creative problem-solving process. For example, current theories of "design thinking," used by IDEO and other leading designers to systematically solve problems, have laid out a process that starts with framing a problem and learning more about it (similar to my Why stage), then proceeds to generating ideas (which corresponds to What If), and eventually builds upon those ideas through prototyping (which could be thought of as the How stage).

A similar progression—moving from understanding a problem, to imagining possible solutions, to then going to work on those possibilities—can also be seen in the creative problem-solving processes of the business consultant Min Basadur (who, in turn, owes a debt to earlier processes developed by the little-known but legendary Creative Problem Solving Institute of Buffalo, New York). Echoes of this are even in the classic four-stage process of creativity—Preparation/Incubation/Illumination/Implementation—developed nearly a century ago by the British psychologist Graham Wallas.

All of which is to say there is good reason why the stages of questioning proceed in the order laid out in this book. It corresponds to what has been learned, through the years, about how best to confront problems and work toward possible solutions. It's also based on observation of how many of the questioners featured in the book cycled through the process of coming up with innovative solutions.

The Why/What If/How progression offers a simplified way to approach questioning; it's an attempt to bring at least some semblance of order to a questioning process that is, by its nature, chaotic and unpredictable. A journey of inquiry is bound to lead you into the unknown (as it should), but if you have a sense of the kinds of questions to ask at various stages along the way, you've at least got some road markers. Indeed, this is the beauty of "process" in general: It may not provide any answers or solutions, but, as one design-thinker told me, having a process helps you to keep taking next steps—so that, as he put it, "even when you don't know what you're doing, you still know what to do."

How do you move from asking to action?

At some point, Van Phillips progressed from Why to What If. Phillips was by now working in the prosthetics industry and doing his own "contextual inquiry" (inquiring up close and in context) in his endeavor to understand how things were done in that business, so that he could question more intelligently.

Yet even as Phillips began to gain expertise in prosthetics, he tried to maintain his original "outsider" perspective. As he was working on his project, he was advised by a mentor to go to the patent office and research everything that had been done on prosthetic foot inventions. "My reaction to that was 'I'm not going to pollute my mind with everyone else's ideas. I'm following my own path, not somebody else's.'"

Phillips was not in a hurry; he was not looking for quick answers from experts. "If you give the mind time and space, it will do its own work on the problem, over time," he said. "And it will usually come up with interesting possibilities to work with." Gradually, those possibilities began to surface in Phillips's mind. At the What If stage the imagination begins to go to work, whether we're conscious of it or not. The mind, if preoccupied with a problem or question long enough, will tend to come up with possibilities that might eventually lead to answers, but at this stage are still speculations, untested hypotheses, and early epiphanies. (Epiphanies often are characterized as "Aha! moments," but that suggests the problem has been solved in a flash. More often, insights arrive as What if moments—bright possibilities that are untested and open to question.)

Exploring What If possibilities is a wide-open, fun stage of questioning and should not be rushed. Today, the idea of "sitting with" and "living with" a question may seem strange, as we've gotten used to having our queries answered quickly and in bite-size servings. Stuart Firestein, in his book *Ignorance*, wonders if we've gotten too comfortable with this. *Are we too enthralled with answers?* he asks. *Are we afraid of questions, especially those that linger too long?*

Often the worst thing you can do with a difficult question is to try to answer it too quickly. When the mind is coming up with What If possibilities, these fresh, new ideas can take time to percolate and form. They often result from connecting existing ideas in unusual and interesting ways. Einstein was an early believer in this form of "combinatorial thinking"; today it is widely accepted as one of the primary sources of creativity. Since this type of thinking involves both connections and questions, I think of it as *connective inquiry*.

As VAN PHILLIPS got, in his words, "knee-deep" into his foot project, he did lots of interesting, offbeat connective inquiry. For example, he'd started thinking about the spring force of a diving board and wondering, *What if you could somehow replicate a diving board's propulsive effect in a prosthetic foot?* Somewhere along the way he learned about animal leg movements—in particular, about how the powerful tendons in a cheetah's hind legs produced remarkable spring-force whenever the legs were bent and the tendons compressed. *What if a human leg could be more like a cheetah's?*

He also made a mental connection with a distant memory. When he was growing up, his father owned an antique Chinese sword with a C-shaped blade. Phillips had always been fascinated by this sword because the curved blade was actually stronger and more flexible than a straight one. This created a fresh possibility in his mind: *Instead of a traditional L-shaped lower leg and foot, what if he dispensed with the heel and created a limb that was one smooth, continuous curve, from leg to toe?* With such a design, and with the right materials, he'd be able to incorporate the elasticity of a cheetah's tendons and the bounce of a diving board. On such a limb, an amputee could not just walk, but run and jump.

> **What if a car windshield could blink?**
>
> In 1902 Alabama tourist Mary Anderson watched her New York streetcar driver struggling to see through his snow-covered windshield and wondered, *Why doesn't someone create a device to remove the snow?* (The "someone," of course, became Mary, designer of the first windshield wiper.) Sixty years later, Bob Kearns brought the windshield wiper into the modern era by posing a new question of his own. Dissatisfied with wipers that moved at one speed whether it was pouring or drizzling outside, Kearns inquired, *Why can't a wiper work more like my eyelid, blinking as much (or little) as needed?* Kearns worked on his "intermittent wiper" idea in his basement, eventually coming up with an elegantly simple three-component electronic sensing and timing device. (The sad story of how the Big Three car companies infringed on his patent is told in the 2008 film *Flash of Genius*.)

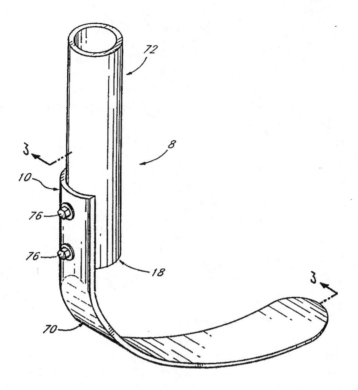

WHAT IF POSSIBILITIES are powerful things; they are the seeds of innovation. But you do not get from idea to reality in one leap, even if you've got spring-force dynamics on your side. What sets apart the innovative questioners is their ability—mostly born out of persistence and determination—to give form to their ideas and make them real. This is the final, and critical, How stage of inquiry—when you've asked all the Whys, considered the What Ifs . . . and must now figure out, *How do I actually get this done?* It's the action stage, yet it is still driven by questions, albeit more practical ones.

How do I decide which of my ideas is the one I'll pursue?

How do I begin to test that idea, to see what works and what doesn't?

And if/when I find it's not working, how do I figure out what's wrong and fix it?

Today, most of us are in a better position to build on our ideas and questions than ever before. We can use computer sketch programs, create YouTube videos of what we're doing, set up beta websites, tap into social networks for help—or even launch a Kickstarter project to fund our efforts to solve a problem or create something new.

PHILLIPS DIDN'T HAVE any of those resources at the time he was working on his foot. He sketched by hand, then built clay prototypes in his basement lab. He would trek up to the kitchen to bake in his oven the ingredients that would go into his superfoot. "I was curing parts between fifty-pound hot plates in my oven, burning myself a lot," he told me.

Phillips created somewhere between two hundred and three hundred prototypes of the Flex-Foot, and "a lot of them broke the first time you put your weight down on them." Every time a foot broke, he dissected the failure through questioning: *Why did it break? What if I change the mix of materials? How will this new version hold up?* Each time Phillips fell, he landed in a place that was further ahead, closer to the breakthrough. He was failing forward, the whole time.

The Flex-Foot prosthetics that Phillips introduced, starting in the mid-1980s and continuing until he sold the line and his company in 2000, revolutionized the prosthetics industry. While the Flex-Foot line had various models for different uses, its most dramatic was the Cheetah—which incorporated various disparate influences (the diving board, the animal leg, the curved Chinese sword). With its curved blades, it changed everything: the way we think about prosthetics, how they're supposed to look, what an amputee can do with them. Using Phillips's creation, an amputee climbed Mount Everest; the runner Aimee Mullins became the first double-amputee sprinter to compete in NCAA track and field, for Georgetown University; and most famously, the South African runner Oscar Pistorius ran on two Cheetahs as he competed in the 2012 Olympics. As for Phillips himself, his prosthetic foot—the decades-long answer to his original question—enabled him to return to one of his deepest passions in life: He now runs every day, on the beach near his home in Mendocino, California.

When he's not running, Phillips is hard at work trying to create new versions of limbs that do even more for less. In fact, almost as soon as he developed the Cheetah, he was asking, *Why does it have to cost so much? What if the design were tweaked in some way— through new materials, different processes—so as to make the limb accessible to more people? How might I make that work?*

It's common for questioners to do this; each "answer" they arrive at brings a fresh wave of questions. To keep questioning is as natural, for them, as breathing. But how did they come to be this way? And why aren't more people like that?

CHAPTER 2

Why We Stop Questioning

Why do kids ask so many questions? (And how do we **really** feel about that?)

Why does questioning fall off a cliff?

Can a school be built on questions?

Who is entitled to ask questions in class?

If we're born to inquire, then why must it be taught?

Can we teach ourselves to question?

Why do kids ask so many questions? (And how do we *really* feel about that?)

A few years ago, the American comedian Louis C.K. wrote a bit for his stand-up act that focused on children and questioning. It starts with a description of a beleaguered mother and her young child, at McDonald's. The child asks why the sky is blue, and the parent snaps, "Just shut up and eat your french fries!" Louis explains to the audience that while this might seem to be harsh, the reality is "You can't answer a kid's question; they don't accept any answer." If you do try to answer, you only end up caught in an endless circle of Why questions—as he then demonstrates by recounting a conversation with his own young daughter.

It starts innocently enough ("Papa, why can't we go outside?"), but eventually Louis is asked to explain why it's raining, why clouds form, why he doesn't *know* why clouds form, why he didn't pay attention in school, why his parents didn't care about his education, and why their parents before that were just as bad. It devolves down to Louis's trying to explain to his child why "we're alone in the universe, and nobody gives a s— about us." It ends, inevitably, with his telling his child, "Shut up and eat your french fries!"

The bit nicely captures a truth that any parent—or anyone who's been around kids of a certain age—has experienced many times over. What makes it funny, though, is the comedian's brutally candid description of how frustrating it can be to be on the receiving end of kids' questions. The adult, in this case, becomes exasperated, insecure, aware of his own ignorance, and reminded of his insignificance—all because of that word *why*. As Louis C.K. makes clear, we may profess to admire kids' curiosity, but at some point we just don't welcome those questions anymore.

Maybe we're simply worn out by the sheer volume of inquiry among young children. According to Paul Harris, a Harvard child psychologist and author, research shows that a child asks about forty thousand questions between the ages of two and five. During that three-year span, Harris says, a shift occurs in the kind of questions being asked: from simple factual ones (name of object) to the first requests for explanations by thirty months. By age four, the lion's share of the questions are seeking explanations, not just facts.

As this is happening, rapid brain growth is occurring. At the University of Washington, advanced brain-scan technology shows connections forming in young brains (some of the lab's work is featured in Tiffany Shlain's fascinating film *Brain Power: From Neurons to Networks*). The lab's scans reveal an explosion of connections (synapses) between neurons in young children's brains—amounting to about a quadrillion connections, or more than three times the number found in an adult brain. Kids' brains are constantly connecting stimuli or thoughts. And as they're making these mental connections, they're seeking more information and clarification by way of questioning.

Not that it's easy for a child to ask a question. Harris has described it as "a series of complex mental maneuvers." It starts with knowing that you don't know. The asking of a question also indicates that the child understands there are various possible answers: "When they ask what's for dinner, they can imagine that it might be soup or pasta," Harris writes in his book *Trusting What You're Told*. "Without the ability to conceive of more than one possible way that things might stand in the world, why ask a question?" Lastly, it means children have figured out an efficient way to fill this gap in their knowledge—by asking someone who might know.

As children venture out into the world—synapses firing in their heads—they constantly encounter things they cannot classify or label. As the children's neurologist Stewart Mostofsky puts it, they have not yet developed "mental models" to categorize things, so part of what they're doing when questioning is asking adults to help them with this huge job of categorizing what they experience around them, labeling it, putting it in the proper file drawers of the brain.

Why is the sky blue?

It may be the ultimate child's question, one that every parent is asked at some point. If you find it hard to answer, you are in good company: Great minds from Aristotle to Isaac Newton grappled with this query over a span of several centuries, notes Nicholas Christakis, writing for edge.org. Christakis credits Newton and his light-refraction experiments with first showing that "white light could be decomposed into its constituent colors." But this only raised another question: *What might refract more blue light towards our eyes?* Scientists eventually learned that the way incident light interacts with gas molecules in the air causes the light in the blue part of the spectrum to scatter more. Meanwhile, biologists identified another contributing factor: our eyes are more sensitive to blue. As Christakis observes, much of the world of science is contained "in a question that a young child can ask."

When innovators talk about the virtues of beginner's mind or *neoteny*, to use the term favored by MIT Media Lab's Joi Ito, one of the desirable things they're referring to is that state where you see things without labels, without categorization. Because once

things have been labeled and filed, they become known quanti-
ties—and we don't think about them, may not even notice them.

Somewhere between ages four and five, children are ideally
suited for questioning: They have gained the language skills to ask,
their brains are still in an expansive, highly connective mode, and
they're seeing things without labels or assumptions. They're perfect
explorers. The physicist Neil deGrasse Tyson talks about young
children being scientists because they turn over rocks and mash
things together; Harvard's Harris points out that they're also like
anthropologists—they don't just conduct experiments, they ask
the people around them questions.

People tend to think that kids don't care much about the
answers—that, as Louis C.K. suggests in his "Why?" routine,
no matter what you answer, they're just going to ask Why again.
But they do, in fact, seem to care very much about the answers
they get. A recent University of Michigan study found that
when preschoolers ask Why, they're not just trying to annoy
adults or simply prolong a conversation—"they're trying to get
to the bottom of things." In the studies, when kids were given
actual explanations, they either agreed and were satisfied, or
they asked a follow-up question; whereas if they didn't get a
good answer, they were more likely to be dissatisfied and to
repeat the original question.

The INSEAD professor and questioning expert Hal Gregersen
says that if you watch closely what's happening when kids ask
adults questions, "the reason kids ask 'why' over and over again
is often because *we* don't understand their questions, or we're just
not listening. And by asking over and over, they're saying to us,
in effect, *'You are not hearing me—you're not understanding what
I'm asking.'*"

As CHILDREN BEGIN preschool, a curious change starts to happen
around questioning. Preschoolers are entering a stimulation-rich
environment, surrounded by other presumably inquisitive kids,
with ready access to an adult question-answerer known as the
teacher—seemingly ideal conditions for questioning. Yet they

immediately begin to ask fewer questions, according to Harris, who cites studies done in various cultures around the world, all showing the same result. He theorizes that a "comfort" factor is at work here; at home with a parent, children are more willing to share their questions than they are at preschool.

But even so, preschoolers are still asking questions at a higher rate than older schoolkids. Most preschool environments are relatively unstructured and allow for more free-form play and exploration—which may be key to helping kids maintain their propensity to inquire and learn at this level.

Interestingly, the more preschool models itself after regular school—the more it becomes a venue for loading kids up with information and feeding them answers to questions they have not yet asked—the more it seems to squelch their natural curiosity. The child psychologist Alison Gopnik has been outspoken in criticizing the trend of turning preschool into school—which, she notes, is driven by overambitious parents and (in the United States, at least) by federal mandates requiring more standardized teaching in preschool.

When we start teaching too much, too soon, says Gopnik, we're inadvertently cutting off paths of inquiry and exploration that kids might otherwise pursue on their own. As Gopnik puts it, "Children are the research and development division of the human species." If they are permitted to do that research—to raise and explore their own questions, through various forms of experimentation, and without being burdened with instructions—they exhibit signs of more creativity and curiosity.

Gopnik says young kids learn in much the same way scientists do, by exploring and experimenting, and that we should beware of trends toward more structured and academic early-childhood programs. That academic rigor comes soon enough, as students begin grade school—which is when questioning by kids really starts to disappear.

Why does questioning fall off a cliff?

In 2010, Professor Kyung-Hee Kim at William & Mary College observed that results of creativity tests given at schools in the United States, using the well-known Torrance system, had begun to decline in 1990—and had been dropping since. This finding triggered a wave of articles in the U.S. media, including a *Newsweek* cover story, "The Creativity Crisis," which focused on the complex question of how to address this problem by doing a better job teaching creativity to children. Amid the article's deep discussion of creativity and neuroscience—covering neural networks, differences between right- and left-brain functions, and the relationship between divergent and convergent thinking—was a throwaway line buried deep in the piece that seemed, to me, to cut to the heart of the matter: "Preschool children, on average, ask their parents about 100 questions a day. By middle school, they've pretty much stopped asking."

If you chart what happens to kids' questioning—and the Right Question Institute has done that, using data from the 2009 U.S. "Nation's Report Card"—it looks as if questioning (denoted by the solid line in the chart) falls off a cliff, even as children's use of reading and writing skills steadily climbs through the school years.

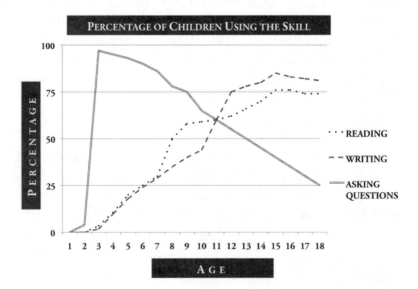

That steep decline in questioning might not be alarming, in and of itself: One might conclude that children just don't need to question as much once they're reading and writing (and texting and googling). But the problem is, as kids stop questioning, they simultaneously become less engaged in school. When the engagement level of students is measured, as in a recent Gallup study, we see the same falling-off-the-cliff phenomenon as students move from elementary school through high school. (When Gallup released this study in early 2013, at the same time as the American "fiscal cliff" crisis, the author Daniel Pink asked on his blog, "Does the 'student cliff' matter more than the fiscal cliff?").

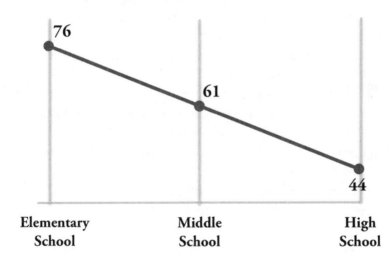

THE SCHOOL CLIFF:
STUDENTS' ENGAGEMENT DROPS OVER TIME

● = % Engaged

76

61

44

| Elementary School | Middle School | High School |

This suggests there may be a relationship—which many teachers could tell you without needing to conduct a formal study—between students asking questions and their being engaged and interested in learning. Admittedly, there's a bit of a chicken-and-egg situation here: Do kids stop questioning because they've lost interest in school, or do they lose interest in school because their natural curiosity (and propensity to question) is somehow tamped down?

I've asked that question of a number of children's neurologists and psychologists, as well as teachers and education experts. Clearly, various factors can influence kids' question-asking and their curiosity levels as they grow up. For instance, at around age five, the brain starts trimming back some of those neural connections that were expanding so rapidly the first few years; this "synaptic pruning" could translate to less questioning and less wondering about the surrounding world. Also, as we develop mental models of that world—with more categorization, more labels—we have less need to ask "What's this?" and "What's that?"

But many educators and learning experts contend that our current system of education does not encourage, teach, or in some cases even *tolerate* questioning. Harvard's Tony Wagner says, "Somehow, we've defined the goal of schooling as enabling you to have more 'right answers' than the person next to you. And we penalize incorrect answers. And we do this at a pace—especially now, in this highly focused test-prep universe—where we don't have time for extraneous questions."

Wagner told me that he often sits in on classes to observe the questioning dynamic. "I was in a seventh-grade science class and this kid started asking all kinds of questions about the universe and stars—and the teacher was just trying to say, 'Look, here are the planets, now memorize this.' And this was powerful to me. The message was that in this class 'we don't have time for questions—because that will take time away from the number of answers I have to cover.'"

To be fair, many teachers feel helpless in the face of this. As one California high school teacher lamented, "I have so many state standards I have to teach conceptwise, it takes away time from what I find most valuable—which is to have [students] inquire about the world."

Dominic Randolph, principal of the Riverdale Country

School in New York, uses the corporate term *product-driven* to describe many of today's schools. Under pressure to improve test scores, they've tried to instill businesslike efficiency into a process designed to impart as much information as possible to students, within a given time frame—leaving little or no time for student inquiry.

When teachers are under this kind of pressure to follow mandated guidelines, it can cause them to be less receptive to students' ideas or inquiries—as one researcher demonstrated in a fascinating study. Susan Engel of Williams College did an experiment with two sets of teachers: One group was not given specific guidelines on how to teach a science class, while the other group was "subtly encouraged" to follow a worksheet. The first group of teachers tended to respond with interest and encouragement when students expressed their own ideas. The second group said things like "Wait a minute. That's not on the instructions." Engel concluded that "teachers are very susceptible to external influences; their understanding of the goal of teaching directly affects how they respond when children spontaneously investigate."

Why do we want kids to "sit still" in class?

As normal twelve-year-olds, the sixth-grade students at Marine Elementary School near Minneapolis tended to squirm, slump, kick, and fidget in their seats—they had an abundance of energy, and controlling it required them to focus so much on sitting still they had trouble concentrating on their schoolwork. Their teacher Abby Brown wondered: *What if they didn't have to sit still?* Brown learned from the latest research at the Mayo Clinic about "activity-permissive education," which advocates letting kids move as they learn. Brown then helped design a new kind of school desk with a raised seat that puts the user in a semi-standing position and allows more freedom of movement. With the new desks, her students' attentiveness immediately improved—and Brown's creation is being looked at as a model for other classrooms.

WHILE SOME OF the problems involving overloaded curriculum and "teaching to the test" seem to have been exacerbated in recent years, the more general problem of schools favoring memorized answers over creative questions is nothing new. Some point out that it's built into an educational system that was created in a different time, the Industrial Age, and for a different purpose.

As a number of education critics have pointed out, schools in many industrialized nations were not, for the most part, designed to produce innovative thinkers or questioners—their primary purpose was to produce workers. The author Seth Godin writes, "Our grandfathers and great grandfathers built schools to train people to have a lifetime of productive labor as part of the industrialized economy. And it worked."

To create good workers, education systems put a premium on compliancy and rote memorization of basic knowledge—excellent qualities in an industrial worker. (Or, as the cartoonist and *Simpsons* creator Matt Groening puts it, "It seems the main rule that traditional schools teach is how to sit in rows quietly, which is perfect training for grown-up work in a dull office or factory, but not so good for education.")

And not so good for questioning: To the extent a school is like a factory, students who inquire about "the way things are" could be seen as insubordinate. It raises, at least in my mind, a question that may seem extreme: *If schools were built on a factory model, were they actually designed to squelch questions?*

LOGICALLY, AS WE move from an industrial society to more of an entrepreneurial one, it makes sense that we would want to trade in the factory/obedience model of schooling for more of a questioning model. But as the world changed and the workplace changed with it, the old educational model hasn't evolved much—and for the most part hasn't adapted to the modern economy's need for more creative, independent-thinking "workers."

Godin and others believe that in attempting to modernize old models of schooling, we should start by asking some basic questions about purpose. Godin offers up this query as a starting point: *What are schools for?* (That question could also be phrased as *Why are we sending kids to school in the first place?*)

With all the current debate around education reform—discussions of conflicting models for schools, competing educational philosophies, differing ideas of how to test, design curricula, evaluate teachers—somehow the fundamental Why questions, which can help frame a larger discussion, don't seem to come up much.

If we do stop to consider Godin's question, although there's no one answer to it, many would agree that at least part of the answer could be summed up as "To prepare students to be productive citizens in the twenty-first century."

That, in turn, raises another fundamental question: *What kind of preparation does the modern workplace and society demand of its citizens—i.e., what kind of skills, knowledge, and capabilities are needed to be productive and thrive?*

The answer to that, again, is not simple, but among those who've studied the needs of the evolving workplace from an educational standpoint—and two people at the forefront are Tony Wagner and John Seely Brown—the consensus seems to be that this new world demands citizens who are self-learners; who are creative and resourceful; who can adjust and adapt to constant change. Both Wagner and Brown put "questioning" at the top of the list of key survival skills for the new marketplace.

(As for skills *not* needed in this new environment? Ability to memorize and repeat back facts—because, as noted in the last chapter, new technology puts many of those facts at our fingertips, eliminating the need for memorization. Indeed, this prompts another of Godin's provocative questions: *Should we abandon the failed experiment of teaching facts?*)

If we simply zoom in on that one Why question regarding the basic purpose of schools, and if we agree that one of their primary purposes is to enable a twenty-first-century citizen to be a lifelong learner, able to adapt to constant change in the modern world . . . and if we also acknowledge that the ability to question effectively is among the most important of the critical skills needed . . . this question naturally arises:

What if our schools could train students to be better lifelong learners and better adapters to change, by enabling them to be better questioners?

How might we create such a school?

To start answering those questions—attempting to envision a school of tomorrow with questioning baked in at its core—it is instructive to glance back at New York's Harlem neighborhood in the 1970s, where a substitute-teacher-turned-principal named Deborah Meier created a radical model for a school designed to foster inquiry.

Can a school be built on questions?

In education circles, Meier, now in her eighties, is seen as a legendary figure. A pioneer of the "small schools" movement that emerged several decades ago, she was the first educator to receive a MacArthur "genius" award in recognition of her work at the groundbreaking Central Park East schools in New York.

Today Meier remains involved with a number of schools she started in the Northeast and writes a popular blog about education, where she poses unfailingly interesting questions:

Is a test-driven education the most likely path for producing an inventive and feisty citizenry?

What would it look and sound like in the average classroom if we wanted to make "being wrong" less threatening?

And this one, which I particularly like: *What might the potential for humans be if we really encouraged that spirit of questioning in children, instead of closing it down?*

I asked Meier about that second question, and she said it originally popped into her head about forty years ago, when a third-grade student at her Harlem school said to her, "What's different about this school is you're interested in what we *don't* know, not just what we do know." Meier was very taken with that comment; it confirmed to her, more than any of the impressive test results her school was achieving, that she was doing what she'd set out to do when she started the Central Park East schools.

Meier opened the first of her schools in 1974 in a dilapidated, old school building in East Harlem, an area that, at the time, "epitomized the collapse of the New York City school system," according to Seymour Fliegel, a former school official in that district. Meier was herself the product of a tony New York private-school education. After getting her master's degree she eventually found herself teaching in a Chicago public school and was dismayed by the conditions. She began working on experimental approaches to education, which brought her to the attention of a New York school superintendent—who, faced with a desperate situation in Harlem, offered Meier a chance to try out some of her ideas.

Meier felt that instead of just pushing information at kids, schools needed to teach them how to make sense of what they were being told so they would know what to make of it and what to do with it. She said in an interview at the time, "My concern is with how students become critical thinkers and problem solvers, which is what a democratic society needs."

Five learning skills, or "habits of mind," were at the core of her school, and each was matched up with a corresponding question:

Evidence: *How do we know what's true or false? What evidence counts?*

Viewpoint: *How might this look if we stepped into other shoes, or looked at it from a different direction?*

Connection: *Is there a pattern? Have we seen something like this before?*

Conjecture: *What if it were different?*

Relevance: *Why does this matter?*

Meier's core questions came out of her own connective inquiry; they blended elements of her early education in an Ethical Culture school with ideas she picked up from other well-known education innovators, including John Dewey, Jean Piaget, and Theodore Sizer.

Before settling on her five habits of mind, Meier started with two particular ways of thinking she wanted to emphasize—skepticism and empathy. "I believe you have to have an open-mindedness to the possibility that you're wrong, or that anything may be wrong," she said. "I've always been very concerned with democracy. If you can't imagine you could be wrong, what's the point of democracy? And if you can't imagine how or why others think differently, then how could you tolerate democracy?"

As Meier established her question-based schools, the classes were run in unorthodox ways, with students given much more autonomy and freedom. Upon visiting in the late seventies, Fliegel encountered "an astonishingly rich educational program," which, for example, "included extensive mapmaking, studies of Native American woodlands culture in seventeenth century Harlem, Egyptian and Roman history, the Dutch settlement of New York, printing and newspapers, the emergence of cities (including a mini-study of the neighborhood around the school) and African American history."

A third-grade class studying medieval society "not only read books but built castles and made armor," while a first-grade class "developed the idea of building a mythical city." Students were taken to the local museums and studied nature in Central Park; Meier felt that "outside the classroom children tend to observe things more keenly and ask more questions."

In some ways, Meier was trying to extend the kindergarten experience through all grades. Teaching kindergarten "was such an extraordinary intellectual experience, and I thought, *Why couldn't we just keep doing that?*" Only in kindergarten, she told me, "do we put up with kids asking questions that are off-topic."

Meier learned to listen carefully to students' questions, finding that they often contained insights that prompted her to rethink her own assumptions and occasionally reconsider the curriculum. "We had one of those world maps with the U.S. right in the middle—remember those? And one of the students looked at it and said, *How come the East Indies are in the west?* And that question got me thinking about the impact of what you put in the center, and what it does to everything else. And it became part of our curriculum. It had so many implications for how you see yourself."

PERHAPS NOT SURPRISINGLY, the students warmed to Meier's approach—but the parents were another story. Some did not know what to make of the unorthodox lessons and the kids' autonomy; an environment such as the one Meier created suggested to some a lack of discipline and structure. As Meier pointed out decades later, however, while it's counterintuitive to many teachers and school administrators, often when you give kids more freedom to pursue what they're interested in, they become easier to control. The much harder thing is forcing them to sit still for five hours and pay attention to information they don't care about.

The complaints at the time led to an inquiry. Fliegel (who wrote about his experience several years later) was sent by the school superintendent to investigate. He came away thoroughly impressed and recommended that the school board back Meier, which it did. In the years that followed, the remarkable success of the Central Park East schools became evident. Over the next decade, in a city with a dropout rate that ranged between 40 and 60 percent, only 1 percent of Meier's students failed to finish secondary school.

MEIER'S QUESTION-DRIVEN SCHOOLS struggled after she left, and there were few imitators—until recently. Today, around the world, a growing number of schools are embracing some of the principles Meier was trying to teach: that students must develop the "habit" of learning and questioning, that knowledge cannot be force-fed to them. But such schools still represent just a "drop in the bucket" in terms of the overall education system, notes Nikhil Goyal, New York–based author of a book on modernizing schools.

Goyal began studying high schools while still attending one himself. A few years ago, when he was a sixteen-year-old junior at a Long Island high school, he became frustrated with his uninspiring school experience and wondered, *Isn't there anything better than this?* So he started examining other schools, across the country. I met him when, at seventeen, he was in the midst of his research; he had found the Beautiful Question website and, since he loves asking questions, offered to be one of the site's inquiry researchers. But he helped me most in providing a crash course on the current state of inquiry-based schools.

Goyal studied schools such as Brightworks and High Tech High, both in California, as well as a handful of others (some public, some private). He was well versed in the approaches of the famously successful schools of Finland and knew that Singapore's schools also were breaking new ground.

Among the schools he studied up close, Goyal was thrilled by what he found. Some of them had no grades, no tests—none of the memorization of facts that dominated his own school experience. Students got to work on interesting projects, sometimes of their own choosing, lasting for months. At Brightworks, "the entire curriculum is based around big questions." Goyal said he thought one of the best things about these project-based or inquiry-based schools is that they got students to ask introspective questions such as *What's interesting to me?* "Nobody's ever asked them that before," Goyal said.

Many of the schools doing inquiry-based learning are still too new to judge whether they are turning out extra successful or productive adults (however one might measure that). But we do know that some of their core principles—the emphasis on letting students explore, direct their own learning, and work on projects instead of taking tests—can also be found at Montessori schools, which have been around long enough to have a track record of adult success stories.

And what a track record Montessori has. Today, so many former students of this private-school system (which only teaches as high as eighth grade) are now running major companies in the tech sector that these alumni have become known as the Montessori Mafia. Their ranks include Wikipedia founder Jimmy Wales, Jeff Bezos of Amazon, and the cofounders of Google, Sergey Brin and

Larry Page. (The former Google executive Marissa Mayer—now the head of Yahoo!—has said that Brin's and Page's Montessori schooling, though long ago, remained a defining influence. "You can't understand Google unless you know that Larry and Sergey were both Montessori kids," according to Mayer. "They're always asking, *Why should it be like that?* It's the way their brains were programmed early on.")

Montessori is private, expensive, and exclusive; so are some of the other inquiry-based schools, and those that are public are few and far between. In terms of schools offering this approach, "we're probably talking about less than one percent of the overall school system," Goyal points out.

At the vast majority of schools, teachers who wish to encourage more inquiry by students must engage in small acts of defiance—going off-script in their lessons, sometimes revising the standard texts and teaching materials. Dan Meyer, a high

Why do movie tickets cost the same for hits or duds?

Challenging students to grapple with real-life questions can help them to grasp abstract concepts, notes Cornell business school professor Robert H. Frank. That's why Frank asks his pupils to "pose an interesting question based on something they have observed or experienced—and then employ basic economic principles in an attempt to answer it." Case in point: Frank's student Peter Hlawitschka asked, *Why do tickets for popular Broadway shows command premium prices, while movie theaters charge the same price no matter how hot the show is?* Hlawitschka's explanation, as shared by Frank in a *New York Times* article, is that unlike on Broadway, additional copies of a popular movie can be inexpensively made and shown many times a day on multiple screens. With low prices, movie theater owners can fill many more seats and generate far more revenue than if they charged premium prices for a more limited number of screenings.

school math teacher in New York, tells a story in a popular TEDx talk about how he had to devise his own methods to encourage his students to ask their own questions and formulate their own problems.

Meyer pointed out that a typical lesson on the problem of "How long will it take to fill a water tank?" provides far too many tips and hints along the way. Meyer decided to "eliminate all the substeps given to kids, so they have to figure it out. Instead of telling them what matters, they need to decide what matters."

At first, Meyer began to strip a lot of the text out of his

teaching materials, giving kids less, so they would have to ask and think more. Then he came up with an even better idea: He showed his class a video of a water tank filling up . . . "agonizingly slowly," he says. Students began to "look at their watches, rolling their eyes. And they're all wondering, at some point, 'Man, how long is it gonna take to fill up?' That's how you know you've baited the hook."

Who is entitled to ask questions in class?

What Dan Meyer did in showing the video and then holding back as he waited for that question to form in students' heads was to transfer ownership: Instead of asking the question himself, he allowed students to think of it on their own—at which point it became *their* question.

This is not insignificant, for two reasons. As Meyer understood, if a student thinks of a question him/herself, it is likely to be of more interest than someone else's question. But this issue of "Who gets to ask the questions in class?" touches on purpose, power, control, and, arguably, even race and social class.

Dennie Palmer Wolf, a professor of education at Brown University, examined the role of questioning in schools for her academic paper "The Art of Questioning" and found that teachers tended "to monopolize the right to question" in classrooms. (To the extent that students shared in that privilege, Wolf cited research showing that it was "the private preserve of the few—the bright, the male, the English-speaking.") Moreover, Wolf's research found that questions were often used by teachers primarily to check up on students, rather than to try to spark interest; such questions were apt to leave a student feeling "exposed" rather than inspired.

John Seely Brown points out that questioning by students can easily come to be seen as a threat by some teachers. "If you come from the belief that teachers are meant to be authoritative, then teachers are going to tend to want to cut off questioning that might reveal what they don't know."

Deborah Meier thinks the desire to control students and maintain order isn't necessarily coming just from teachers. At one point in my talk with her, I mentioned that today's business culture—with its ad messages promoting "break the rules" and "think different" messages—seems to embrace the same independent-thinking ethos that Meier tried to instill in the grade schoolers in Harlem several decades ago. But when I suggested to Meier that perhaps the establishment had caught up with her ideals—that, with our new hunger for innovation, we might be more willing today to tolerate, and possibly even teach, questioning—she had her doubts.

She believes we continue to live in a society that wants questions to be asked by some, but not others. "Yes, we want a Silicon Valley," she said, "but do we really want three hundred million people who actually think for themselves?"

When Meier started teaching in urban schools, she was dismayed to find that low-income children, in particular, "were trained *not* to ask questions in school," and she doesn't think that has changed much in the ensuing years. The discouraging may not be deliberate in most cases. Teachers under pressure to cover more material, and particularly those in under-funded, overcrowded urban schools, can face formidable challenges in trying to manage large classrooms. The imperative to maintain order and "just get through the lesson" can be at odds with allowing kids to question.

What is a flame?

It seems such a simple question, but do you know the answer? Actor Alan Alda had been fascinated with that question as a child. Nearly seventy years later, Alda started the Alan Alda Center for Communicating Science at Stony Brook University in New York and he started off by organizing a contest to see who could best explain *What is a flame?* The kicker: Kids age nine to twelve would serve as the judges. More than eight hundred scientists or science buffs took up the challenge; the winner, physicist Benjamin Ames, made a seven-minute animated music video explaining oxygen, carbon, hydrogen, incandescence, and oxidation (with atoms represented by Legos). You might say Alda and Ames answered another beautiful question: *How do you make science enjoyable for kids?* The next question Alda's contest will take on: *What is time?* (See the winning answers at centerforcommunicatingscience.org.)

But other, subtle forces may be conspiring against student

questioning. For instance, children may be self-censoring their questions due to cultural pressures. Joshua Aronson of New York University has studied some of the difficulties that low-income minority students face, such as the disproportionate tendency of schools to suspend African-American boys. But Aronson has also conducted interesting research on what he calls "the stereotype threat." It zeroes in on the psychology of stigma, in particular "the way human beings respond to nega-tive stereotypes about their racial or gender group." Aronson studied standardized test performances among black, Latino, and female college students, and his findings suggest that when a person perceives him/herself as the target of a well-known stereotype (e.g., girls aren't good at math), it can have an adverse effect on performance in school.

Would students who are battling against stereotypes be less inclined to interrupt lessons by asking questions, revealing to the rest of the class that they don't know something? "Absolutely," Aronson said. "Fear is the enemy of curiosity. Unfortunately, if you're in that situation, you may feel pressure to look a certain way to others." That can cause students to act as if they already know or just don't care. "You're inclined to play it safe," Aronson says, rather than risk the possibility of confirming the stereotype.

Parents, too, undoubtedly play a role in determining which kids ask questions in school. A recent study of fourth- and fifth-grade students by Indiana University sociologist Jessica McCrory Calarco found that students from families with higher incomes were more likely to be encouraged by their parents to ask questions at school, whereas children from modest backgrounds were encouraged by their parents to be more deferential to authority—and to try to figure things out for themselves, instead of asking for help. "Even very shy middle-class children learned to feel comfortable approaching teachers with questions, and recognized the benefits of doing so," Calarco reports. "Working-class children instead worried about making teachers angry if they asked for help at the wrong time or in the wrong way, and also felt others would judge them as not smart if they asked for help." These differences, Calarco found, stemmed directly from what "children learn from their parents at home."

Deborah Meier, however, bristled at those findings. "The study makes it sound as if those lower-income parents are wrong, but they're *not* wrong," she said. "They know that if their kids ask questions, they might get in trouble. They're telling their children to be careful in school." The middle-class kids are in a different situation, Meier notes. "They go to school feeling safe." And because they feel safe, they can take the risk of raising their hands.

BUT EVEN THE "safe" middle-class student who has been encouraged by parents to question may still find that the typical classroom environment doesn't stimulate curiosity or inspire inquiry. One of the "master questioners" I interviewed was a fifteen-year-old high school student, Jack Andraka, who, through his own remarkable journey of inquiry, was able to develop a new, highly effective, and inexpensive way to screen for certain types of cancer. (The full story of how Andraka used questions to solve the problem is in the next chapter.) I was curious whether someone such as Andraka, who clearly is inclined to question, learned to do so in school, and whether he tended to ask a lot of questions there.

He said his parents taught him to question. "They would ask me questions, and they would get me to ask them questions— but then they would never answer the questions they guided me to," Andraka told me. "They would instead have me go and explore through experiments or personal experience and make a hypothesis."

At school—which Andraka described as "your ordinary public high school," located in Maryland—"we really do not have students ask enough questions and do enough exploration by themselves. The teacher tells you what to do and you do it. You're really restricted with these tight guidelines. In my opinion, that's not the best way to learn."

I asked Andraka whether his classmates asked a lot of questions. "In my high school, to be quote-unquote cool, you're typically very quiet and sit in the corner, and you might snicker among your friends every now and then. So that, to me, is pretty boring." As for himself, Andraka said, "Either I'm extremely quiet and working on something else like trying to find a new way to test for pancreatic cancer, for example, or I'm basically answering every single question. But I don't ask questions like 'What would happen if this happens?' I do that on my own—I do all of my exploring outside of school. Because in school it's not allowed and that just . . . really sucks."

IF EVEN A born-and-bred questioner such as Andraka isn't asking questions in school, it suggests a fundamental problem. Dan Rothstein and Luz Santana of the Right Question Institute say it's no mystery what's going on: Even in the most progressive schools, questioning is still primarily the domain of the teacher. "Questions are used a lot in the classroom but it's mostly one-way," says Rothstein. "It's not about the student asking, it's about the teacher prompting the student by using questions that the teacher has formulated." By taking this approach, Rothstein says, teachers "have inadvertently contributed to the professionalization of asking questions—to the idea that only the people who know more are allowed to ask."

After two decades of studying and teaching questioning, Rothstein and Santana hope their three-year-old Right Question Institute—young as a toddler, and just as enamored of questions—can help shift the balance of power in classrooms by putting the kids in charge of the questions.

If we're born to inquire, then why must it be taught?

When the Boston high school teacher Ling-Se Peet used the Right Question Institute's "Question Formulation Technique" for the first time in her humanities class, she began by laying out a provocative premise to her twenty-five students: *Torture can be justified.*

In the parlance of Rothstein and Santana, this opening statement is known as a Q-focus because its purpose is to provide a focal point for generating questions from the students. Peet's class was divided into small groups, and each group's initial task was to come up with as many questions as possible, within a time limit, pertaining to that statement.

After reviewing a set of rules (write each question down, don't debate or try to answer questions, just keep trying to think of more questions), the students in each group began to come at that premise from a variety of angles. Some questions aimed at bringing clarity to the issue: *How do you define torture? When is torture used?* Some were offbeat yet intriguing: *Can torture make you happy?* Other questions expanded the scope of the discussion: *Does torture have anything to do with justice? Who are most likely to be tortured?*

The kids had no experience doing this type of questioning exercise, but according to Peet, after some initial reservations about the rules (some felt that questions ought to be answered as soon as they were raised), the questions began to flow freely within each group, with each written down by a group member. Then the students were directed to the second stage of the exercise: They were instructed to change open questions to closed ones, and vice versa—so that, for example, an open question that began as *Why is torture effective?* might be changed to a closed one: *Is torture effective?* The purpose of this part of the exercise, according to Rothstein, is to show that a question can be narrowed down in some cases, or expanded in others. As students do this, he says, they begin to see that "the way you ask a question yields different results and can lead you in different directions."

Next, the students were asked to "prioritize" their questions: to figure out which three were the most important to move the discussion forward. Rothstein and Santana stress the importance of this "convergent" part of questioning. They feel it's not enough to encourage students to toss out questions endlessly; to question effectively, they must learn how to analyze their own questions and zero in on ones they would like to pursue further.

Some of the questions from the student groups that made it through to this final stage included *Why does torture work? Who decides whether torture should be justified or not? How can someone's pain be the price for the outcome you want?*

By the end of the session, Rothstein observed, some of the kids "looked spent." The process is difficult, he acknowledges, because "it requires them to do something they've never done—to think in questions." But in this class, and in others where the Right Question Institute's technique has been tried, a high level of engagement among students has been observed. This may be partly because Rothstein and Santana cleverly designed the process with gamelike rules (only questions allowed; any nonquestion must be turned into a question) that inject an element of play into it. And perhaps questions, by their very nature, invite and allow for more participation by more kids throughout the class. You don't have to know the answer to ask a question, so the smart kids don't dominate. Rothstein thinks it also has something to do with the students' tendency to quickly become invested in the questions they've thought of on their own. "The 'ownership' part of this is very important," he said. "We've had kids say that when you ask your own question, you then feel like it's your job to get the answer."

THE QUESTION PROCESS Rothstein and Santana developed was years in the making. It didn't start out being for kids in school—it was originally intended to help adults use questioning more effectively in their dealings with government bureaucrats, doctors, landlords, and school officials.

Luz Santana knew from firsthand experience that those who don't know how to ask the right questions are vulnerable to being denied that which they might need or are entitled to have. Santana migrated to the United States from Puerto Rico when she was in her twenties and, after initially being on welfare, found a job working in a factory. "Then I got laid off," she told me, "and as I tried to navigate the social services system to get into a job training program, I was denied."

Santana didn't know how to properly inquire as to *why* she was turned down; "I didn't know how to advocate for myself," she says.

She was fortunate that as she was being denied, another social worker intervened on her behalf, pointing out that Santana actually *was* qualified for the program. Santana entered the training program, got a job, simultaneously went back to school, and eventually earned a master's degree. But she never forgot that early lesson about the need for people, especially those disadvantaged, to be able to effectively speak up for themselves. She ended up going into social services work herself, as a housing advocate in the city of Lawrence, Massachusetts.

There she met Rothstein—who had a very different background (Kentucky bred, Harvard educated) but similar interests. Rothstein had gotten his doctorate in education at Harvard, where he was intrigued by this question:

What can the people thinking about social problems or making social policy learn from the people who are actually affected by those problems?

As Rothstein gravitated toward urban policy work, he became a director of neighborhood planning in Lawrence and met Santana at a gathering on housing problems in the city. Toward the end of the meeting, from the periphery of the room, Santana raised her hand and asked whether the city was getting enough input from the people actually affected by the housing problems being discussed. "And I thought that would have been a great question to *start* the meeting with," Rothstein recalls.

Subsequently, Rothstein asked for Santana's help with the launch of a high school dropout-prevention program in Lawrence. While working on the program, they became aware of a particular obstacle: parents clearly needed to be more involved in their children's education and in school policies affecting those kids—yet many of the parents refused to attend school meetings.

Rothstein and Santana logically asked, *Why?* "They told us they didn't go to the meetings because they didn't even know what questions to ask," Rothstein recalls.

This was a lightbulb moment for the two of them: *What if we could find a way to help parents ask better questions at school meetings?*

They had their What If question, but as they proceeded to the

How stage of trying to act on it, they took a wrong turn. Rothstein and Santana thought the most efficient way to help parents ask better questions at school meetings would be to supply them with those questions. So the two of them began compiling questions for various situations (questioning school budgetary decisions, questioning why a child was being suspended, etc.) and gave them to the parents to take to the meetings.

"We went to one of the meetings where the parents had these question lists," Santana recalls, "and they'd go up to the microphone and read questions from the list. But as soon as *they* were asked a question by someone from the school, they'd turn back to us, like, *What do I do now?*" Santana says she and her partner quickly understood their mistake: "We realized that the parents needed to think on their own—and come up with their own questions."

Rothstein and Santana began coaching parents how to do that. In particular, they taught them how to inquire about school decisions that most affected them—which meant probing the reasons behind the decisions, the process that led to those decisions, and the role parents could play in that process.

As the program went along, a few parents revealed something surprising: They were using these same questioning techniques in other situations, outside the school meetings—while trying to get information from a doctor in the emergency room, or in settling a dispute with a landlord.

This led Rothstein and Santana to begin to expand their question-teaching process and try it out in a variety of situations. They began working with health clinics, social services agencies, and adult education programs around the country. They found that their questioning techniques were being used by immigrant parents in New Mexico, residents at a homeless shelter in Louisville, and sugarcane-plantation workers in Hawaii. Rothstein and Santana formed a nonprofit organization, which, in 2011, came to be known as the Right Question Institute.

As their questioning technique was slowly gaining traction in adult education programs, something interesting happened: Adult-ed teachers reported that some adult students, upon learning the technique, were wondering, *Why didn't I learn this in high school?* Which, in turn, led to another What If moment for Rothstein and Santana:

What if we take our adult question-formulation program and adapt it for school-age kids?

Rothstein and Santana then designed a program for K–12 classrooms, broken down into a series of steps:

1. **Teachers design a Question Focus** (e.g., "Torture can be justified").
2. **Students produce questions** (no help from the teacher; no answering or debating the questions; write down every question; change any statements into questions).
3. **Students improve their questions** (opening and closing them).
4. **Students prioritize their questions.** They are typically instructed to come to agreement on three favorites.
5. **Students and teachers decide on next steps,** for acting on the prioritized questions.
6. **Students reflect on what they have learned.**

The process is designed to be simple enough that teachers can learn it in an hour, and students can grasp it immediately. However, making it simple was hard—that basic formula took about a decade to produce.

The RQI technique has drawn widespread praise from teachers. When her students start thinking in questions, observes the Boston high school teacher Marcy Ostberg, it "seems to unlock something for them." Rothstein says teachers have been lining up for RQI sessions at teacher conferences. "When they come to the sessions and learn about it," he said, "they're slapping their heads and saying, *How come we've never done this before?*"

THE SOCIAL CRITIC Neil Postman wondered about this more than two decades ago, when he wrote about the importance of questioning in education and posed this query of his own:

"Is it not curious, then, that the most significant intellectual skill available to human beings is not taught in schools?"

Rothstein was asked in a newspaper interview why there has been a long-standing failure to teach questioning, and whether it's because:

- We don't think it needs to be taught, or
- We don't know how to teach it.

"My answer to that is yes and yes," he said. Regarding that first rationale, Rothstein says that questioning is thought of simply as "a natural part of speech" and something people do instinctively. Many, including Deborah Meier, feel that kids are born questioners, and that we don't need to teach it—we just have to stop discouraging it. But Rothstein maintains that questioning is a more subtle and complex skill than many realize, involving three kinds of sophisticated thinking—divergent, convergent, and metacognitive. Some of it comes naturally to kids, but some must be learned and practiced. Since questioning seems to drop off at around age five, the innate questioning skills we start out with have long been neglected by junior high and high school. By that time, "the question-asking muscle," as Rothstein calls it, has atrophied and needs to be built up.

Can we teach ourselves to question?

If the question muscle has atrophied by junior high, imagine its condition by the time a student goes to college. Indeed, Rothstein's downward-sloping question-asking chart continues to plummet right through the college years. University professors I interviewed confirmed a dearth of student questions, even among bright Ivy Leaguers.

"For twenty years I've been teaching at the Harvard Business School," professor Clayton Christensen told me. "And I love this place, but the intuition to ask questions, the curiosity, is much less than twenty years ago." As to the cause: "If all you do as you're growing up is watch stuff on a screen—or go to school, where they give you the answers—then you don't develop the instinct for asking questions," Christensen said. "They don't know how to ask because it's never been asked of them."

William Deresiewicz, the acclaimed author and essayist who teaches at Yale University, cited another factor. "The college education that students are getting now, particularly at elite institutions, tends to be technocratic," he said. "They're trained to develop expertise in a particular area—trained to solve the problems that are particular to that area. It's about jumping through hoops, and mastering what's on the test. There's no time where students are asked to step back and think about what they're doing—and why they're doing it. What I'm seeing is a failure among these students to ask big questions about values and meaning and purpose. What we really need is for these kids—our future leaders—to learn how to ask those kinds of questions and not just technocratic ones."

How might parents make their kids better questioners?

In studying "master questioners," Hal Gregersen inquired about their childhoods and found that most had "at least one adult in their lives who encouraged them to ask provocative questions." The Nobel laureate scientist Isidor Isaac Rabi was one such child; when he came home from school, "while other mothers asked their kids *'Did you learn anything today?'* [my mother] would say, *'Izzy, did you ask a good question today?'*" Clayton Christensen thinks parents can help their kids be more inquisitive by posing what if questions "that invite children to think deeply about the world around them." But Christensen thinks it's also important to encourage kids to solve problems in a hands-on way, via challenging household tasks and chores. That worked for IDEO cofounder David Kelley. His career as a problem-solving designer was forged in a childhood home where "if the washing machine broke, you went and tried to make a new part to fix it."

Deresiewicz says the best professors can inspire that kind of inquiry, but they're rare. He cites as an example a favorite professor and mentor of his own, about whom Deresiewicz has written elegantly ("He had a young person's ability to see the world with fresh eyes. His white hair shot up off his forehead like a jolt of discovery"). I asked Deresiewicz what his professor did to spark inquiry.

"He had an ability to reframe things—to ask questions that got at something fundamental. Sometimes the questions almost seemed stupid; there's the idea of 'the holy fool' who asks the questions no one else will, and that was part of what he was doing." In doing this, Deresiewicz has written, his professor "was showing us that everything is open to question, especially the things we thought we already knew."

Importantly, the professor was also "willing to ask questions without knowing the answer. Teachers and professors, we think our authority rests on having answers. But students find it really liberating to have a teacher say, 'I don't know the answer—so let's figure this out together.'"

Is it possible the kind of Socratic teaching that Deresiewicz's professor did could make a comeback in the online world? That's what Sebastian Thrun is hoping. Thrun, known for developing Google's self-driving car and other tech breakthroughs, says he was never comfortable asking disruptive questions in his native Germany but found a much more receptive environment in Silicon Valley. While working at Google he also taught at Stanford University; in 2011, an artificial intelligence course he co-taught was offered online, and Thrun was surprised to see that tens of thousands signed up for it. Soon after, he made the jump from self-directed cars to self-directed learning. The online university he launched, Udacity, is one of a growing number of such programs that have been attracting attention (and mixed reviews) in the past few years. But one of the interesting things Thrun is trying to do with Udacity is to bring the Socratic method to online teaching.

The Udacity courses are designed not just to broadcast lectures but to inject thoughtful questioning at critical junctures, to get students thinking about what they're learning. As for encouraging students to ask their own questions, Thrun and one of his partners in the start-up, a former Google designer named Irene Au, insist that questioning is actually easier online—because anonymity helps. You don't have to be "that person" in the back of the huge lecture hall, trying to shout out a question at the end of class while others in the room are itching to exit. (One college professor recently observed that he'd never gotten as many student questions as when he began teaching online.)

Yale's Deresiewicz is skeptical. He points out the big difference between typing a question into your computer and asking a real, live professor (he also thinks the online college revolution is the first step in dismantling universities to get rid of the overhead of actual classrooms and teachers). He sees no substitute for the collaborative and unpredictable give-and-take between an assembled group of students and a learned master: "You can't improve on Socrates's invention," Deresiewicz concludes.

WHETHER OR NOT online courses provide an answer in and of themselves, they are part of a larger phenomenon in which more people of all ages are beginning to direct their own learning, exercising their questioning muscles—and doing so outside the established institutions of learning.

Nikhil Goyal thinks this is where the future of learning-by-inquiry is going to happen—not in schools ("I have no hope that the schools, for the most part, will change," he said), but in makeshift classrooms, often held in "maker" or "hacker" spaces where people come together to build and create.

John Seely Brown holds a similar view: "The kids who actually drop out of school or who view that the real learning happens after school, they're becoming part of this massive network of maker movements that is forming." The maker movement is mostly about building things (whether low-tech or high-tech), as well as creating art and music. But it's driven by project-based, peer-to-peer learning, which tends to happen as novice "makers" in the group question the more experienced ones. This is going on in basements, playgrounds, museums (San Francisco's Exploratorium recently established a maker space), and, perhaps most surprisingly, libraries. "Libraries are being remade as interesting maker spaces, with the librarian playing more of the role of the teacher of inquiry-based learning," Brown says.

Brown believes that young people may be honing better new-economy skills outside the classroom than in it; they're learning to create, experiment, build, question, and learn. So it may turn out that in a world of exponential change, "these are the kids who will have the skills to rise to the top."

In a sense, we're all "makers" now, or, at least, we would do well to think of ourselves that way. Whether or not we were ever properly taught how to question, we can develop the skill now, on our own, in our own spaces. One way to start is by looking at how other practiced questioners do it—focusing, in particular, on how they employ fundamental Why, What If, and How questions to solve problems and create change.

CHAPTER 3

The Why, What If, and How
of Innovative Questioning

Why . . .

WHY do we have to wait for the picture?

WHY does stepping back help us move forward?

WHY did George Carlin see things the rest of us missed?

WHY should you be stuck without a bed if I've got an extra air mattress?

WHY must we "question the question"?

What if . . .

WHAT IF we could map the DNA of music?

WHAT IF your brain is a forest, thick with trees? (And what if the branches touch?)

WHAT IF you sleep with a question? (Will you wake with an answer?)

WHAT IF your ideas are wrong and your socks don't match?

How . . .

HOW can we give form to our questions?

HOW do you build a tower that doesn't collapse (even after you put the marshmallow on top)?

HOW can you learn to love a broken foot?

HOW might we create a symphony together?

WHY . . .

Why do we have to wait for the picture?

Edwin Land was a brilliant inventor, sometimes described today as the Steve Jobs of his time. He was capable of seeing new possibilities—at times coming to him as detailed, fully formed visions—that others could not begin to imagine. Yet even Land couldn't see the life-changing opportunity he held in his own hands on a sunny winter's day in 1943. Rather, a question from a precocious three-year-old suddenly brought the future into focus.

Land was on vacation with his family in Santa Fe, New Mexico. He had taken some photographs of his young daughter, Jennifer, using his favorite camera. In those days, film had to be taken to a darkroom or a processing lab for development; Land knew this, as did any adult. But young Jennifer had a different take. She asked her father why they couldn't see the picture he had just taken without having to wait.

Land found he had no good answer for her. He took this as a challenge, a "puzzle she had set for me," as he described it.

"Stimulated by the dangerously invigorating plateau air," Land recalled in a speech years later, "I thought, *Why not? Why not design a picture that can be developed right away?*"

Land, then in his midthirties, was already used to tackling big questions. The two-time Harvard dropout had parlayed his fascination with light polarization into a modestly successful business. His technology, which allowed for filtering light and reducing glare, was used on sunglasses and photo filters. Land had bigger ambitions, hoping it could actually save lives: *What if we could reduce automobile accidents through polarized headlights and windshields?*

This idea, which Land explored during the 1930s and early 1940s, was to use polarization so that headlights, while still fully lighting the road ahead, would no longer blind drivers coming the other way. But Land couldn't get backing from the automakers, and by 1943 his company was slowing down and in need of a fresh innovation.

After Land spent a couple of hours thinking about Jennifer's query, he began to build upon her initial Why with a series of What If questions of his own. The fundamental challenge he faced could be summed up as *What if you could somehow have a darkroom inside a camera?*

According to Christopher Bonanos, author of *Instant: The Story of Polaroid*, Land knew that "it wouldn't do to have a tank of chemicals sloshing around inside a camera." But what if those chemicals "could be contained in little pouches, and then spread over the negative somehow?" This was one of a series of questions Land worked through during a feverish couple of hours spent walking by himself. He wondered, *How would one print a positive? How would you configure both negative film and positive paper in the back of the camera?*

Land wasted no time in giving form to the questions, and partial answers, swirling in his head. That very day he summoned a colleague and began to write out a detailed plan for an instant camera. He began creating prototypes so quickly that he produced the first instant test photo (a picture of himself) within a few months. But, facing hurdles and setbacks, too, Land's team had to struggle to get the first black-and-white instant camera to market by a promised introduction date four years later.

Land's own questions weren't even fully answered by then. From the outset, he had envisioned something greater than what he was able to deliver in 1948 in a splashy introduction. Land grappled with questions like *How can we do this in color? Why can't the camera be easier to use?* Another thirty years would pass before he answered those questions with his masterpiece: the color, one-button, even faster-printing SX-70.

The journey to answer his daughter's beautiful question may have been long and arduous at times, but Land was primed and ready for the trip. A year before Jennifer's question and Land's feverish walk, in December of 1942, he had said to Polaroid employees, "If you dream of something worth doing and then simply go to work on it . . . if you think of, detail by detail, what you have to do next, it is a wonderful dream even if the end is a long way off, for there are about five thousand steps to be taken before we realize it; and start making the first ten, and stay making twenty after, it is amazing how quickly you get through those five thousand steps."

THE POLAROID STORY is a favorite of innovators and questioners because it shows a number of interesting things about the dynamics of questioning. To begin with, it demonstrates that a game-changing question can come from anyone, even a naïve child. This underscores a point made earlier, that nonexperts or outsiders are often better at questioning than the experts. No one would argue that expert knowledge isn't valuable—but when it's time to question, it can get in the way.

The Polaroid tale also nicely illustrates the sequential inquiry process that can be triggered by a certain kind of catalytic question. This Why–What If–How progression—which can be identified in many stories of innovative breakthroughs—is clearly evident in the Polaroid example.

Land's worldview began to shift as soon as he (with prompting from Jennifer) looked at an existing, less-than-ideal reality and asked, in effect, *Why does it have to be that way?* This led to a blizzard of What If hypothetical queries as Land worked through many smaller questions in service of a larger one: *What if you could have a darkroom inside a camera?* He connected ideas and pieces of knowledge from his work in chemistry, optics, and engineering— the author Bonanos observes that everything Land knew seemed to come together. But all of that clever connective inquiry would have come to nothing if Land hadn't eventually proceeded to the How stage: getting his ideas down on paper, getting feedback on the idea, then beginning to create early, tangible versions of his camera-with-darkroom-inside; then testing those early versions, failing, revising, testing again.

I'M SURE LAND never thought of his creative process as being divided into Why, What If, and How stages. But the logic in this sequence reflects how people tend to approach and work through problems—progressing from becoming aware of and understanding the problem, to thinking of possible solutions, to trying to enact those solutions.

Each stage of the problem solving process has distinct challenges and issues—requiring a different mind-set, along with different types of questions. Expertise is helpful at certain points, not so helpful at others; wide-open, unfettered divergent thinking is critical at one stage, discipline and focus is called for at another. By thinking of questioning and problem solving in a more structured way, we can remind ourselves to shift approaches, change tools, and adjust our questions according to which stage we're entering.

If What If is about imagining and How is about doing, the initial Why stage has to do with seeing and understanding. The "seeing" part of that might seem easy—just open your eyes and look around, right? But Edwin Land couldn't see a problem that was right in front of him; at first only Jennifer could see it. That suggests those who would like to get better at asking Why have two options. You can conduct all business, including the business of everyday life, constantly accompanied by a curious and vocal three- or four-year-old, who will see what you miss. Or you can attempt to adjust the way you look at the world so that your perspective more closely aligns with that of a curious child. That second option is by no means easy—it takes some effort to see things with a fresh eye.

That's only part of what's required to ask powerful Why questions. To do so, we must:

- Step back.
- Notice what others miss.
- Challenge assumptions (including our own).
- Gain a deeper understanding of the situation or problem at hand, through contextual inquiry.
- Question the questions we're asking.
- Take ownership of a particular question.

While a fairly straightforward process, it begins by moving backward.

Why does stepping back help us move forward?

The term *stepping back* is often used when we talk about questioning—*step back and ask why, step back and reconsider*, and so forth. But what are we stepping back from?

It's not insignificant that Edwin Land was on vacation when the big Why question surfaced. He was removed from the day-to-day rush of his work. He had the time and the distance from practical business matters to entertain a question that was highly impractical. Meanwhile, Land's daughter, in asking her question, inspired him to pause briefly to consider reality from a naïve perspective. This points to a second, different kind of back step—his distancing himself from his own assumptions and expertise. For a moment, he stopped knowing and began to wonder.

To question well—in particular, to ask fundamental Why questions—we don't necessarily have to be on vacation, accompanied by a precocious three-year-old. But at least temporarily, it's necessary to stop *doing* and stop *knowing* in order to start asking.

The "doing" part would seem to be more in our control to stop than the "knowing"—yet it might be even harder. In a world that expects us to move fast, to keep advancing (if only incrementally), to just "get it done," who has time for asking why?

This is particularly true in the workplace. A good way to become unpopular in a business meeting is to ask, "Why are we doing this?"—even though the question may be entirely justified. It often takes a thick-skinned outsider to be willing to even try. George Lois, the renowned designer of iconic magazine covers and celebrated advertising campaigns, was also known for being a disruptive force in business meetings. It wasn't just that he was passionate in arguing for his ideas; the real issue, Lois recalls, was that often he was the only person in the meeting willing to ask why. The gathered business executives would be anxious to proceed on a course of action assumed to be sensible. While everyone else nodded in agreement, "I would be the only guy raising his hand to say, 'Wait a minute, this thing you want to do doesn't make any sense. Why the hell are you doing it this way?'"

Others in the room saw Lois to be slowing the meeting and stopping the group from moving forward. But Lois understood that the group was apt to be operating on habit—trotting out an idea or approach similar to what had been done in similar situations before, without questioning whether it was the best idea or the right approach in this instance. The group needed to be challenged to "step back" by someone like Lois—who had a healthy enough ego to withstand being the lone questioner in the room.

The pressure to keep moving forward—and the accompanying reluctance to step back and question—is not just a business phenomenon. As everyday life becomes more jam-packed with tasks, activities, diversions, and distractions, "stepping back and questioning" is unlikely to get a slot on the schedule. Which means some of the most important questions—about why we're engaging in all those activities in the first place—never get raised.

Gretchen Rubin, author of *The Happiness Project*, says that it's becoming increasingly difficult for people to find time "to step back and ask a large question like, 'What do I want from life, anyway?'" Rubin says that for a long time, she was caught up in this same cycle herself. "I was so focused on my daily to-do list that I didn't spend any time thinking about whether I was

Why does it pay to swim with dolphins?

Stepping back from everyday work and activities can allow for the kind of reflection and deep questioning that occasionally leads to career-changing (and even industry-changing) insights. Such was the case with Marc Benioff, an executive at the tech company Oracle who took an extended break from his job so he could just think. Benioff journeyed to India and then continued on to Hawaii, where, as he told the authors of *The Innovator's DNA*, he went swimming with dolphins in the Pacific Ocean. Out there in the water, he thought of a question: "I asked myself '*Why aren't all enterprise software applications built like Amazon and eBay?*'" This inspired Benioff to launch Salesforce.com, which set out to use the Internet to radically change the design and distribution of business software programs. Within eight years, Benioff's company had $1 billion in sales and was credited with "turning the software industry on its head."

actually happy or how I could be happier." As previously noted, Rubin's "back-step" moment came during a bus ride on a rainy day, at one of those rare times when everything slowed down enough to allow her to ask, *Why am I not happy? (And what if I were to do something about that?)*

So perhaps the first rule of asking why is that there must be a pause, a space, an interruption in the meeting, a halt of "progress," a quiet moment looking out the window on the bus. Often, these are the only times when there is time to question.

IF ASKING WHY requires stepping back from "doing," it also demands a step back from "knowing." Whether in life or in work, people become experts within their own domains—generally confident that they already know what they need to know to do well in their jobs and lives. Having this sense of knowing can make us less curious and less open to new ideas and possibilities. To make matters worse, we don't "know" as much we might think we do.

Robert Burton, a neurologist and the author of the book *On Being Certain*, contends that we all suffer from a common human condition of thinking we know more than we do. For years, Burton has been grappling with the question *What does it mean to be convinced?*

He told me he has concluded, based on extensive research, that the feeling of "knowing" is just that—a feeling, or a sensation. However, the feeling is so strong that it creates what Burton calls a "certainty epidemic"—wherein many people overestimate their knowledge, put too much faith in their "gut instinct," and walk around convinced they have more answers than they actually do. If you feel this way, you're less likely to ask questions.

Furthermore, we also get in the habit of not paying much attention to the world around us. Neurologists have found that our brains are hardwired to quickly categorize, filter, and even ignore some of the massive amounts of stimuli coming at us every moment. A nice description of this phenomenon comes from Maura O'Neill, the chief innovation officer for USAID, a government agency focused on social problems. In her writing, O'Neill observed, "Our brains have evolved to dump most of what we see, quickly categorize the rest, and file it away in our long term memory using our brain's equivalent of the Dewey Decimal system."

As O'Neill notes, this behavior developed for practical reasons. Our ancestors needed to quickly determine if something coming at them was friendly or harmful; today, we still need to do that at times, though we're more often concerned, in this info-rich environment, with trying to sort what's new and important from what's known or extraneous. We make judgments in fractions of a second: *This* I'll pay attention to, everything else I'll ignore because (a) it doesn't concern/interest me or (b) I already know about it.

We make that judgment about what's "known" based on everything we've experienced already—and as O'Neill notes, "the more we see, hear, touch, or smell something, the more hard-wired in our brain it becomes." We routinely "default to the set of knowledge and experience each one of us has."

This works well under most circumstances, but when we wish to move beyond that default setting—to consider new ideas and possibilities, to break from habitual thinking and expand upon our existing knowledge—it helps if we can let go of what we know, just temporarily. You have to be adventurous enough (and humble enough) to enter the "know nothing" zone of a constant questioner such as Paul Bennett.

BENNETT IS A longtime creative director at the innovation firm IDEO. A native of the United Kingdom who grew up in Singapore, he originally headed up IDEO's London office, then helped open branches in Asia. A globe-trotter, he is constantly observing and wondering why, for instance, people in certain parts of China hang their dried fish on the line right next to their washed clothes. Bennett shares many of his observations and questions in a blog titled The Curiosity Chronicles.

"I position myself relentlessly as an idiot at IDEO," Bennett observes. "And that's not a negative, it's a positive. Because being comfortable with not knowing—that's the first part of being able to question."

Having grown comfortable in that role, Bennett says, he is able to ask "incredibly naïve questions" without feeling the least self-conscious. For example, when Bennett was called in to speak at the parliament in Iceland during the country's financial meltdown, "I asked stupid questions like 'Where's the money?' Not because I was trying to be disrespectful but because no one seemed to be able to give a straight answer to this basic question."

Part of the value in asking naïve questions, Bennett says, is that it forces people to explain things simply, which can help bring clarity to an otherwise complex issue. "If I just keep saying, 'I don't get it, can you tell me why once more?,' it forces people to synthesize and simplify—to strip away the irrelevances and get to the core idea."

Sometimes, he says, his naïveté gives others permission to step back and rethink in ways they might not normally be comfortable doing. In some parts of Asia, for example, rigid hierarchical structures in business and government tend to discourage questioning. "In those cultures, people sometimes welcome outsiders coming in and asking basic questions because they may be wondering about these things themselves—but they don't want to ask because they can't afford to look foolish or disrespectful."

Bennett says that within IDEO, the company recognizes it's important to create an environment where it's safe to ask "stupid" questions. "You need to have a culture that engenders trust," he says. "Part of questioning is about exposing vulnerability—and being okay with vulnerability as a cultural currency." So at the firm, no question is too basic to ask; and co-workers are encouraged to support and build upon others' questions, rather than dismissing them or giving pat answers. Bennett says, "We allow people to fall backwards and be caught by one another."

IN SILICON VALLEY, IDEO and other innovation-driven firms go out of their way to protect and encourage naïve questioning because they know, from experience, that it can lead to valuable insights that result in breakthrough ideas and successful products.

The valley is a place where everyone, it seems, is racing nonstop to get to "what's next." This would seem an unlikely place for slowing down, stepping back, and asking fundamental questions. Yet a number of the best minds in the tech sector have embraced this approach, led in recent years by the late cofounder of Apple, Steve Jobs, who was a proponent and practitioner of the Zen principle known as *shoshin*, or "beginner's mind."

Jobs was determined to reimagine and re-create the ways we integrate technology into our everyday lives. This required asking fundamental questions (Jobs was known to be a dogged questioner of everything from current market practices to the ideas of his employees, many of whom were subject to deconstructive interrogation). One of his tools in challenging conventional wisdom was a bit of ancient wisdom, brought to Northern California in the 1960s by a Japanese Zen master named Shunryu Suzuki. Author of the book *Zen Mind, Beginner's Mind*, Suzuki immigrated to the area and taught there until his death in 1971.

In his book, Suzuki writes, "The mind of the beginner is empty, free of the habits of the expert." Such a mind, he added, is "open to all possibilities" and "can see things as they are."

Suzuki also made an important point that underscores the potential value of this way of thinking to a would-be innovator: "In the beginner's mind there are many possibilities, but in the expert's there are few."

Beginner's mind, along with other Zen principles of deep thinking, mindfulness, listening, and questioning, gradually caught on with others in Silicon Valley, beyond Jobs and Apple. Les Kaye is a Zen abbot whose Kannon Do Zen Meditation Center is located in Mountain View, California, just down the road from Google. His followers include folks from Google and Apple, as well as various tech-start-up entrepreneurs and the venture capitalists who fund them. Kaye is aware that some of these people may be motivated by the notion that a "question-everything" Zen mind-set could be used to help spark new ideas and innovations (one recent book coined the term *Zennovation* to describe the merging of Zen principles and innovation strategies).

Kaye is quick to point out, "It would be a mistake for people to think, 'If I do Zen practice, I'll become more creative.' It's not a magic pill." Moreover, Kaye's center cites "no striving" as a guiding Zen principle; it's considered inappropriate to lust after material gains and business success. When I pointed out to Kaye that Steve Jobs seemed to successfully use "beginner's mind" to envision new products as he simultaneously "strived" for greater market share, Kaye, who once studied with Jobs at the same Zen center, remarked, "Steve had an unusual relationship with Zen. He got the artistic side of it but not the Buddhist side—the art, but not the heart."

Still, Jobs proved that, for better or worse, you can be both a questioner and a conqueror. Indeed, you can extract practical lessons from beginner's mind, whether or not you choose to go "full Zen." Randy Komisar, a partner in the renowned Silicon Valley venture capital firm Kleiner Perkins Caufield & Byers, and a Zen practitioner, says the key to adopting this manner of observing and questioning is to make an effort to become, in his word, "detached"—from everyday thoughts, distractions, preconceived notions, habitual behaviors, and even from oneself. "Basically, you begin to observe yourself as if you were a third party." If you can achieve that sense of detachment, your thinking becomes more "flexible and fluid," Komisar maintains, and "you find yourself in a better position to question everything."

TED founder Richard Saul Wurman says it helps him, when approaching any new situation or subject, to think of his mind as "an empty bucket." The job is to slowly and methodically fill that bucket, Wurman says, and you begin by asking the most basic of questions.

Beginner's mind is akin to adopting a more childlike mindset. That's not as fanciful as it might sound. I mentioned previously that Joichi Ito, director of the prestigious MIT Media Lab—which has had a hand in creating everything from the Kindle electronic reader to futuristic cars that can fold in half—favors the term *neoteny* to describe the phenomenon of maintaining childlike mental attributes as an adult. Ito says one can train oneself to think this way.

The Media Lab has a "kindergarten for adults" atmosphere, where constant play is encouraged. The lab is also designed so that people from different disciplines work together, which means "we are often looking at a problem we're not an expert in," says Tod Machover, a cutting-edge musical composer and MIT professor who, in his experimental work at the lab, helped create the popular interactive video game *Guitar Hero*. Machover says it's not uncommon for breakthrough ideas to come from people who are working outside their area of expertise because the novices are "able to see a problem with a fresh eye, forget about what's easy or hard, and not worry about what other people in that field have done."

For those who doubt whether "serious" adults can actually be encouraged to think more like children, a study conducted by the researchers Darya Zabelina and Michael Robinson at North Dakota State University indicates that it's actually easy for people to "think young," with a little nudge.

Zabelina had noticed, in previous studies, that young children tended to perform well on creativity tests because they are uninhibited. So Zabelina and Robinson took two groups of adults and instructed one group to think of themselves as "seven-year-olds, enjoying a day off from school" (the other group just thought of themselves as the adults they are). When the two groups were given a creativity test, the "think young" group came up with better, more original ideas and exhibited "more flexible, fluid thinking."

Zabelina believes that "mind-sets are flexible. It is possible to tap into the more open way of thinking of a child." All that's needed, it seems, is to be given permission (by others or by ourselves) to take that step back in time.

Why did George Carlin see things the rest of us missed?

When we do step back, what do we then see? We're seeing essentially the same realities and situations. But with more distance, a bigger picture comes into view. We may now be able to see the overall context; we might notice the patterns and relationships between things we'd previously thought of as separate. This can change everything. Upon stepping back and reexamining something you've been looking at the same way for years, you might suddenly feel as if you're seeing it for the first time.

If you've ever experienced this, it feels a bit like déjà vu in reverse. With déjà vu, you go somewhere you've never before been yet it seems oddly familiar; conversely, when you look at something familiar and suddenly see it fresh, this is a case of *vuja de*, to use a quirky term favored by Stanford University professor and author Bob Sutton.

Sutton has argued that if we train ourselves to look at the world around us through a vuja de lens, it can open up a range of new possibilities—fresh questions to ask, ideas to pursue, challenges to tackle, all previously unnoticed because they were camouflaged in overly familiar surroundings. Adopting this view, business leaders and managers are more apt to notice inconsistencies and outdated methods—as well as dormant opportunities. Someone working on social issues or even personal ones is likely to notice more and to ask fundamental questions about what he or she notices.

It isn't easy, Sutton notes: "It means thinking of things that are usually assumed to be negative as positive, and vice versa. It can mean reversing assumptions about cause and effect, or what matters most versus least. It means not traveling through life on automatic pilot."

As with beginner's mind, Sutton's vuja de idea has resonated in various corners of the innovation sector, having been picked up by, among others, IDEO, whose general manager, Tom Kelley, has written that vuja de provides the ability to "see what's always been there but has gone unnoticed."

But years before IDEO or even Sutton talked about vuja de, the term was mentioned, albeit briefly, in a stand-up comedy routine by the American comedian George Carlin. In the midst of his act, Carlin paused, as if he'd just had an epiphany—then announced to the audience that he'd experienced vuja de, which, as he explained, was "the strange feeling that, somehow, none of this has ever happened before."

Carlin died in 2008, but his daughter, the comedian and radio host Kelly Carlin, feels the vuja de way of looking at the world—of observing mundane, everyday things as if one were witnessing something strange and fascinating—is exactly the way Carlin went through his life and got his material. "When the familiar becomes this sort of alien world and you can see it fresh, then it's like you've gone into a whole other section of the file folder in your brain," she said. "And now you have access to this other perspective that most people don't have."

Carlin used that perspective to develop a style of observational humor that could be thought of as the Why school of comedy. "It was observing our everyday life—baseball, dogs and cats, the way someone stands in front of the refrigerator—and asking, *Why do we do things the way we do them?*" Kelly Carlin says. George Carlin studied routine behaviors that most of us take for granted, mapping the inconsistencies, searching for some kind of rationale (and usually not finding one). *When we've lost our keys and are searching for them,* he wondered, *why do we keep looking in the same few places, over and over?*

Kelly Carlin, who often interviews other comedians on her podcast series *Waking from the American Dream*, thinks comedians in general are more apt to have a vuja de perspective. "Most comics grew up feeling like they didn't belong," she says. "They were the class clowns, the outsiders—maybe the one who had the learning disability and didn't do well in an academic setting. As outsiders, it's natural for them to stand back and observe, and to wonder about what everyone is doing. And eventually, that's where they get their material."

George Carlin once said that he could not help noticing the irrational behaviors, all the things that just don't make sense—and that he sometimes wished he didn't notice all of it because it agitated him so much.

MOST OF US have the opposite problem—we don't notice enough. IDEO's Kelley thinks it's because we don't generally take the time required for close observation. When people fail to see what's right in front of them, it's often because "they stopped looking too soon."

The Dartmouth University business professor Vijay Govindarajan and the consultant Srikanth Srinivas have devised an exercise that nicely illustrates what Kelley is talking about. In their seminars, they briefly show attendees the figure below:

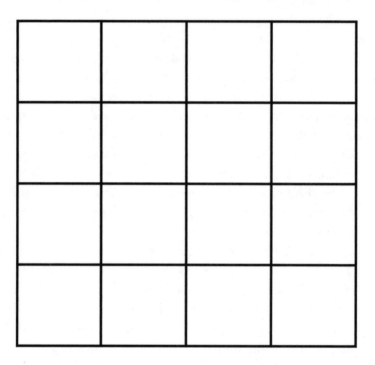

Then, Srinivas told me, the figure is covered up and he asks, "How many squares did you see?"

The easy answer is sixteen. But the more observant people in the group are apt to notice—especially after Srinivas allows them to have a second, longer look—that you can find additional squares by configuring them differently. In addition to the sixteen single squares, there are nine two-by-two squares, four three-by-three squares, and one large four-by-four square, which brings the total to thirty squares.

"The squares were always there, but you didn't find them until you looked for them," Govindarajan and Srinivas wrote on the *Harvard Business Review* blog, after they published the puzzle there. (They got hundreds of responses from readers, whose answers to "How many squares?" ranged from sixteen to thirty up to sixty—if you count the thirty squares with black edges as well as the thirty with white edges—and all the way to infinity.)

Srinivas told me he uses the exercise to illustrate that we often fail to see all the possibilities available to us because we simply haven't spent enough time looking. He said the exercise particularly resonates with people who are in a difficult situation: "Sometimes people feel like they have nowhere to go and they've run out of options, and my point is, 'There is always another square, another possibility, if you just keep looking for it.'"

Great questioners "keep looking"—at a situation or a problem, at the ways people around them behave, at their own behaviors. They study the small details; and they look for not only what's there but what's *missing*. They step back, view things sideways, squint if necessary. In Sutton's writings on vuja de and how to see the familiar, he advises "shifting our focus from objects or patterns in the foreground to those in the background."

Such close observation demands patience and persistence. After seeing the first sixteen squares, we're inclined to move on and look elsewhere;

Why can't computers do more than compute?

In the 1950s it wasn't clear how computers could be used outside of mathematics. Conway Berners-Lee, a British mathematician who worked on the early commercial electronic computers, was fascinated by the question, *Could computers be used to link information rather than simply compute numbers?* The question was later refined by his son, software engineer Tim Berners-Lee. Overwhelmed by massive amounts of research data, Berners-Lee wondered if there were a way to combine the nascent Internet with linked hypertext documents to better find and share information. In 1989, he proposed the global hypertext project to be known as the World Wide Web. His prototype included the now familiar architecture of web browsers, HTML, HTTP, and URLs.

but the thirtieth square, the one you notice later, can turn out to be a window of opportunity that others haven't yet seen. Einstein talked about looking for the needle in the haystack and finding it—at which point most people stop looking. The secret, he said, is to keep looking, in search of an even better needle.

Why should you be stuck without a bed if I've got an extra air mattress?

In the fall of 2007, Joe Gebbia and Brian Chesky had one question uppermost in their minds, and it wasn't a beautiful one. "How were we going to pay the rent? *That* was the main issue at the time," Gebbia recalls. He and his roommate, Chesky, had no jobs, and not much money. But they did have a decent San Francisco apartment with a place to sleep and a roof over their heads. Which was more than could be said for many of the people coming to town for a local business conference—the city's hotels were all booked, and conference-goers were desperate for a place to stay.

This situation (which Gebbia and Chesky had experienced first-hand as visitors to prior conferences) didn't make sense to them: *Why can't we find a place for these people to crash for a night or two?* Which then led to *Why not our place?*

Gebbia and Chesky got hold of three inflatable air mattresses. They could simply have run a cheap classified ad, rented out their airbeds for a modest fee during the conference, and picked up enough money to cover a small portion of that month's rent. But almost immediately, they started to think bigger about this idea and asked all kinds of What If questions, such as *What if we provide more than just a mattress to sleep on?* They didn't have much to offer, but they threw in a modest breakfast (how modest? Pop-Tarts!) and sightseeing tips. And rather than just put a listing on Craigslist, Gebbia and Chesky (who both had a design background) thought, *What if we create our own website?*

They did all of this, rented out the three mattresses to three individuals who didn't know each other, and everyone enjoyed the experience. Gebbia says, they now started to think, *Why not make a business out of this? What if we could create this same experience in every major city?*

Here is where the two dreamers ran headfirst into conventional wisdom. Initially, no one, outside of Chesky, Gebbia, and a third partner they brought on, thought this was an idea that made business sense or was worth supporting. Paul Graham, a renowned angel investor in Silicon Valley who runs the start-up incubator firm Y Combinator, believed quite simply, "No one would want to stay in someone else's bed."

The idea that would eventually become Airbnb was challenging a basic assumption: that you needed established, reputable hotels to provide accommodation for out-of-town visitors. Those paying close attention might have noticed that just a few years prior to this, lots of people held similar assumptions about cars—you could buy them, you could rent them, but there was no practical way to *share* them. Then an entrepreneur named Robin Chase asked, *Why not?*—and subsequently introduced Zipcar.

Gebbia told me that part of the reason he and Chesky believed this was a problem worth solving—the reason, he suspects, that they saw what others missed—was that they had been on both sides of the problem. "We knew what it was like to come to town needing a place to stay, and we knew what it was like to have extra space that we needed to rent," Gebbia said. "So we connected those two dots. In retrospect it makes complete sense—but at the time, no one else had connected those dots."

Gebbia and Chesky had a kind of "rebel" attitude that goes with successful questioning. It's one thing to see a problem and to question why the problem exists—and maybe even wonder whether there might be a better alternative. It's another to keep asking those questions even after experts have told you, in effect, "You can't change this situation; there are good reasons why things are the way they are."

Gebbia and Chesky had to overcome that initial resistance by continuing to push forward on their original question (about whether they could expand that first hosting experience into a business), and they were propelled by new questions at each step of the way. They wondered, *What if we take this idea on the road and test it in another city?* With the 2008 Democratic presidential convention in Denver, they found the perfect place to launch—lots of people coming into town, not enough hotels. *But how would those visitors, and the people with space to rent, learn about Airbnb?* Gebbia and Chesky couldn't afford ads; so they had to make news. The founders knew that the news channels would be doing stories about how crowded and overbooked Denver was. They pitched Airbnb as a "solution story" to news producers and ended up on CNN. The bookings came in and the Denver launch was a success.

But Gebbia says they kept questioning, kept iterating and refining the model for another year before they felt they had it right. They used the site themselves, stayed in rentals, and asked, *What's working here and what's not?* When they noticed, for example, that exchanging money with apartment hosts was awkward—"It just felt like the whole experience was relaxed and fun, until it came time to pay," Gebbia recalls—this spurred them to ask, *What if you could pay online?* When they noticed that many of the visitors to their site were asking about foreign cities, this led to a big question: *Why are we limiting this to the U.S.? What if we go global?* Within less than two years, they were in more than a hundred countries, doing a million bookings, and flush with more than one hundred million investment dollars. They had even won over early skeptics such as Y Combinator's Graham, who became one of their seed investors.

These days, Gebbia and Chesky are asking a whole new set of questions about whether it's feasible to create a "sharing economy." At the core of this idea is the fundamental question *Why should we, as a society, continue to buy things that we really don't need to own?* (Consider, for example, that the average power drill in the United States is used a total of thirteen minutes in its lifetime.) As Gebbia notes, we've spent decades accumulating "stuff" in the modern consumer age. *"What if we spent the next hundred years sharing more of that stuff? What if access trumped ownership?"*

WHETHER OR NOT Airbnb, joined by others, will be able to successfully lead that ambitious "sharing economy" movement is an open question, and one that—even more than the earlier questions about whether people would be willing to share homes and beds—aggressively challenges assumptions about how our economy works, the extent to which people are willing to change ingrained behavior, and whether sharing even makes sense as a viable business model.

Clearly, though, the success Gebbia and Chesky have already achieved is rooted in their willingness to challenge assumptions and to believe that everything is subject to change—regardless of what conventional wisdom holds. I think of this brand of questioning as a subcategory of Why questions that could be considered "challenger questions." They have a certain attitude about them: restless, rebellious, skeptical of convention and authority. As in:

> *Why should we settle for what currently exists?*

> *And why should I believe you when you tell me something can't be done?*

Why can't India have 911 emergency service?

This was the question Shaffi Mather tackled, following a health emergency involving his mother. He started with one ambulance and a simple number (1298) that people could dial in a crisis. But the toughest question was, *How much should we charge?* Mather wanted the service to be available to everyone, so he tried a pay-what-you-can honor system—but everyone claimed to be poor. So he inquired, *How can we get those with money to pay more?* The answer: The better the hospital you requested, the more you were charged for the ride. With backing from the Acumen Fund, Mather's service became Asia's largest ambulance company, transporting nearly 2 million people. Mather kept questioning along the way, with occasional misfires: Once, to try to cut costs, he asked, *What if the ambulance doctors also carried the cots?* The lesson learned: people assume that any doctor who has to carry cots must not be a very good doctor.

Asking challenger questions is inherently uncomfortable—"it creates dissonance," notes Paul Bottino, who directs Harvard University's student-innovator program. The program draws some of the brightest, most creative college students—yet even those students arrive with a tendency to accept much of what they're told without question, Bottino says. One of his chief tasks is to teach them "to understand that the incumbency has an interest in maintaining the status quo. To question well, you must have the ability to say, 'It doesn't have to be that way.'"

That goes against what many are taught in school: that each

question has one right answer and you'd better accept it (and memorize it). When Deborah Meier established her Central Park East School designed to encourage questioning, the first "habit of mind" she taught her students was to ask, *How do we know what's true?* Meier wanted them to question everything they were taught and all they were told. George Carlin had a lifelong mistrust of authority, Kelly Carlin noted, and his advice to parents was "Don't just teach your children to read. Teach them to question what they read. Teach them to question everything."

After years of being conditioned to think that "answers" coming from "experts" should be accepted, the only way to get more comfortable questioning the expert assumptions of others is to do it repeatedly and over time, Bottino says. Among the things one must get used to, in asking challenger questions, is that you're likely to be asked the classic antichallenger question: *What makes you think* you *know more than the experts?* (The answer is that you don't know more, you know less—which sometimes is a good thing.)

Another common counterquestion that challengers can expect to be hit with is some version of *Okay, genius, how would* you *do it better?* An interesting assumption is built into this question: that if someone is going to challenge the existing ways, then he/she had better have an alternative ready. But it's important to ask Why and What If questions even if we don't yet know the How. Getting to a better alternative may be a long process, but it has to start somewhere—and that starting point often involves questioning the status quo.

Why must we "question the question"?

Questions that challenge the prevailing assumptions are useful and sometimes catalytic—but they can also be flawed themselves. Assumptions and biases of our own may be embedded in the questions we ask. One of the ways to find out is to subject those questions to . . . questioning.

Robert Burton, the aforementioned neurologist who writes about the "certainty epidemic," the widespread tendency of people to question less than they should, says that even when people do ask questions, they're often relying on those same unreliable gut instincts and biases. "Everything that's ever happened to you or occurred to you in your life informs every decision you make—and also influences what questions you decide to ask. So it can be useful to step back and inquire, *Why did I come up with that question?*" Burton adds, "Every time you come up with a question, you should be wondering, *What are the underlying assumptions of that question? Is there a different question I should be asking?*"

Questioning one's own questions—as in, *Why am I asking why?*—might seem like a circular exercise, bound to lead nowhere and yield dizziness. But there are practical, constructive ways to do this, and they can help produce a more insightful or more informed question. They range from simple practices such as "the five whys" to more exhaustive methods such as contextual inquiry, wherein we take our questions out into the larger world to see how they survive contact with reality.

The five whys methodology originated in Japan and is credited to Sakichi Toyoda, the founder of Toyota Industries. For decades, the company used the practice of asking why five times in succession as a means of getting to the root of a particular manufacturing problem. When, for example, a faulty car part came out of a factory, asking why the first time would yield the most obvious answer—say, that someone on the assembly line had made a mistake. By then asking why that mistake occurred, an underlying cause might surface—such as insufficient training on a task. Asking why again, the company might discover the training program was underfunded; and asking why about that could lead back to fundamental company priorities about where money should be spent and what was most important in the end.

The value of this kind of excavation-by-inquiry is becoming more widely recognized in the business world, most recently as part of the Lean Startup methodology taught by the author/consultant Eric Ries, who is a big proponent of the five whys. I asked Ries why a simple, almost-childlike practice seems to work so well. "It's a technique that's really designed to overcome the limits of human psychology," Ries explained. By this he means that people are inclined to look for the easiest, most obvious explanation for a problem. On top of that, "we tend to personalize things that are really systemic." It's easier to just blame that poor assembly-line worker than to consider all the complex, interrelated factors that may be contributing to the problem.

The five whys can be used outside of business, as well. IDEO has used it to address a number of behavioral issues. The firm offers this example of how it can be applied to a lifestyle issue.

Why do you exercise?
Because it's healthy.
Why is it healthy?
Because it raises my heart rate.
Why is that important?
So that I burn more calories.
Why do you want to do that?
To lose weight.
Why are you trying to lose weight?
I feel social pressure to look fit.

One might ask, *Why stop at five?* That designated stopping point does seem arbitrary (in actual practice, you may get to something important after three whys, other times it might take six—and, admittedly, sometimes the technique doesn't work at all). But if you don't stop asking why at some reasonable point, you may end up, like Louis C.K. in his "Why?" comedy bit, lost in cosmic questions about why the universe is the way it is.

However many times you do it, asking "Why?" repeatedly does seem to have value in all kinds of endeavors that require getting at deeper truths. The Hollywood character actor and author Stephen Tobolowsky uses this kind of sequential questioning to burrow down to the core of each character he plays—and said it usually takes "three levels of questions, three assaults on the fortress, before you get to something useful and specific as an actor."

If Tobolowsky is playing, say, a doctor, he may start by questioning the character's current motivations, but he'll gradually use levels of inquiry to go deeper and deeper: "I'll ask myself, *As a doctor, what am I really good at and not so good at?* Then I'll go to a deeper level of questioning: *Why did I want to become a doctor in the first place?*" When told about the five whys methodology, Tobolowksy hadn't heard of it—but said he's been doing his own version of the three whys for many years because it works.

THERE ARE VARIOUS other ways to "work on" a question you have chosen to pursue—to deconstruct it, or to alter its shape and scope. At the MIT Media Lab, Tod Machover teaches students to broaden their questions in some instances, and narrow them in others. You might broaden a question to make it more applicable to more people, and therefore more significant. For example, the Airbnb founders could have limited the scope of their question to *Can we set up an online accommodation-sharing system in San Francisco?*—but they quickly broadened it to *Can this idea work worldwide?* On the other hand, as Machover notes, to move forward on a big question sometimes it's necessary to break it down into smaller, more actionable questions—as in, *Before we try to do this thing worldwide, how might we make it work in our own backyard?*

Another method of tinkering with questions has been developed by the Right Question Institute, which has discovered,

---

Why isn't the water reaching the people who need it?

With the creation of Water.org, the engineer/activist Gary White teamed up with actor Matt Damon to tackle the problem of nearly one billion people lacking access to safe water. The conventional approach was to raise charitable donations to drill wells "and basically give water projects away." Seeing this wasn't working, White and Damon inquired, *Why aren't charitable efforts succeeding in getting water to where it's most needed?* Turns out the subsidies were going to local middlemen who ran the utilities—while the poor were still left having to overpay or walk great distances to get water. Eventually, White and Damon focused on this empowering question: *What if local communities could have the means to create their own sources of water?* Water.org's innovative "Water Credit" makes small loans available to people (mostly women) who can then develop or acquire their own water sources. So far it has helped more than a million people worldwide.

through its research, that you can improve a question by opening and closing it. For instance, suppose one is grappling with the question *Why is my father-in-law difficult to get along with?* Like most Why, What If, and How questions, this question is open-ended because it has no one definitive answer. But note what happens when we transform this into a closed, yes-or-no question: *Is my father-in-law difficult to get along with?*

Worded this way, the question almost forces one to confront the assumption within the original question—and to consider that it might not be valid (because the father-in-law, in this scenario, might have other relatives and friends with whom he gets along swimmingly). So this might cause me to go back and revise that original question to make it more accurate: *Why is my father-in-law so difficult* for me *to get along with?* In its research, the RQI has found that this process works both ways—closed questions can also be improved by opening them up.

While you can do much tinkering around the edges of a question using such methods, perhaps the best way to question a question is to take it out into the world with you—and see if the assumptions behind it hold up when exposed to real people and situations. Often, what seems to be the right question in one context proves to be the wrong one in another.

The developing world has a shortage of incubators for infants. For years, health organizations and philanthropic groups asked the logical question: *How can we get more incubators to the places that need them?* A relatively straightforward answer to that question was—donate them. But that was the right answer to the wrong question. This led to thousands of incubators being donated to poor nations, "only to end up in 'incubator graveyards,'" as the *New York Times* reported. This was part of a larger problem that went far beyond incubators; one study found that 96 percent of foreign-donated medical equipment ended up being used for a short time, then abandoned.

The better question, which was eventually asked by health officials working on the problem, was *Why aren't people in developing countries using the incubators they have?* On-the-ground observation revealed that the incubators were prone to breaking down and locals didn't have the parts or know-how to fix them. Having answered the Why, the health officials moved to the What If, specifically, *What if we could provide incubators that were easy to maintain and fix?*

One doctor working on the initiative, Jonathan Rosen, knew from his own study of the problem that cars and car parts were readily available in many of the areas with incubator problems. So the ultimate question became *How can we make an incubator out of car parts?* A nonprofit design group was brought in to tackle that question, and they eventually pieced together the "car-parts incubator," which was inexpensive, easy to use, and could be fixed by anyone with basic mechanical skills, using parts from a local junkyard.

In the philanthropic world, as well as in business, medicine, and science, there are many stories like the car-parts-incubator story— in which the wrong question is asked, based on incomplete information or faulty assumptions, often because those formulating the questions are too far removed from the problem they're trying to solve. One of the best ways to overcome this is to try to close the distance between the questioner and the problem.

Contextual inquiry is about asking questions up close and in context, relying on observation, listening, and empathy to guide us toward a more intelligent, and therefore more effective, question.

In the business world, IDEO has been a pioneer of this type of research. As the design firm was being formed twenty-odd years ago, its founders, including the designer David Kelley and his brother Tom, realized that to solve human engineering problems (such as, *How do we make gadgets that fit into people's lives?*), the company would have to employ the kind of psychological and behavioral inquiry normally done by social scientists. So the firm hired psychologists and other students of human behavior and began to develop its own methods of observing people.

IDEO understood that to question effectively, one couldn't do it from inside the bubble of the company, or in artificial settings such as focus groups. To understand how people live, you have to immerse yourself in their lives—watch them in their kitchens, follow them as they go to the supermarket, and so forth. The company's researchers sometimes go to great lengths to experience things firsthand.

One classic example involved a hospital group that hired IDEO to help answer the question *What is our patient experience like?* The hospital executives were surprised when IDEO, instead of doing a snazzy PowerPoint presentation, showed them a long, deadly dull video of a hospital ceiling. The point of the film: "When you lie in a hospital bed all day, all you do is look at the ceiling, and it's a really shitty experience," IDEO's Paul Bennett explained. The firm understood this because someone from IDEO actually checked into the hospital, was wheeled around on a gurney, and then lay in a hospital bed for hours. This kind of "immersive" approach enables the firm to consider a question or problem from the inside out, instead of from the outside looking in. (Soon after seeing the video, the hospital's nurses took it upon themselves to decorate the ceiling tiles in each room.)

To do contextual inquiry well, you don't need a team of trained researchers. What's required is a willingness to go out into the world with a curious and open mind, to observe closely, and—perhaps most important, according to a number of the questioners I've interviewed—to *listen*. Listening informs questioning. Paul Bennett says that one of the keys to being a good questioner is to stop reflexively asking so many thoughtless questions and pay attention—eventually, a truly interesting question may come to mind. The Acumen Fund's Jacqueline Novogratz, whose nonprofit group tackles social problems by first spending extensive time on the ground in the villages and communities they're trying to help, talks about "listening with your whole body"—using all senses to absorb what's going on around you.

Contextual inquiry requires a commitment to the question you're exploring. It's one thing to ponder questions in your room, or within your own company's offices, or in online surveys; it's another to go out there and, as Novogratz says, "spend time sitting on the floor with people, listening to them as they tell you about their lives." Deciding to go to that level is part of taking ownership of a question. It's about pausing, before jumping in headlong, to ask, *Why is this* my *problem? And if it's not my problem, why* should it be?

While I was interviewing Srikanth Srinivas—the man who asks people to count squares and look for unseen windows—he asked an interesting question. We were discussing how breakthroughs often start with a question and were focused on stories such as those of Netflix and Polaroid. Srinivas noted that the questions that were asked (*Why should I have to pay late fees? Why do we have to wait for the picture?*) were ordinary questions that could have been asked by anyone. Then he added, "But most people would have asked a question like that and then not acted on it. So the question is, *why do some people act on a question?*"

There's no one answer to that; you could say it has to do with imagination, determination—or sometimes desperation, as in the case of Van Phillips and his prosthetic foot. But this much can be said of Phillips, Polaroid's Land, Netflix's Hastings, Acumen's Novogratz, the Airbnb founders, and others in this book: Confronted with a problem that was larger than themselves, they decided to make that problem—and the question that defined the problem—their own.

The difference between just asking a question or pursuing it is the difference between flirting with an idea or living with it. If you choose the latter, the question will likely become what the psychotherapist Eric Maisel calls a "productive obsession." It will surface, recede, then surface again. It will invade your dreams as it embeds itself in your subconscious. You'll wrestle with it, walk with it, sleep with it. And all of this will prove helpful during the What If stage of inquiry.

WHAT IF . . .

What if we could map the DNA of music?

Before he changed the way many listen to music, Tim Westergren was himself a musician, playing in a rock band that, like most bands and musicians Westergren knew back then, struggled to find an audience. Many of the musicians he knew were talented, but found themselves in that classic catch-22: they couldn't build a sizable following unless they were played on the radio, and they couldn't get played on the radio unless they had a sizable following.

So this prompted the initial Why question—*Why can't good musicians find the audience they deserve?*—that lodged in Westergren's head. He eventually quit the band to get a job in the film industry as a music composer. But his question stayed with him.

In his new line of work, Westergren's job was to create music that reflected someone else's tastes. "As a film composer, your job is to profile your director's tastes and give them what they want," Westergren told *The Street*. But he didn't just ask directors what they liked; instead, he played various types of music for them to see how they reacted. Then, he would create what he called "an informal genome of musical tastes in my head."

This led to what some would call an epiphany, though it was actually a moment of connective inquiry. Westergren was reading a magazine article about the folk musician Aimee Mann—a talented artist with a modest following who, in Westergren's words, "was sort of stuck in this no-man's-land . . . she was being shelved, and her records weren't being released."

Reading about Mann resurfaced the question Westergren had contemplated before about why musicians couldn't find audiences, but now something different happened; the question didn't just hang in the air. Westergren began to connect what he had recently learned—"this process I'd developed to profile music taste"—to the problem faced by Aimee Mann and so many other musicians.

What if there was a way to use music profiling to somehow

connect Aimee Mann with an audience inclined to like the kind of music she makes?

Westergren knew the technology existed to create algorithmic engines capable of making fairly straightforward and predictable recommendations ("If you liked that murder-mystery book, here is another murder-mystery book you might like"). But what he was envisioning was something far more sophisticated: a system that could analyze why you liked the music you liked, based on dozens, perhaps hundreds, of subtle musical characteristics and attributes. He would have to find a way to break music down to its most basic elements—or, to use the biological analogy that Westergren was thinking of, its genes. So this was the real question he had to tackle:

What if we could map the DNA of music?

Once he had his What If question, the How stage began, as it often does, with sharing the idea and trying to drum up support. Westergren secured enough backing (in part from maxing out his own credit cards) to hire a team of musicians and techies. Then they began to work on their experiment.

Every day, a group of musicians hired by Westergren would come in to work, put on a pair of headphones, and listen to music. They analyzed every song, breaking the music down into some four hundred attributes—starting with broad categories such as melody, harmony, rhythm, instrumentation, vocal performance. Each of those categories was further subdivided into basic building blocks, or "genes"; voice, for example, could have as many as twenty-five to thirty attributes, from raspy to smooth. While the musicians dissected the music, the tech engineers developed a specialized search engine. Both parts were critical; Westergren felt the "secret sauce" he was developing relied on a blend of human judgment and algorithm.

It took the better part of a year to build a prototype—"because it takes a while to analyze music that way," Westergren explained. "It's actually completely f---ing ridiculous to do it like that, but it was the only strategy I could think of."

The first time he tested the prototype, Westergren typed in a

Beatles song and the system offered up a recommendation: a Bee Gees song. Westergren, thinking of 1970s, disco-style Bee Gees songs, panicked briefly. But Westergren's creation was, on this musical point at least, smarter than he was—early Bee Gees songs were actually similar, musically, to the Beatles song he had input.

Today, Pandora Radio has seventy million listeners. Westergren is proud that it answers not only the question of whether music can be mapped genetically, but also that original query of his—about finding a way to match up musicians with listeners. Every day, Westergren says, Pandora takes the music of relatively unknown bands and feeds that music to listeners most apt to enjoy it. Those listeners may not care about musical genes or the career prospects of obscure musicians, but the service answers a different question for them: *What if a radio station could know what songs you would like before you knew?*

THE PANDORA STORY, like many stories of inquiry-driven start-ups, started with someone's wondering about an unmet need. It concluded with the questioner, Westergren, figuring out how to bring a fully realized version of the answer into the world.

But what happened in between? That's when the lightning struck. In Westergren's case, ideas and influences began to come together; he combined what he knew about music with what he was learning about technology. Inspiration was drawn from a magazine article, and from a seemingly unrelated world (biology). A vision of a new possibility began to form in the mind. It all resulted in an audacious hypothetical question that might or might not have been feasible—but was exciting enough to rally people to the challenge of trying to make it work.

The What If stage is the blue-sky moment of questioning, when anything is possible. Those possibilities may not survive the more practical How stage; but it's critical to innovation that there be a time for wild, improbable ideas to surface and to inspire.

If the word *why* has a penetrative power, enabling the questioner to get past assumptions and dig deep into problems, the words *what if* have a more expansive effect—allowing us to think without limits or constraints, firing the imagination. John Seely Brown has written, "In order for imagination to flourish, there must be an opportunity to see things as other than they currently are or appear to be. This begins with a simple question: What if? It is a process of introducing something strange and perhaps even demonstrably untrue into our current situation or perspective."

The Pandora What If question certainly introduced something "strange" into the world—Westergren's notion that you could take the whole vast universe of music and break it down in a genetic manner struck many (especially musicians) as an off-the-wall idea. But the beauty of the What If stage of questioning is that it's a time when off-the-wall ideas are welcome.

WHERE DO THOSE wild, speculative ideas come from? Obviously, if we knew the precise location of the source, and how to access it, then creativity wouldn't be as mysterious and unpredictable as it is. But we do know that coming up with original ideas or insights—the kind of lightbulb moments that can lead to imaginative What If questions—often involves the ability to combine ideas and influences, to mix and remix things that might not ordinarily go together. Einstein and others have referred to this as "combinatorial thinking"; in this book, I've been using the term *connective inquiry* to focus on the questioning aspect. Whatever one calls it, this mix-and-match mental process is at the root of creativity and innovation.

It can be a relief to know that, in coming up with fresh ideas, we don't have to invent from scratch; we can draw upon what already

---

What if we combine three snacks into one? (And then add a prize?)

In the 1890s, Frederick Rueckheim, fresh from his native Germany to seek his fortune in Chicago, had a flash of connective inquiry: Observing the growing popularity of candy, peanuts, and popcorn snacks, Rueckheim wondered: *What if I combine all of those into one?* He vended his mixture at the 1893 Chicago World's Fair, but it wasn't quite right yet; the candy-coated popcorn tended to clump together, and the name—Candied Popcorn and Peanuts—was accurate but not compelling. On the question of *How to keep it all from sticking together?* Rueckheim added oil to the mix. As for the name, it arrived unexpectedly in 1896, when someone sampled the snack and declared, "That's crackerjack!" An inveterate questioner, Rueckheim kept wondering, *What can be added to Cracker Jack to make it even more appealing?* In 1913 he inserted the final ingredient—small prizes.

exists and use that as raw material. The key may lie in connecting those bits and pieces in a clever, unusual, and useful way, resulting in (to use a term that seems to have originated with the British designer John Thackara) *smart recombinations.*

Smart recombinations are all around us. Pandora, for example, is a combination of radio station and search engine; it also takes the biological model of genetic coding and transfers it to the domain of music (a smart recombination often takes ideas or influences from separate domains and mashes them together). In today's tech world, many of the most successful products—Apple's iPhone being just one notable example—are hybrids, melding functions and features in new ways.

Companies, too, can be smart recombinations. Netflix was started as a video-rental business that operated like a monthly membership health club (and now it has added "TV production studio" to the mix). Airbnb is a combination of an online travel agency, a social media platform, and a good old-fashioned bed-and-breakfast (the B&B itself is a smart recombination from way back).

People have been combining and recombining ideas for as long as there have been ideas, but in the Internet age, the opportunities and possibilities for creating "mashups" seem limitless. "The creative act is no longer about building something out of nothing but rather building something new out of cultural products that already exist," according to *Wired* magazine.

Smart recombinations are inspired in all sorts of ways. Sometimes they are the result of cold calculation (*How can we combine* this *moneymaking thing with* that *moneymaking thing to make even more money?*); sometimes they're a product of serendipity. In the case of the hit book *Abraham Lincoln, Vampire Hunter,* it was a little of both. The book's author, Seth Grahame-Smith, was in a bookstore and noticed one "bestseller table" full of vampire books, while a nearby table was piled high with Lincoln biographies. As Grahame-Smith later confessed to the *New York Times,* he looked at those two piles, and "sort of shrewdly, from a cynical standpoint, I thought, 'Wouldn't it be great if you could combine these two things?'"

While many recombinations are not particularly "smart," the

ones that stand out take preexisting elements and remix them to form something original, surprising, interesting, and useful. That seems to happen when we combine ideas or influences that, on the surface, have no logical or natural connection—yet, once combined, form something powerful.

DAVID KORD MURRAY, a former rocket scientist who worked on projects for NASA and later became the head of innovation at Intuit, made a study of connective creativity in his book *Borrowing Brilliance*. According to Murray, "The nature of innovation [is that] we build new ideas out of existing ideas." Murray cites Einstein, Walt Disney, George Lucas, and Steve Jobs as prime examples of innovators who "defined problems, borrowed ideas, and then made new combinations." They did it, Murray says, by combining things that didn't seem to go together and by borrowing ideas "from faraway places."

Innovators who are good at connecting are inclined to take something they're working on—say, Walt Disney's planning a new amusement park—and begin to think analogously: *What if this amusement park could be like a movie, brought to life?* "In doing this," Murray explains, "Disney takes his original subject, an amusement park, and lays a metaphor on top of it and begins to see the whole thing through that 'movie' metaphor—so he creates it with storyboards, and the employees become cast members, and so on." Creating theme parks now seems like an obvious combination—but it was a fresh, surprising, and compelling mixture when Disney introduced it.

If, as Murray notes, the most creative ideas result from "long distance" connections (bringing together ideas that seem unrelated and far apart), then that means the most promising connective inquiries do not merely ask, *What if we combine A and B?*, but rather, *What if we combine A and Z?* (Or better yet, *A and 26?*) To forge those illogical connections, Murray advises, "You must quiet the logical mind." This is confirmed by the latest neurological research, which suggests that the human brain is a connective-inquiry machine that never sleeps. It is constantly sorting through seemingly unrelated bits and pieces and inquiring, *What if I put this together with that?*

What if your brain is a forest, thick with trees? (And what if the branches touch?)

When we entertain challenging questions—*Why does X have to be the way it is? What if I try to think of a different way of doing it?*—it's a form of divergent thinking, and it triggers some interesting activity in the brain, says Dr. Ken Heilman, professor of neurology at the University of Florida's College of Medicine.

To get a picture of what's going on, Heilman says, start by thinking of the brain as a forest full of trees. "Think of a neuron, or a nerve cell, as one of those trees," he says. In this analogy, the cell body forms the tree trunk; there are major branches, known as axons, and smaller branches, dendrites, that extend out to the farthest reaches. "In the brain, some of those trees are closer together than others, and the branches communicate with each other." As this happens, "neural connections" are formed, which can produce new thoughts, ideas, and insights.

Not all connections are equal, in terms of yielding creative insights. More obvious mental connections and associations—as when we associate a table and a chair—are more commonplace and tend to occur in the brain's left hemisphere, notes the neurology professor John Kounios of Drexel University. But remote associations—"like when we think of 'table' and the idea of 'under the table'"—require more of a neural reach. The brain's right hemisphere, made up of cells with longer branches, is better suited for this task.

Heilman, Kounios, and others have found that mental breakthroughs, the big insights that can solve problems or come up with highly creative new ideas, often involve those remote connections that happen in the right hemisphere. We arrive at originality because the dendrites have reached out and made contact with the branches of faraway "trees," thereby enabling us to combine thoughts, bits of knowledge, and influences that normally do not mix.

JUST ASKING WHY and What If will not necessarily cause these neural connections to occur—but questioning can help nourish the trees and extend the reach of those branches. Chen-Bo Zhong, a professor at the University of Toronto's Rotman School, has done extensive research on connective or associative thinking—why it can produce insights and creative ideas, what encourages the brain to engage in this type of thinking, and so forth. Zhong's research has found that we can't necessarily control the brain's search for remote connections—much of which happens in the unconscious mind—but we can provide impetus and help guide that search by focusing on a problem to be solved, a challenging question to be answered. "Having that goal or that question you're working on is very important," Zhong confirms. If your conscious mind puts a big question out there, chances are good that your unconscious mind will go to work on it.

Moreover, if you have a curious mind—and if you actively ask questions and gather knowledge to sate that curiosity—this also can aid in connective inquiry by providing "a plethora of raw materials to be connected," as Zhong puts it. In particular, if your curiosity has been focused on a particular problem, and you've been doing deep thinking, contextual inquiry, questioning the problem from various perspectives and angles, asking your multiple Whys—it all becomes fodder for later insights and smart recombinations.

What if dots and dashes could sort the world?

In 1948, a Philadelphia supermarket executive visited Drexel University's campus to see if students could develop an efficient means of encoding product data. As the *New York Times* recounts, two grad students tried but were stymied at first. Then one of them spent the winter at his grandparents' place in Miami Beach, thinking about the challenge. To represent information visually, he realized he would need a code. Being a former Boy Scout, Joseph Woodland wondered, *What if Morse code, with its elegant simplicity and limitless combinatorial potential, could be adapted graphically?* That connective inquiry took on life at the beach when he raked his fingers through the sand and had the revelation that wide lines and narrow lines could work instead of dots and dashes. Woodland and his fellow student developed and patented the idea, which eventually led to creation of the bar code.

So even though it can initially be beneficial to approach a problem with a beginner's mind, as you progress to imagining What If
solutions, it's useful to have some acquired knowledge on the problem—preferably gathered from diverse viewpoints. It also helps to
have a wide base of knowledge on all sorts of things that might
seem to be unrelated to the problem—the more eclectic your storehouse of information, the more possibilities for unexpected
connections. (Heilman points out that people who are well read
and well traveled, those who have diverse interests and a broad
liberal arts education, are developing "a whole series of different
modules that can enable more connectivity and more creativity.")

That storehouse of eclectic knowledge can help you begin to
brainstorm What If ideas; and various exercises can help you do
that. But before undertaking conscious efforts to spark connective
inquiry, bear in mind that it seems to thrive when we're distracted
or even unconscious. So the best thing may be to take your question for a walk. Or take it to the museum. Or, if you're feeling
lucky, take it to bed.

What if you sleep with a question?
(Will you wake with an answer?)

Long before he delved deep into the forest of neuron trees and
their dendrite branches, Dr. Heilman, while still a student, made
a firsthand discovery about creativity and brain function. "When
I used to take tests in college, I would be very anxious," he told
me. "So I came up with a process whereby I would always answer
the more obvious questions first. Then, as my anxiety would
lessen, I'd start to answer more of the questions that required real
thinking."

Heilman didn't know it at the time, but his approach made
sense for a biological and chemical reason. When you're anxious,
he learned later in his professional research, your brain tends to be
less creative and imaginative. "You want to attend to the outside
world, not the inside," he said. "And you're trying to get to answers
that are the simplest. But when you're relaxed, you go the other

way—you're able to go to the inside world." In the more relaxed state, neural networks open up and connections of all kinds form more freely.

For a questioner, it's important to spend time with challenging questions instead of trying to answer them right away. By "living with" a question, thinking about it and then stepping away from it, allowing it to marinate, you give your brain a chance to come up with the kinds of fresh insights and What If possibilities that can lead to breakthroughs.

A growing body of research, including Zhong's studies, finds that people often come up with more novel ideas or solutions when they're relaxed or distracted—in what Zhong calls a state of inattention. This prompted Zhong to ask, *Should artists or scientists simply engage in daydreaming to produce groundbreaking discoveries or trailblazing creations?*

Obviously, as Zhong acknowledges, daydreaming alone is not the answer. More likely, it can help in the in-between stages of creative problem solving. Zhong theorizes that it may be best to move back and forth between focused attention and inattention. As an example of this, consider the teenager Jack Andraka as he came up with his idea for an innovative cancer-screening test.

Andraka first became focused on early cancer detection after a family friend died from pancreatic cancer. He did some research and learned that a hundred people a day were dying from that same disease—and that many people were not even finding out they had it until it was too late. Given the scope of the problem and the importance of early detection in potentially saving lives, Andraka wondered, *Why isn't there a fast, inexpensive test for pancreatic cancer?*

Andraka was not a trained scientist, but he was a serious buff who devoured science journals. He understood, early on, that a better screening test would probably require combining ideas from different branches of science—and Andraka was well suited for this task because he was constantly connecting bits of information picked up in one place to something discovered in another place.

"What I do is, I'll pick up, for example, the *Cancer Journal* and then I'll pick up a physics article and then some random chemistry article, and I'll read them all," Andraka told me. At some point after doing all of his research, Andraka says, "I'll just relax on the couch or walk around and do a lot of thinking: *What if I combine these different ideas to solve this one problem?* I just let it incubate and see if I can connect these different ideas somehow."

As Andraka was doing his culling, connecting, and occasional "chilling on the couch," he began making connections with carbon nanotubes—he had been learning about them in various articles. He was fascinated to discover that "carbon nanotubes have this one property that, when you pull them apart, they change their electrical properties. There's an antibody that grows inside when you attach a protein module to it." This led Andraka to his big What If question (which was a mouthful): *"What if I exposed a single-wall carbon nanotube with an antibody to a protein overexposed in pancreatic cancer?"*

His epiphany was not quite an aha moment; it was a hypothetical question, albeit a promising one, with, he figured, "about a fifty-fifty chance of being right." Then, as he started doing more research into antibodies and their properties, "everything was matching up and my confidence was growing. Of course, my parents thought I was crazy." He then checked with his brother, a chemist. "I said to him, 'Hey, does this sound right?,' and he said, 'Oh, no, that would never work!'"

Andraka then e-mailed two hundred professors, and one was interested enough to give him access to a lab. That's when Andraka had to figure out, *How am I going to make this thing real . . . and affordable . . . and reliable?* Those answers didn't come easily, but he developed (at age fifteen, mind you) a paper sensor that detected cancer a hundred times faster than anything on the market, with four hundred times the sensitivity. It was also twenty-six thousand times less expensive than current tests . . . and 100 percent accurate. Andraka's innovation earned him an international science fair award and an invitation to be a special guest at President Obama's 2013 State of the Union address.

HEARING ANDRAKA DESCRIBE his thought process—including closing his eyes and allowing all those various bits of information he'd absorbed to coalesce—reminded me of something Google's scientist-in-residence Ray Kurzweil revealed in an interview. He said that when he is working on a difficult problem, he sets aside time, right before going to bed, to review all the pertinent issues and challenges. Then he goes to sleep and allows his unconscious mind to go to work.

A growing body of research describes what happens when we allow the unconscious mind to work on a problem. Writing recently on the site Big Think, Sam McNerney pulled together a number of recent studies showing that sleeping can help people to perform better at solving difficult problems requiring a creative solution. (McNerney quoted an old John Steinbeck line: "A difficult problem at night is resolved in the morning after the committee of sleep has worked on it.")

Similar research exists on daydreaming and its value in producing original, creative ideas. And everyone knows about the clichéd (but only because it's true) idea-in-the-shower moment. The same neurological forces seem to be at work in all of these instances. The sleeping or relaxed brain cuts off distractions and turns inward, as the right hemisphere becomes more active, leading to periods of greater connectivity.

Some of the same effects can be seen during walks (remember Edwin Land, pacing the grounds of his resort?), long drives, or other activities that distract the mind a little, but not too much. (Watching a movie is too much of a distraction and shuts down creative thinking.)

The neurologist Kounios reports "striking anecdotal evidence" that tinkering or doodling can also induce an inattention that is conducive to having insights. "And it's possible you may get different results depending on which hand you doodle with," Kounios says. "Using the left hand may stimulate the brain's right hemisphere."

If you're looking to take a break and simultaneously stimulate connective inquiry, a visit to the museum might be just the ticket.

It engages the imagination, yet leaves room for thinking; it offers up as inspiration the many creative connections and smart recombinations that others have produced in the past; and it exposes the visitor to so many ideas and influences that it provides abundant raw material for making new mental connections. (The designer George Lois, who claims some of his best ideas have come while meandering through the Metropolitan Museum, says, "Museums are the custodians of epiphanies.")

The point about connective inquiry—and the What If stage in general—is that when you take on a challenging question, if you spend time with that question, your mind will keep working on it. This doesn't mean there aren't conscious ways to trigger What If ideas, including some of the exercises to follow. But be willing to slow down, go quiet, and let the question incubate. If nothing else, this provides a handy excuse when it's time to get out of bed in the morning: "Give me another ten minutes, I need to do some more connective inquiry."

What if your ideas are wrong and your socks don't match?

If sleeping or daydreaming doesn't yield enough lightbulb ideas and What If queries, there are ways to encourage more of this kind of thinking. One way is by purposely trying to "think wrong."

This idea's roots can be found in the work of the creativity guru Edward de Bono; more recently, it has been embraced by innovation firms such as Frog Design and the designers Stefan Sagmeister and John Bielenberg. All are practitioners of divergent thinking—which calls for trying to generate a wide range of ideas, including offbeat ones, in the early stages of creative problem solving.

This is not easy to do because the conscious brain is resistant to wide-open idea generation and far-reaching connective inquiry. The mind is inclined to try to solve problems by doing the same things over and over, following familiar and well-worn neural paths.

The idea, then, is to force your brain off those predictable paths by purposely "thinking wrong"—coming up with ideas that seem to make no sense, mixing and matching things that don't normally go together. Proponents of this approach say it has a jarring effect on creative thinking; in neurological terms, when you force yourself to confront contrary thoughts or upside-down ideas, you "jiggle the synapses" in the brain, in the words of author and adult learning expert Kathleen Taylor. In so doing, you may loosen some of the old, stale neural connections and make it easier to form new ones.

John Bielenberg, a designer best known for running an experimental problem-solving workshop known as Project M, has been teaching people to "think wrong" for about two decades. As Bielenberg explains it, truly gifted innovators and creative geniuses have no difficulty connecting ideas in surprising and unusual ways. "Picasso and Steve Jobs were natural 'wrong thinkers,'" he says, "but the rest of us have to work at it."

To that end, Bielenberg uses exercises in his workshop that require participants to make "random connections" between unrelated ideas, or even just words. Here's a simple word exercise, and all you need is a dictionary: Choose a high number and a low number (say 342 and 5); go to page 342 in the dictionary and find the fifth word. Try to come up with ideas based around that word; take the word apart and rearrange letters to find other words; then repeat the process to come up with a second word, and see if you can form an interesting combination with those two words; you can even advance to a three-word combination if you like.

A number of creative artists use word-combination exercises like this to get their creative juices flowing. It's become so popular that you don't even need a dictionary anymore—the Idea Generator app will randomly select and combine three words for you when you shake your smartphone.

In his workshop and with some of his clients, Bielenberg takes this random-combination exercise up a notch—for example, by asking a bank to consider offbeat What If scenarios in which their business is combined with another, completely unrelated one, as in, *What if your bank was run by the makers of Sesame Street? Would there be puppets in place of tellers?*

THERE ARE LOTS of variations on the exercises Bielenberg does. Some years back I attended a workshop run by the creativity consultant Tom Monahan, who teaches an exercise he calls 180-degree thinking—which is "thinking wrong" with a different name. In his exercises, Monahan encourages participants to come up with ideas for things that don't work—an oven that can't cook, a car that doesn't move. It sounds crazy, but when you do the exercise, interesting things can emerge; you come up with offbeat, alternate uses for the oven or the car.

But the goal of such exercises is not necessarily to generate lasting ideas on the spot; if you do come up with an idea worth pursuing, that's a bonus. The real point is to begin to train the mind to think differently when confronted with a problem or a challenge—to consider a wide range of possibilities, including offbeat ones, and to connect ideas that don't normally go together. It's an attempt to develop and strengthen the What If muscle.

As JOHN SEELY Brown noted, What If questions tend to free up the imagination because they allow you to "see things as other than they currently are"—they allow you to shift reality, if only briefly.

Luke Williams, a former creative director at Frog Design and author of the book *Disrupt*, talks about ways that What If questions can be used to "invert" reality. If the current reality is that restaurants provide people with a menu upon arrival, the inverse hypothesis is *What if a restaurant provided customers with a menu only when they leave?* Williams has worked with clients who have used hypothetical questioning to challenge the most basic assumptions about customer behavior. He cites the example of Jonah Staw, who, over dinner with friends, was exchanging wild, implausible business ideas with others in the group. Someone asked, *What if some company started selling socks that didn't match?* This classic example of "thinking wrong" could have come straight out of a workshop by Bielenberg or Monahan. Today, the company LittleMissMatched—which sells colorful, mismatched pairs of socks to young girls who consider it a fun fashion statement—is a thriving business.

We can use What If questions to erase the past and make a fresh start. One of the favorite questions of Airbnb's Joe Gebbia is *What if we could start with a blank page?*—a question that works as well in personal relationships or life choices as it does in business. We can also use What If questions to remove the possibility of failure simply by asking, *What if we could not fail?* We can use them to envision doing the impossible.

At some point, however, we must contend with reality. An innovation or creative breakthrough can start with thinking wrong, but along the way impossibilities must be made possible, as we move from speculation to something more tangible—something that exists in the real world. Divergent, anything-goes thinking must begin to converge around what's doable. For this to happen, What If questions must give way to How questions.

> **What if prisons had no walls?**
>
> There are many differing views on how to reform prisons, but on one point there's a consensus: conventional incarceration is not working, as evidenced by high recidivism rates and soaring costs. In search of an alternative way of dealing with prisoners that might cut crime, reduce costs, and be more humane, one interesting question being asked is: *What if prisons could be turned inside out, with the convicts released instead of incarcerated?* New technology—in particular, GPS tracking devices—offers the possibility that non-violent offenders could be released from prison with enhanced high-tech supervision via wearable devices that broadcast prisoners' real-time locations and flag any backsliding consistently and immediately (two failures of current parole systems). The system has already been tested successfully in Hawaii; if adopted on a broader scale, as the *Atlantic* notes, it would empty half of our broken, expensive prisons in one fell swoop.

HOW . . .

How can we give form to our questions?

Unconscious creativity, wherein all of those mental connections come together to form What If possibilities as you daydream or sleep, is a welcome gift. But there comes a time to awake and go to work. This was a problem for Gauri Nanda.

She was having trouble getting out of bed in the morning. She started with Why: *Why am I oversleeping, why isn't my alarm clock getting me up?* The answer to that was simple: She'd gotten into the habit (like many of us) of hitting the snooze button again and again. Nanda was a design student at MIT with a knack for problem solving, so she analyzed her situation and asked, *What if it was harder to turn off the alarm clock? What if your alarm clock forced you to get out of bed and chase after it?*

This led to a question that could be considered a classic in connective inquiry: *What if I put wheels on it?* Nanda had a vision of creating the first alarm clock on wheels. Her What If question set things in motion—but then again, anyone can speculate about putting wheels on something. How do you actually put them on?

Nanda began by doing something that tends to be a starting point of the How stage—she solicited feedback on her speculative idea, asking a few trusted friends what they thought of the notion of an alarm clock on wheels that would roll off a night table and force you to chase it down to turn it off. "They laughed," Nanda said, "but in a good way." They also said it was the kind of thing they might buy.

Nanda made her first test versions of a rolling clock using materials she had handy, combined with what she could borrow from the lab at her college. Parts from LEGO toys, including LEGO motors and wheels, formed her early versions of what she called the Clocky. To create a protective covering for the clock, to cushion its regular fall from a night table to the floor, Nanda used shag carpeting. "It almost made it look like a furry animal," she recalls.

While testing her invention, Nanda realized "this was going to be much harder than I thought." Getting the clock to roll was easy; enabling it to survive those suicide dives off the night table was another matter. "It's an unusual thing to expect a clock to go through," she acknowledged. *How might that shock be absorbed?* Nanda used reinforced electronics inside the clock, along with bigger wheels designed to take the brunt of the fall. These lessons were learned through repeated testing—dropping the clock over and over to see how it held up. Nanda also realized during testing that the runaway clock moved predictably and thus was easy to catch. She had to figure out how to make it more elusive. She put in a microprocessor that enabled the clock to move at different speeds, following various routes.

Nanda's quirky project drew the attention of technology blogs, which generated Internet buzz that led to an invitation for Nanda to show her still-unfinished invention on a television program. Now Nanda faced the challenge of how to make her rough prototype ready for prime time. Visible wires connecting the clock to a circuit board had to go. The shag-carpet covering needed to be replaced, eventually by a tough silicon skin.

The Clocky cleaned up well, and after a few media appearances, customer interest in the product was growing. Thus Nanda now had to figure out *How do we gear up production? How do we handle the orders? How do we launch a full-fledged business?*

Nanda worked through all of those issues, launched her business, Nanda Home, in 2006, and sold more than a half million units of the Clocky over the next three years. While the product originated with Nanda's connective-inquiry skills and her willingness to ask What If, it would never have come into existence if Nanda hadn't taken that far-out idea and turned it, step by step, into a practical reality.

THE HOW STAGE of questioning is where the rubber meets the road or, in Nanda's case, the clock hits the floor. It's the point at which things come together and then, more often than not, fall apart, repeatedly. Reality intrudes and nothing goes quite as planned. To say it's the hard part of questioning is not to suggest it's easy to challenge assumptions by asking Why, or to envision new possibilities by asking What If. Those require difficult backward steps and leaps of imagination. But How tends to be more of a slow and difficult march, marked by failures that are likely to be beneficial—but don't necessarily seem that way at the time.

One of the difficult early challenges at this stage is to make a commitment to one idea. At the wide-open What If stage of inquiry, one tends to ask many questions, to explore multiple possibilities—from practical to far-out ideas. But when it comes time to act on an idea, you have to narrow possibilities and converge on the one deemed worthy of being taken to the next level.

In committing to an idea, it becomes critical to find a way to share it in order to get feedback. We all have ideas that live in our own head and never go beyond that. Even just by telling other people about a question you're working on, you've begun to form a commitment. "The important thing about telling everyone your idea is that it puts you on the hook for following through, because you're going to look foolish if you do nothing," observed the designer Sam Potts.

Nanda did this simply by asking those friends, *What would you think of an alarm clock on wheels—would you ever want something like that?* That kind of verbal pitch is useful up to a point. But you haven't really committed to an idea until you've given actual form to it. The question or idea must be made tangible and shareable—the better to be considered, passed around, perhaps tested in some way.

The most basic way to give form to an idea is to put it on paper (Nanda created rough sketches of what a Clocky might look like before she started building). Depending on the idea, putting it in writing—a summary, a proposal—may be sufficient, but keep in mind that visuals have great power. "If you want everyone to have the same mental model of a problem, the fastest way to do it is with a picture," according to the visualization expert David Sibbet.

That image could be drawn on the back of a napkin, or on an iPad using various available sketch programs, or with stock art off the Internet. As the representation of an idea becomes more complex—a test website, say, or a three-dimensional early model of a product (such as Nanda's shag-carpeted clock)—it moves into the prototype stage.

That's an overly technical term for something that can be done by anyone, in almost any endeavor. A prototype could be a short YouTube video that serves as the first step in making a film; it could be a pilot program or a trial run; a rudimentary model that may be taped or glued together; a sophisticated 3-D rendering using computer-aided design software; or just about anything that can be made to represent an idea in a preliminary form. The

IDEO designer Diego Rodriguez once remarked, "A prototype is a question, embodied." Given a body, the question becomes harder to ignore. Nanda's question—*What if a clock had wheels?*—became much more compelling to people when they actually saw a clock with wheels.

Technology has made it much easier to create prototypes quickly, inexpensively, in all shapes and forms. (This book started with a prototype: a blog called A More Beautiful Question, which began to advance some of the ideas of the book and solicited feedback from readers.) Some programs now can turn anyone into a sketch artist or website designer; more advanced software also allows users now to create highly sophisticated models that can be tested in all kinds of what-if scenarios (so that, for example, a digital prototype of a building can be subjected to simulated earthquake-level stress, to see how the building would hold up).

How might we roll it instead of lugging it?

The question *What if we put wheels on it?* has been the basis of countless "smart recombinations." For example in 1970 Bernard Sadow, a luggage company executive, was dragging two heavy suitcases through an airport when he noticed workers easily transporting a large machine on a wheeled skid. Sadow wondered, *What if I put wheels on these suitcases?* That led to a protracted How stage, which began with Sadow attaching four wheels to a suitcase laid flat—providing a way to drag one's bags. But that idea was later improved by an airline pilot, Robert Plath, who thought of using a long upright handle to pull a suitcase propped up on two wheels (instead of laying flat on four). The end result of all that questioning by Sadow and Plath: the now-ubiquitous Rollaboard suitcase.

The possibilities for prototyping will be greatly expanded as 3-D printing becomes widely available and affordable over the next few years. The technology, which makes it easy to sketch an idea for an object on a computer screen and then manufacture a physical version (usually made of plastic or steel), is "enabling a class of ordinary people to take their ideas and turn those into physical, real products," according to J. Paul Grayson, chief executive of the design-software company Alibre. It provides just one more way to bring our questions into the physical world.

Still, technology doesn't necessarily ease the trepidation many people feel about going public with ideas—particularly at the rough, early stages. As the writer Peter Sims noted in *Harvard*

Business Review, most of us, throughout our school years and even in the business world, have been taught to hold back ideas until they are polished and perfect. That tendency toward overthinking and excessively preparing, rather than quickly trying out ideas to get feedback and to see what works and doesn't, is a behavior that becomes ingrained over time.

But it's not the natural, instinctive way of exploring and creating. If you look at the way children act on their questions and ideas, you see a much better example of how to move quickly and fearlessly from What If to How.

How do you build a tower that doesn't collapse (even after you put the marshmallow on top)?

A software designer shared a story about an interesting experiment in which the organizers brought together a group of kindergarten children who were divided into small teams and given a challenge: Using uncooked spaghetti sticks, string, tape, and a marshmallow, they had to assemble the tallest structure they could, within a time limit (the marshmallow was supposed to be placed on top of the completed structure).

Then, in a second phase of the experiment, the organizers added a new wrinkle. They brought in teams of Harvard MBA grad students to compete in this challenge against the kindergartners. The grad students, I'm told, took it seriously. They brought a highly analytical approach to the challenge, debating among themselves about how best to combine the sticks, the string, and the tape to achieve maximum altitude.

Perhaps you'll have guessed this already, but the MBA students were no match for the kindergartners. For all their planning and discussion, the structures they carefully conceived and constructed invariably fell apart—and then they were out of time before they could get in more attempts. (I was told by my friend that the MBA grads also spent too much of their time arguing about who should be in charge.)

The kids used their time much more efficiently by constructing right away. They tried one way of building, and if it didn't work, they quickly tried another. They got in a lot more tries. They learned from their mistakes as they went along, instead of attempting to figure out everything in advance.

The point of the marshmallow experiment was not to humble MBA students (if anything, that was a side benefit), but rather to better understand how to make progress when tasked with a difficult challenge in uncertain conditions. What we learn from those kids is that there's no substitute for quickly trying things out to see what works.

Looking at this through the questioning prism: The MBA students got stuck too long contemplating the possible What Ifs, while the kids moved quickly from What If to How. As soon as they thought of a possible combination, they tried it to see how it would work.

So WHAT DOES an offbeat test involving marshmallows and kindergartners mean to those of us operating in the real world? One way to think about it is that in today's increasingly dynamic environment, we're all being challenged (or will soon be) to take some version of the marshmallow test: we'll be expected to quickly adapt to using new and unfamiliar tools, as we try to construct new businesses, new markets, new careers, new life plans—using ever-changing technology, without clear instructions, and with the clock ticking. All of which requires people to be not only better questioners, but better experimenters.

When you take a look at how adults in innovative environments work, they tend to operate much like the kids in the marshmallow test. At IDEO, the firm's designers quickly move from coming up with ideas to building and testing those ideas. The same is true at MIT Media Lab, where, as the director Joi Ito explains, the researchers and students don't spend a lot of time wondering about the questions they're pursuing, or debating how best to proceed. They quickly start doing what you're supposed to do in a lab—experimenting. As Ito puts it, "These days it's easier and less expensive to just try out your ideas than to figure out *if* you should try them out."

What Ito is doing in his lab is also happening at companies such as Google and Facebook, and throughout much of the tech industry worldwide. At Facebook, founder Mark Zuckerberg has elevated the idea of quickly building and testing ideas to a sacred principle that Zuckerberg has described as the Hacker Way. In a letter to potential Facebook investors at the time of the company's 2012 IPO, Zuckerberg explained that while the word *hacking* has some negative connotations, at Facebook it means "building something quickly or testing the boundaries of what can be done." This means constantly trying out new ideas in rough form. "Hackers try to build the best services over the long term by quickly releasing and learning from smaller iterations rather than trying to get everything right all at once . . . Instead of debating for days whether a new idea is possible or what the best way to build something is, hackers would rather just prototype something and see what works."

The rapid test-and-learn approach has caught on throughout the entrepreneurial world, fueled in part by Eric Ries's Lean Startup phenomenon. Ries maintains that entrepreneurs, existing companies—or anyone trying to create something new and innovative—must find ways to constantly experiment and quickly put new ideas out into the world for public consumption, rather than devoting extensive resources and time to trying to perfect ideas behind closed doors. Ries urges businesses to focus on developing what he calls "minimum viable products"—in effect, quick, imperfect test versions of ideas that can be put out into the marketplace in order to learn what works and what doesn't.

But this is more than a business strategy. The basic principles of the test-and-learn approach apply in almost any situation where people are trying to solve problems in dynamic, uncertain conditions.

For example, New York City under former Mayor Michael Bloomberg used test-and-learn pilot programs on everything from creating more pedestrian areas to implementing bike-rental programs to setting up a citywide 311 phone call-in system for providing information to residents. Bloomberg's administration was adept at bringing about change by tackling basic Why questions; Bloomberg acted as a kind of "pilot program mayor." It made it more possible to enact large-scale change—because if a pilot program wasn't panning out, it was easier to adjust it or just scrap it without having invested in full implementation.

How can you learn to love a broken foot?

Test-and-learn doesn't sound all that painful. However, baked into this approach of acting on questions via constant experimentation is the near certainty of failure—and not just one failure, but quite possibly many, each bringing some level of disappointment if not actual pain.

How do you make a hard-boiled egg's shell disappear?

The household kitchen is a hotbed for innovative questioning—both by professional kitchenware designers and inquisitive homemakers simply asking, *Why is this chore done this particular way?* and *How might it be done better?* For Betsy Ravreby Kaufman the task in question involved making deviled eggs for parties: Kaufman hated the drudgery of egg-peeling as well as having to throw away eggs due to stuck shells or gouges. Standing over a boiling pot of eggs, she thought, *Wouldn't it be cool if you could hard-boil an egg and not have shells to peel?* Which then morphed to, *What if you could boil an egg in a hard-boiled egg shape, but with the shell off?* She pitched her idea to Edison Nation, which backs invention ideas, and a year later a plastic "hard boiled egg system" called Eggies could be found not just in Kaufman's kitchen, but on store shelves, as well.

Van Phillips tried many prototypes of his prosthetic foot, starting off full of hope each time—and ending, in some instances, on the ground, his broken foot beside him. Yet none of this slowed his progress. As Winston Churchill once said, "The trick is to go from one failure to another, with no loss of enthusiasm." But how does one learn to perform that "trick" of "failing enthusiastically"?

"Every time a prototype breaks, it's heartbreaking," Phillips said. But it's also an opportunity: *How do I learn to learn from failure?* The answer is, through questioning. Rather than run from a failure or try to forget it ever happened, hold it to the light and inquire, *Why did the idea or effort fail? What if I could take what I've learned from this failure and try a revised approach? How might I do that?*

Stanford University's Bob Sutton says that when analyzing a misstep, in addition to asking what went wrong, you should also ask, *In this failure, what went* right? (Conversely, when you try out something and it seems to have succeeded, look for what went wrong or could have been better, Sutton says. The best learning comes from looking at successes and failures side by side.)

In analyzing a series of setbacks, a key question to ask is *Am I failing differently each time?* "If you keep making the same mistakes again and again," the IDEO founder David Kelley has observed, "you aren't learning anything. If you keep making new and different mistakes, that means you are doing new things and learning new things."

In sharing early versions of an idea with the world at large, one is likely to receive negative feedback—which some people interpret as evidence of a failure. But that's not necessarily true, says Harvard's Paul Bottino, who points out that when it comes to feedback, "dissonance can actually be more valuable than resonance." As people push back on your idea, it can be a good indication that you're entering uncharted, potentially important territory—because you're more likely to get negative feedback ("That could never work!") on ideas that challenge common assumptions. "Dissonance is the most misunderstood kind of feedback," Bottino says. "We really should welcome it and learn to make the most of it."

As Bottino points out, it's critical when taking on a challenging project to know how to solicit outside input and help, and to know how to engage with potential advisers, supporters, and collaborators. If you're pursuing a truly ambitious question, you probably can't answer it alone. Collaborative inquiry begins with asking others, *Do you find this question as interesting as I do? Want to join me in trying to answer it?*

THE INTERNET AND social networking has made it easier to find and connect with those who share our interests—and who may be exploring similar questions and challenges. Even if they're not, you might still be able to stoke their curiosity and garner their support.

Jack Andraka could not have gotten far with his question—*What if we could create a simpler, faster screening test for pancreatic cancer?*—without help. He particularly needed materials and tools with which to conduct experiments—he needed a lab. Andraka had gotten some early dissonant feedback from his own parents and brother, who thought his idea "would never work." But he forged ahead anyway. He gave form to his idea by laying out a basic plan: "I wrote up a procedure, budget, and timeline—that was really just trying to get a concrete representation of my idea," he said. Then he e-mailed "anyone in my area who knew something about pancreatic cancer," including experts at the National Institutes of Health, at Johns Hopkins, the University of Maryland, and others. His outreach to two hundred people brought more dissonant feedback. "Some of them just said, 'This won't work.' Others went through each and every step of my procedure saying this was wrong and that was wrong. It was pretty harsh." But one professor saw an intriguing possibility in Andraka's overarching question, as well as his more technical one (*What if I exposed a single-wall carbon nanotube with an antibody to a protein overexposed in pancreatic cancer?*). That professor responded, "'Yeah, sure, it might work,'" Andraka recalled. More important, the professor opened up his lab to Andraka.

The teenager had never been in a professional laboratory before.

> How do you fit a large golf course on a small island?
>
> When pro golfer Jack Nicklaus was hired in the 1980s to design a golf course on Grand Cayman Island, he faced a difficult challenge: The island, a mere six miles wide and twenty-two miles long, was too small to accommodate a full-size course. In his first whack at the problem, Nicklaus and his team cleverly designed a nine-hole course that can be played twice from different tees. Still, golfers couldn't shorten their swings, and balls were too easily sailing out into the surrounding water. At this point, instead of continuing to focus on the size of the course, Nicklaus reframed the problem: *What if golf balls didn't travel as far?* After heavy testing and research, Nicklaus and the MacGregor Golf Company developed the limited-flight "Cayman ball," which drives half the distance of a regular golf ball with the same amount of swing. Small island hotels and backyard duffers everywhere rejoiced.

"I was like, 'Wow, this is a centrifuge!' It was like being in a candy shop." But as Andraka began running tests, he started to experience failures. "In the first month I blew up the cell that I was carefully growing," he said. "Nothing was working."

Andraka's success came slowly, step by step, as he broke down the overall challenge into smaller problems and questions. With each solution, he could proceed to the next question. The first obstacle—Andraka's attempt to optimize the antibody he wanted to use in his paper sensor—stymied him for three months, but he kept tweaking the experiment until he found his antibody. Then he started working on his carbon nanotubes. Then he had to figure out how to combine the antibody and the nanotubes in his sensor. Finally he had to test it to see if it could detect pancreatic cancer. After seven months, he was done.

Asked about the experience of getting through the How stage—dealing with real-world complications, failures, lack of progress—Andraka recalled, "I would say coming up with the question—that's fun. Then arriving at a theoretical solution is even more fun." Then, as he was testing and learning in the lab, there were extreme ups and downs, he said. "At certain points, I was starting to think, 'Maybe all of those people are right. I'm a fifteen-year-old. What do I know about cancer?'"

But finally getting to an answer "is the best experience you can ever have." Andraka used the word *elegant* to describe the solution he arrived at—an odd word for something that looks like a mundane paper-strip test kit. "It's pure elation that you found this elegant way to solve a problem."

How might we create a symphony together?

That a fifteen-year-old kid with a far-fetched idea for detecting cancer could send out a batch of e-mails and thereby gain full access to a world-class lab shows that resources exist to aid in tackling almost any problem, and that people will help if you just ask (and ask well: Andraka had a powerful question, buttressed by a reasonable plan).

As the *New York Times* observed in an article headlined "Don't Know How? Find Someone Who Does," today anyone with a good idea can easily link up with experts who can help develop the idea, build it, and, when it's done, figure out what to do with it. "When we think of inventors," the *Times'* Nicole LaPorte wrote, "we think of a solitary soul hunkered down in a basement lab for weeks or months before emerging to claim an unshared victory." However, the reality is that "drawing on other people's experience and resources" is often far better than going it alone.

This shouldn't be surprising: When looking at a challenging problem or question, the more perspectives that can be brought to bear, the better. According to Scott Page, author of *The Difference: How the Power of Diversity Creates Better Groups, Firms, Schools, and Societies*, we all get "stuck" when trying to answer tough questions, but "if we have people with diverse tools, they'll get stuck in different places." As you look for potential collaborators, aim for people with backgrounds, cultural experiences, and skill sets that differ from your own: diversity fuels creativity.

Whereas in the past one might have been inclined to look for collaborators locally (as Andraka did, initially), today there's no need to put geographical limits on your outreach. Now, for anyone looking to tackle big questions, "we all have two amazing things available to us," said the film producer and part-time inventor Mick Ebeling. "We have a near-infinite resource of information at our fingertips—no other generation has had access to that. And we have this immediacy of human connection [through social networking and the Web in general]. You combine all of that information and that connection with people, and what we have is a global brain to tap into."

Ebeling himself tapped into the "global brain" when he decided to take on an ambitious project, with the goal of helping a paralyzed artist continue to create his art. The story began when Ebeling visited an exhibition of artwork by Los Angeles artist Tony "TemptOne" Quan, a legend in the graffiti world. Though Quan had once been a prolific artist, he became afflicted with ALS (aka Lou Gehrig's disease) and gradually lost use of his hands and legs, making it increasingly difficult to work. At first, Ebeling thought about writing a check to Quan and his family, but then, over a conversation with his wife at dinner, this question surfaced: *If Stephen Hawking can communicate through a machine, why don't we have a way for an artist like Quan to draw again?*

That Why question started Ebeling on a journey that eventually led him to a What If moment: When Ebeling learned about laser-tagging projection technology—which uses a laser and a pointer to write graffiti on the sides of buildings—he wondered if there might be an affordable way to enable someone to communicate and even create art by manipulating a laser through eye movements. Ebeling had no idea how this might be achieved, but now at least he had a good working question: *Knowing that laser technology can be used to create art, hands-free, what if we can figure out a way for Quan to control the laser with his eyes?*

Ebeling had no expertise in any of the technology involved. He made his challenge even more ambitious by deciding that anything he developed would have to be extremely affordable—the idea was not to replicate a high-priced, Hawking-like personal communication system, but rather something much simpler and accessible even to a paralyzed person of limited financial means.

"I felt that the way to attack this was in a communal way," Ebeling said. He approached Graffiti Research Lab, a company that specialized in laser-tagging technology, and asked if anyone there wanted to help him answer his question. He also searched among his own broad network of contacts for people with expertise in computer coding and engineering. "Today, we're all hackers and makers," Ebeling said; you have to find the right mix of people to bring together around a question that interests them all. After a year of planning and organization, Ebeling brought together in his house a team of seven international hackers and programmers for two and a half weeks of all-day programming sessions. By the end, they had cobbled together the Eyewriter.

The device was remarkably simple, at least on the surface: an inexpensive pair of sunglasses connected by wire to a small packet that incorporates ocular-recognition technology and lasers. The

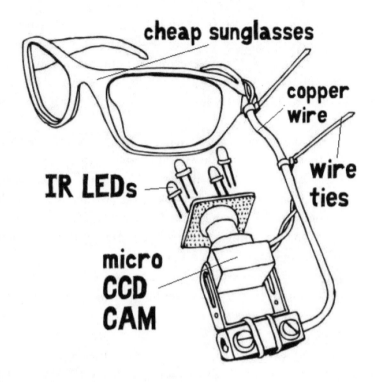

first true test of the system came when it was brought to Quan, who was in the hospital at the time. Ebeling's crew set up outside the hospital a projector that was wirelessly linked to the Eyewriter they gave to Quan. That night, for the first time in six years, Quan was able to create graffiti—using eye movements to control the laser in his Eyewriter as he began to "draw" on a building wall outside the hospital.

The DIY design and the software for the Eyewriter are downloadable for free. "Anyone who is paralyzed now has access to draw or communicate using only their eyes," Ebeling announced at a recent TED Conference, drawing a standing ovation from the crowd. (Ebeling closed his talk with two questions that he urged audience members to ask themselves every day: *"If not now, then when? If not me, then who?"*)

Ebeling is so sold on the power of collaborative inquiry that he launched a website, Not Impossible Labs, designed to help innovators connect with each other and find great problems to work on together. The name derives from his belief that "it is naïve now to think that anything, any problem we might be looking at, is impossible to solve." Whatever ambitious question you might come up with, people are out there with the knowledge, skills, and imagination to help you work toward an answer—if you can connect with them.

Reaching out to potential collaborators can require a leap of faith for those accustomed to trying to solve problems on their own. (I'm a case in point: As an author I've always written books pretty much alone. But with this book, I tried a different approach, using my blog to ask if anyone wanted to contribute ideas, research, or thoughts on questioning. As a result, I ended up with more than a dozen collaborators who contributed immensely to the project.) Among the concerns/questions that may arise: *Will the idea still be "mine" if I share it? Why would anyone care enough to actually help? If I'm used to coming up with ideas alone, will I be able to do so working with others?*

Tod Machover of MIT Media Lab has emerged as an advocate for, and a master of, collaborative inquiry in his work. Machover is both an engineer and a musical composer, whose work has ranged from creating the popular *Guitar Hero* interactive music game to composing operas and symphonies in which the audience actively participates in creating the musical performance. While almost every large-scale project he works on ends up being a collaborative endeavor, Machover stresses that it's critical to find a balance between working alone on ideas and working with others. "There are times, especially early in the creative process, when I want to slow down and think about a challenging question by myself," he said. (At such times, he retreats to the solitude of a barn converted into a music studio.) "As a composer I love the act of imagining a question—and even a whole world—and being able to make it real in your mind over a long period, before you share it with others."

But there's also a time, he said, when you must take your question "out of the barn" and begin to work with others. The Media Lab is designed to be an ideal collaborative environment, bringing together people from a wide range of disciplines. "Everyone is comfortable saying to others in the lab, 'Here's something I'm passionate about—would you help me to think about this question?'"

But Machover doesn't just collaborate with other members of the lab. On one of his most recent projects, he was invited by the Toronto Symphony to compose an original piece of music for them. He decided to invite the whole city of Toronto to cocreate a symphony with him, by capturing and sharing sounds representing everyday life in Toronto. "I wanted to see what happens when you try to answer a question working with *a lot* of people," Machover said. The collaborative query he raised: *What does Toronto sound like?*

For years, Machover has been exploring different variations on what is essentially the same question: *How might we turn music into a more participatory experience?* It springs from his sense that most people have become passive consumers of music—"it's everywhere, on everyone's headphones, but fewer people are studying music, making it, or participating in the full experience of music," he said. In the midnineties, Machover created an experimental music event called the *Brain Opera*—featuring a whole orchestra of instruments the general public could play. These "hyperinstruments" were scattered around New York's Lincoln Center, and as people wandered through the collection, they were invited to play with them (the instruments created sound in response to the user's movements). Those sounds were then edited together for a stage performance whose composition "was half-mine and half-created

How might we cut the cord?

Increasingly, it's a wireless world—so why are we still tethered to an outlet when recharging our devices? This was the question Israeli entrepreneur Ran Poliakine asked in 2006, and his quest to answer it led him to Nikola Tesla's 1890s work on wireless power. Poliakine created the "wireless charging" category with the October 2009 launch of the Duracell Powermat, which works by magnetic induction. Separately, in 2010, astrobiologist student Meredith Perry was searching for a way to beam power directly to electronic gadgets without using cords, and her Google-fueled research led her to the concept of "piezoelectricity" (electricity resulting from pressure). This dictated Perry's next question: *How do I create vibration in the air without actually moving something?* Her uBeam recharging device, which CrunchFund's Mike Arrington called "the closest thing to magic," combines the fields of sound, electricity, and battery technology, and is currently under development backed by millions of dollars in venture capital.

by the public," Machover said. "The point was to say, 'If you like listening to music, you'll like it even more if you can be part of it, touch it and shape it.'"

The idea for *Guitar Hero*—which also responds to body movement, enabling nonmusicians to create their own guitar riffs just by going through the motions—came out of the *Brain Opera* experiment. And the Toronto Symphony experiment was another attempt to pose his question about collaborative music in a fresh way. Thousands participated in the project, with many writing their own musical vignettes (using melodies and chords provided by Machover) incorporating the sounds of the Toronto subway, the harborfront, etc. Machover wove the many sounds together into a single musical piece, performed by the Toronto Symphony in 2013.

Machover was surprised at first that so many participated in the experimental attempt to answer his question. "But what I've become convinced of is that if you're willing to lay out something in public that you care about, people will be interested in participating. And they're capable of remarkable things."

Sharing a question with others is akin to issuing a challenge that a certain type of curious-minded person may find hard to resist. Just by formulating the question, you've taken a critical and difficult first step that others can now piggyback on. As the author Clay Shirky has noted in his writing, many people are drawn to an existing idea they can join in on and help to improve or advance, rather than starting from scratch on their own. Machover observes that in appealing to others with a shared question, "you are involving collaborators as equals in a project." What may start out seeming as if it's "your" question quickly becomes theirs, too; questions belong to everyone.

As for the answer, it belongs to whoever gets to it first. Holding back ideas—hoarding your beautiful questions—is usually pointless because it's hard to make headway on something hidden in a drawer. Better to bring a question out into the light of day and trust that, with help from others, you'll get something out of it—a solution, a learning experience, an insight, a fresh perspective, a sense of purpose—that will be yours.

WHILE THE How stage is positioned here as a third and final stage of innovative questioning, there really is no final stage—because the questions don't end, even when you arrive at a solution.

Many successful questioners, having arrived at an "answer," quickly return to asking questions. Often, they're questioning the very answers they found, which may not have been definitive. There is invariably room (and the need) to find ways to improve those solutions, to expand upon them, take them to another level.

Van Phillips might have been content with the high-level prosthetic limb he designed, but from his perspective, it solved a problem for some amputees—those who could afford to pay thousands of dollars for a replacement limb—but not others. Phillips had a vision for a high-performance replacement limb that would sell for a hundred dollars, making it affordable to amputees in the developing world; he was particularly focused on helping landmine survivors. So he began, some years ago, cycling through new Why and What If questions on a new and affordable prosthetic, and he was deep into the How stage of this line of questioning at the time of this writing. He'd already figured out how to make it, but he was still working through the details of how to bring the product to market.

Mick Ebeling, too, found himself quickly moving on to a new set of questions about his Eyewriter. The system initially worked well for Tony Quan, who controlled the mechanism through rapid blinking. But a new problem developed: As his medical condition led to degeneration of Quan's ocular muscles, it became difficult for him to blink quickly. So Ebeling's new question was *What if we found another way to control the laser? What if it could be done by thinking, not blinking?*

To that end, Ebeling began pulling together a new team of collaborators to work on the Brainwriter—an advanced version of the Eyewriter. The idea is to create a drawing tool powered by electrical brain activity, as measured by EEG. This would seem to be even more complex and challenging than the creation of the Eyewriter, though Ebeling insisted, "It's very doable if you have the right people involved."

The notion of a need to keep moving ideas forward, to keep pursuing new opportunities and responding to change by way of constant, cyclical questioning is particularly relevant in today's dynamic business environment, where companies find that "answers" are transitory and increasingly short-lived. The next chapter considers why constant questioning is more important to business than ever before.

CHAPTER 4

Questioning in Business

Why do smart businesspeople screw up?

Why are we in business? (And by the way—what business are we *really* in?)

What if our company didn't exist?

What if we could become a cause and not just a company?

How can we make a better experiment?

If we brainstorm in questions, will lightning strike?

Will anyone follow a leader who embraces uncertainty?

Should mission statements be mission questions?

How might we create a culture of inquiry?

Why do smart businesspeople screw up?

Clayton Christensen is today considered one of the foremost experts on business innovation. A veteran professor at the Harvard Business School, Christensen introduced the term *disruptive innovation* into the business lexicon two decades ago, and it has become both a cliché and a driving force in business ever since. His ideas have been embraced by the likes of Intel leader Andy Grove and Apple cofounder Steve Jobs.

But back in the late 1990s, Christensen was a relatively unknown professor with a question he couldn't shake—a Why question that sprang from a phenomenon that was happening more and more in business and didn't make sense to Christensen. He saw that a number of successful, market-leading companies in the tech sector and other industries were getting blindsided by newcomers offering products or services that may not have been as good, but were simpler, more convenient, and more affordable. Even more puzzling, the companies suffering these sudden reversals of fortune seemed to be doing all the right things: serving their customers better, improving their products, increasing their profit margins. "They were doing exactly what they were taught in business school," Christensen says.

Christensen wondered, in particular, why the established business leaders weren't able to respond to these challenges. "For me, it always starts with a question," Christensen told me. "I knew the failure could not be attributed to managers' being stupid. So I framed the question as *Why are the smartest people in the world having this problem?* Just thinking of it that way made me look in different places."

What Christensen discovered was that while most of the companies getting in trouble were focused on innovation that aimed to make good products even better, the real potential for breakthrough innovation was at the low end of the market—this was true in business offerings that ranged from disk drives to automobiles. In an increasingly technical marketplace, if you could take a product that was expensive, complex, and exclusive and make it affordable and accessible, you could open up a mass market and change the game—toppling the established leaders. But why were only the newcomers seizing this opportunity? Why weren't the established leaders, with all their know-how and resources, able to dominate the low end of the market as well as the high end?

Christensen came to see this as a dilemma: To pursue disruptive innovation at the low end, companies would have to move away from all they had worked so hard to build. As Christensen puts it, they faced this deceptively tricky question: *Should we make better products that we can sell for higher profits to our best customers—or make worse products that none of our customers would buy, and that would ruin our margins?*

If you were a smart business leader, you naturally opted for the former. And in making that seemingly logical choice, you sealed your company's fate.

After Christensen published his theory in the bestselling book *The Innovator's Dilemma*, the idea of focusing on "disruptive innovation" at the low end of markets became standard business practice, particularly in Silicon Valley, where Christensen's book was, for a time, a kind of innovator's bible. While it's a testament to Christensen's keen questioning ability that he was able to find and pursue the Whys and What Ifs that led to his discovery, nevertheless one can't help wondering:

Why didn't others—particularly the smart people running those companies he studied—see the "innovator's dilemma" themselves?

Why did it take a business professor to point out what was going on in their businesses, their industries, under their own noses? Why weren't they asking the questions Christensen was asking?

CHRISTENSEN HAS A theory on this, as well: They hadn't been trained to question. In business school these future chief executives were armed with management theory that was perfectly serviceable and sensible—up to the point at which the world changed and the old theory failed. When that point was reached, most leaders weren't able to step back and ask:

Why isn't this working anymore?

What if the business market is now upside-down—and the bottom has risen to the top? And if that's the case . . .

How should my business respond to this new reality? How do we rewrite the old theories?

Today, while market conditions and challenges have become even more complex, uncertain, and subject to radical disruption across industries, Christensen feels that business leaders, for the most part, still aren't asking enough questions, and especially the right kinds of questions.

Keith Yamashita, a longtime consultant to top companies such as IBM and Coca-Cola, observes that in the business world at large "we're coming off a twenty-five-year posteighties period of efficiency, efficiency, efficiency. I think the unintended consequence of that entire efficiency era is that people diminished their questions to very small-minded ones. In this quest for incremental improvement, it became all about asking, *How can we save a little bit of money, make it a little more efficient, where can we cut costs?*"

But Yamashita says the era of "small-minded questions" is ending. "Company leaders are realizing that if they're only asking the small questions, it's not going to advance their agenda, their position, or their brands. In order to innovate now, they have to ask more expansive questions."

What Yamashita is talking about is an evolution in business questions themselves. The old, closed questions (*How many? How much? How fast?*) still matter on a practical level, but increasingly businesses must tackle more sophisticated open questions *(Why? What if? How?)* to thrive in an environment that demands a clearer sense of purpose, a vision for the future, and an appetite for change.

This affects new companies as much as the established ones. Start-ups have always had to ask tough questions about their reason for being (*Why does the world need another company? Why should anyone care about us? How in the world are we going to break through?*), and that's truer than ever in a market now crowded with newcomers.

But established companies in old-line industries may need questioning even more. Many are dealing with new threats and volatile changes that are suddenly calling into question why they're needed, what they do, and how they do it. Small wonder, then, that for top business consultants such as Dev Patnaik of Jump Associates "questioning is now the number one thing I spend my time on with clients."

IT'S NOT EASY to bring questioning to companies; most of them weren't built for it. American businesses in particular, and many major post–World War II European companies, "were designed on a military model that came out of the war, built by people who'd been through that war, and the businesses were organized around that mind-set," Patnaik says. Central to that was the idea of a formal hierarchy and chain of command that didn't leave much room for calling into question the accepted practices and procedures.

That old model doesn't lend itself particularly well to a business market that favors speed, flexibility, and collaborative inquiry. But changing that established business model—specifically, to allow for more questioning—requires difficult shifts in ingrained policies and approaches. For example, Eric Ries, the pioneer of the Lean Startup movement, which teaches entrepreneurs and other companies how to adopt more agile, flexible approaches, points out that an incentive system has been built through the years to encourage answers, not questions. "The industrial economy was all about knowing the answer and expressing confidence," Ries said. "If you did your homework, you were supposed to *know*. If you had unanswered questions, that meant you did a bad job and wouldn't get rewarded."

Another challenge is that while rapid change makes it necessary for businesses to question more, it also causes businesspeople to feel as if they don't have time to question what they're doing. Tony Wagner, the Harvard education expert who has studied the role of questioning in business, notes, "The pressure on short-term results tends to drive questioning out of the equation."

For those inclined to question, the difficulty may be in knowing what to ask. "With all the uncertainty out there," Patnaik says, "organizations don't even know what they don't know." Figuring out the questions that are most critical for a particular company to consider, given current challenges and market conditions, may be the first order of business. While the key questions vary depending on the individual business, a good place to start is at the most fundamental level—with questions of purpose.

Why are we in business? (And by the way—what business are we *really* in?)

Almost every company would acknowledge that it is in business to make money so that it can *stay* in business. But most companies, if you trace their origins, were started for more complex reasons than that. Many of the companies featured in this book—Patagonia, W. L. Gore, Nike, Airbnb, Panera, Netflix—started out on a quest to fill an unmet need, to make some aspect of our lives a bit easier, more convenient, more enjoyable. Most good companies are born trying to answer a question and solve a problem, which provides an early sense of purpose.

But that motivating principle gets buried over time. Asking Why questions can help to unearth it. (And if, after being dug up, that sense of purpose needs to be revitalized, freshened up, and made relevant again, questioning can help with that, too.)

There are different ways of thinking about purpose. A furniture retailer might choose to think its purpose is to sell people furniture. But it could also approach the business in a very different way. Its higher purpose might be that the company brings a sense of style into the lives of those on a budget; or that it enables people to express their creativity through home furnishings. Getting this right is subtle; advertising sometimes attaches generic or artificial purposes to companies. But if the leaders of a company think hard enough, and question well enough, about where the company came from, what it does best, and whom it serves, they will often uncover a more meaningful and authentic purpose in the company's origins.

Yamashita uses a set of questions when he works with companies to try to identify purpose. One of the main ones is fairly straightforward, if a bit grand:

What is our company's purpose on this earth?

Yamashita acknowledges that this may sound high-minded for a company. But the new business environment increasingly demands that companies think in terms that go beyond mundane corporate concerns. To arrive at a powerful sense of purpose,

QUESTIONING IN BUSINESS   141

Yamashita says, companies today need "a fundamental orientation that is outward looking"—so they can understand what people out there in the world desire and need, and what's standing in the way. At the same time, business leaders also must look inward, to clarify their core values and larger ambitions.

To figure out the internal values, Yamashita urges company leaders to look back in time and consider this question:

Who have we (as a company) historically been when we've been at our best?

At the finest moments in a company's history, Yamashita holds, its core values usually came shining through. But from time to time it may be necessary to revisit that past to reaffirm the company's higher purpose.

Casey Sheahan, the CEO of the outdoor-apparel company Patagonia, admits that even a company such as his—with a strong, well-defined mission that is tied to encouraging outdoor activity and protecting the environment—has to revisit questions about purpose and mission regularly. "There is great tension every day in the company between being successful in terms of growth, and what this means in terms of our environmental impact." The bigger Patagonia gets, the more challenging this becomes. Sheahan grapples constantly with the question *How can we minimize the environmental impact of the tremendous carbon footprint of operating a $570 million business?*

What helps guide the company at all times, he said, is the knowledge of how it began. "When the company was started by the founders, it was basically about protecting what they loved, nature, and trying expand the sphere of influence in order to inspire others."

Not only is that the reason Patagonia exists—it's also the reason people come to work there, to this day. "It's why they're going up the stairs two steps at a time to get to their jobs," Sheahan says. The company has enjoyed strong financial growth in recent years, but that's not the Why factor for most people working there. When Sheahan talks about financial results, there is mild interest; "but when I say something like, 'By the way, we're sending fifty people

down to the Gulf to help with the cleanup efforts down there'—
suddenly people are on their feet cheering. *That's* why they're here."

Not every company has a clear environmental mission like
Patagonia's, but Sheahan maintains, "For any organization, it is
galvanizing to have a strong purpose and values, no matter what
they might be." A good way to surface that is by looking back to
when the business was founded and asking, *What was that higher
purpose at the outset? And how can we rally people around that today?*

At the same time, as Yamashita points out, it's just as important
to look forward when asking big questions about purpose. He
urges clients to work on *Whom must we fearlessly become?* That can
be a difficult challenge, he says, because it requires "envisioning a
version of the company that does not exist yet."

PURPOSE QUESTIONS ARE important because if you can answer
them, that frees up company leaders to pursue all kinds of far-
reaching opportunities and questions, knowing all the while that
they are on firm footing. "Products come and go, leaders come and
go, trends come and go," says Yamashita, "but through all of that,
you need to know the answer to the question *What is true about us,
at our core?*"

Knowing that answer becomes especially critical when a
company finds itself in the midst of dramatic change. The digital
revolution has forced many companies to rebuild and rethink,
sometimes pushing them into unfamiliar territory. A company
that has figured out the basic questions of identity and purpose is
in a better position to handle unsettling new questions such as
What business are we in now?

Nike provides an instructive example of how a company can
continually adapt through constant questioning of its most basic
approaches. The company tends to guard its secrets closely, but a
few years ago I had an opportunity to talk to a design researcher
who'd done some work with Nike and got an up-close look at how
it ventures out into the ball fields, courts, and running tracks with
athletes (both pros and the weekend jocks) to study their movements and to detect their needs.

About a decade ago, Nike's researchers observed a profound change that digital technology was having on athletes such as runners. The many more ways to measure, improve, and enrich the running experience also created complications. Runners were fumbling with various gadgets—stopwatches, heart monitors, music players—as they ran. Nike went into classic Why mode (*Why does this problem exist? Why hasn't anyone addressed it?*). Then, in considering What If possibilities, the idea emerged of creating a hybrid, networked tool, somehow connected to a Nike running shoe, that could encompass many of the new needs a runner has: from measuring distances, to charting progress, to getting pumped up by music, to connecting with other runners. In effect, Nike was proposing:

What if a running shoe could run your life?

But getting to the How of this was another matter; Nike was a sneaker company, not a digital-device maker. The company figured that the only way to pull off something as audacious as this was through a partnership with a tech company. Striking a collaborative deal with Steve Jobs and Apple wasn't easy. (According to a press report, Jobs initially berated Nike chief executive Mark Parker for trying to expand into digital; *stick to the sneakers* was Jobs's message, with a profanity or two thrown in.) But eventually, Nike won over Jobs and produced a hybrid product, Nike+, which wirelessly connected a Nike running shoe to an Apple iPod device, which was in turn connected to a website. A classic "smart recombination," it enabled the runner to program music, track running and

Are we really who we say we are?

In the mid-1990s, the premium cable channel HBO was in a creative rut when, according to *Fast Company*, then-chief programmer Chris Albrecht sat down with other HBO executives and asked the question above. Albrecht wanted his colleagues to step back and take a hard look at the channel's creative output—and consider whether it actually lived up to the high-quality image HBO was projecting. The consensus answer to Albrecht's question: "We're not quite there yet." The group then proceeded to apply a set of additional questions to each of its shows, asking, *Is it distinctive? Is it good?* They focused in on the central idea behind each show: *Was it an original and worthwhile idea? And was this show the very best realization of that idea?* Subsequently, the results of that rigorous inquiry materialized in the form of groundbreaking series like *Sex and the City* and *The Sopranos*.

health data, communicate with other runners, find running partners, share tips, and so forth.

But it did something more important for Nike—it helped
them begin to think outside the shoebox. Nike now has a line of
digital products, including its highly successful FuelBand wrist
tracker. It is gradually becoming a digital company as much as it
is a shoe company. So if you ask, *What business is Nike really in?*,
the answer is constantly changing—though it's grounded in the
core purpose of serving an athlete's lifestyle needs, in whatever
form they might take.

Nike isn't the only company going through these kinds of
core changes of late. A recent article in *Fast Company* pointed
out that a number of today's leading companies—Nike, Apple,
Netflix—have increasingly been finding success by moving
outside their primary area of expertise. The article, with the
provocative headline "Death to Core Competency," suggests
that whatever a company's specialty product or service might
be—whatever got you to where you are today—might *not* be the
thing that gets you to the next level. Even newer companies
must make these kinds of major shifts: In 2008, Facebook—
having already achieved remarkable early growth in terms of
attracting nearly 100 million users—brought in a new executive,
Sheryl Sandberg, who reportedly posed a fundamental question
to the company's leaders and employees: *What business was
Facebook in?* With all of its rapid subscriber growth, the company
had yet to settle on a model for making money. Sandberg's question prompted internal debate—and resulted in a new strategy
that was much more advertising-focused.

It's a sobering realization for many businesses: They can't rest on
what they've already done, or what they know. The need to bring a
"beginner's mind" to business may make it necessary to—if only
temporarily—set aside all history, and all notions of what has
worked in the past, in order to ask questions from a fresh
perspective.

What if our company didn't exist?

Early in its history, the microprocessor company Intel found itself facing a difficult decision. The company had started out making computer memory chips, and its success with that product established Intel. But as the memory-chip business began to slow down, Intel's cofounders, Andrew Grove and Gordon Moore, had to decide whether to shift the company's focus into more promising areas. Yet they were torn: Chips were central to their identity—and Intel wouldn't have gotten to where it was without them.

Then Grove posed an interesting question to his partner:

If we were kicked out of the company, what do you think the new CEO would do?

Grove and Moore reasoned that a new leader would feel no emotional attachment to the declining memory-chip business and would probably leave it behind. So they did likewise, shifting Intel's focus to microprocessors—which set the stage for remarkable growth in the years to follow.

When companies are facing disruptive change (and these days, what company isn't?), old habits and traditions can sometimes get in the way of progress. One of the things hypothetical What If questioning can do is remove those constraints, if only briefly, to allow for more fresh thinking.

You could ask, as Grove and Moore did, *What if different leaders were brought in?*, but Clay Christensen suggests a bolder version of this question: *What if the company didn't exist?* That question allows you to take a clean-slate approach in thinking about the industry and your place in it. Christensen points out that thinking about your company as if there were no history enables leaders to stop focusing on preexisting beliefs and structures—"the stuff they've already invested in"—and consider new possibilities. That's particularly useful "if, at any point in the future, you see the possibility that the core business might slow down," Christensen says. (While contemplating a world in which your company did not exist, another question worth considering is *Who would miss us?* The answer to that can help clarify who your most important custom-ers are and what your real purpose is.)

It's not easy for a company to move away from what it has done in the past. The consultant Jack Bergstrand of Brand Velocity thinks one of the most important questions companies should ask regularly is *What should we* stop *doing?* Company leaders naturally tend to focus on what they should *start* doing. Bergstrand notes that coming to terms with what you're willing to eliminate is always harder. Yet if you can't answer that question, he maintains, "it lessens your chances of being successful at what you want to do next—because you'll be sucking up resources doing what's no longer needed and taking those resources away from what should be a top priority." Moreover, if you can't figure out what you should stop doing, it might be an early warning sign that you don't know what your strategy is.

Bergstrand explains that it's difficult for most companies to stop doing things—especially putting an end to programs or products that were once successful—because "we don't like to kill our babies." In addition, corporate politics can get in the way; individuals or groups within a company are naturally inclined to protect their own projects. "Even asking the question about 'what should we stop' makes people inside a company uncomfortable," Bergstrand says. For that reason, it may be necessary to adopt the *What if the company didn't exist?* mind-set—so that you can then be willing to cut ties with old programs, products, and practices.

HISTORY AND ROUTINE aren't the only things that can impede a company's forward movement. Various real-world constraints can also inhibit a company's ability to adapt and innovate; for example, being overly concerned with practical issues such as costs and budgets tends to limit the scope of creative thinking. That's why some business leaders (including Steve Jobs when he headed Apple) have been known to use What If hypothetical questioning to temporarily remove practical constraints. One such approach is to encourage teams working on projects to ask themselves, *What if money were no object? How might we approach the project differently?*

By temporarily removing these restrictions, people's imaginations are freed up to find the best idea, cost notwithstanding. You might end up with a groundbreaking possibility that can then be scaled back to make it more affordable.

Conversely, using What If questions to *impose* constraints can also be effective. By challenging people to think about creating or achieving something within extreme limits—*What if we could only charge ten bucks for our hundred-dollar service?*—it forces a rethinking of real-world practicalities and assumptions. Sometimes the fantasy becomes reality. As the business consultant and Dartmouth University professor Vijay Govindarajan notes, hospitals in India have developed incredibly inexpensive (yet still safe and reliable) surgical approaches to provide operations for a fraction of their cost in other countries—in part because they were forced by market pressures to question the prevailing assumptions about surgical costs.

> **What if we were to compete against ourselves?**
>
> In 2007, the 150-year-old *Atlantic Monthly* was suffering along with many other advertising-starved magazines. Publisher David G. Bradley brought in new editorial and business teams and, the *New York Times* reports, they brainstormed as if they were launching a Silicon Valley startup whose mission was to attack the magazine, asking: *What would we do if the goal was to aggressively cannibalize ourselves?* Answer: they'd launch an assault on the digital front. Knowing that news aggregation was killing magazines, they started their own "killers," TheAtlantic Wire.com, TheAtlanticCities.com, and Quartz. They gradually merged the previously separate digital and print staffs, ended the paywall for Atlantic.com readers, and even officially dropped "monthly" from their name. By late 2012, traffic to web properties was up 2500 percent and revenue doubled; the company was profitable for the first time in decades. They essentially ate their own lunch, and now are dining out on that great decision.

What if we could become a cause and not just a company?

As businesses throw off constraints and imagine bold What If possibilities, some may consider an ultra-ambitious one: Can a company transform itself into a cause? And why would it want to do so?

The answer to the second question partly has to do with a new dynamic in the relationship between consumers and business. Because of the Internet and social media, people know more about companies and brands than ever before. And they care more than ever about how companies are behaving, what a company's values are, what that company stands for.

Employees feel this even more strongly. Younger workers, in particular, have shown they want to align themselves with companies that support principles and values similar to their own, and companies that are contributing to a greater good. "The modern worker is not the salary worker of old," says Tim Ogilvie of the consulting firm Peer Insight. "Increasingly, they're saying, 'I want to do something I really believe in.'" So to the extent a company can stand for something more than just what it sells or creates, it can develop a deeper relationship with both consumers and employees.

Keith Yamashita says companies can try to find their cause by asking, *What does the world hunger for?* This may require some contextual inquiry—venturing beyond the corporate bubble to spend time with the people who are your customers—to figure out what they care about or feel passionate about. The next step is to identify what may be standing in their way—an obstacle, a problem. To the extent you can alleviate that problem, your company can be seen as more than just a business out to make money.

A case in point is Panera Bread, the growing U.S.-based chain of bakery/restaurants. Panera CEO Ron Shaich recalls that as the company sought to find a more meaningful role in communities, it looked for a problem that matched up well with its capabilities and resources. At one point, Shaich had a conversation that questioned:

What does the world need most . . . that we are uniquely able to provide?

Shaich says he wrestled with that question for a while, then worked his way to an answer with the launch of Panera Cares—an initiative to open a number of pay-what-you-can cafés that are identical to the chain's other restaurants, except customers pay what they wish or can afford (based on suggested donation amounts).

With so much fresh-baked bread in so many outlets, Panera has always been "uniquely able" to provide leftover bread to people in need—and the company has, for years, been a contributor to community food pantries. But there's a difference between donating to charity (something many companies do, almost by rote), and fully committing to a cause. "We started asking ourselves, *What more can we do?*" Shaich says. "I felt like, I want to put our bodies on the line." What gradually became clear was that Panera could provide not just bread giveaways, but a more complete dining experience for those going hungry. That extra level of involvement— "putting bodies on the line," to use Shaich's words—made the effort bigger and more distinctive than a standard corporate charity program.

How can we drive more ounces into more bodies, more often?

During the years Jeffrey Dunn was a top executive at Coca-Cola, the "unbeautiful question" above was central to the marketing of Coke's sugary soft drinks. Coke wasn't alone, of course: Author Michael Moss has revealed that companies throughout the snack food industry have been similarly focused on ingenious questions and methods aimed at increasing consumption of products loaded with salt, sugar, and fat— even as America's obesity epidemic has steadily worsened. Today, Dunn has moved on to a more healthful product, as the head of the carrot company Bolthouse Farms (which pioneered the marketing of "baby carrots" after a local grower, tired of throwing away misshapen or gnarly carrots, wondered, *What if I peel off the skin and cut them into perfect mini-carrots?*). At Bolthouse, Dunn has been promoting baby carrots as crunchy treats available in snack-packs—an endeavor to answer his new question, *What if we marketed baby carrots like junk food?*

The first Panera Cares café opened about two years ago. Now, the five cafés around the country serve over a million people a year (and for the most part cover costs, as high donations from some customers tend to balance out lower ones by others).

SHAICH NOTES THAT as the company was developing the Panera Cares idea and putting it into practice (with the CEO himself working at the first café), a number of tough choices were made to ensure the integrity of the program: offering a full menu instead of a limited one, using donation boxes at the cafés instead of cash registers (Shaich was concerned that the latter could create psychological pressure on customers to pay). At each step, Shaich says, the company had to ask, *Do we want to take a short-cut on this or do it right?*

As Peer Insight's Tim Ogilvie observes, being true to a cause often requires making tough decisions and sacrificing at times. "When you come to the point where you can't serve both the bottom line and the cause, one or the other must suffer," says Ogilvie, pointing to the Whole Foods supermarket chain, which stopped selling live lobsters for an extended time until it found a supplier that did humane harvesting. "Those are hard choices, but when you opt for the cause over the bottom line, employees can see that, and then they believe in the company and the cause even more."

One of the challenges for marketers in becoming a cause is that while they may be used to saying they're "for" certain things, they rarely go the other way and ask themselves, *What are we against?* As part of its stand against excess consumerism, Patagonia went out on a limb when it considered:

What if we asked people not *to buy from us?*

The company decided it was willing to risk losing sales in support of a larger cause and ran ads urging people *not* to buy its clothing (or at least, not to buy a new jacket if they didn't actually need it). Says Patagonia's Sheahan, "Those ads were just asking people to question their consumerism and maybe be a little more mindful about the stuff they're purchasing." Still, it was a high-risk message, though Sheahan says it actually helped the brand gain market share by attracting more customers—who presumably admired the stand Patagonia was taking with the ads.

How can we make a better experiment?

Questioning also has an important role in everyday business matters such as product development. As Lean Startup's Eric Ries points out, it is central to testing out new ideas to see what works. Ries believes one of the most important questions businesses need to ask today is the one above. It's somewhat counterintuitive for most managers—who tend to think in terms of "making products," not "making experiments." But as Ries points out, anytime you're doing something new "it's an experiment whether you admit it or not. Because it is not a fact that it's going to work."

So how do companies get better at experimenting? Ries says you start with the acknowledgment that "we *are* operating amid all this uncertainty—and that the purpose of building a product or doing any other activity is to create an experiment to reduce that uncertainty." This means that instead of asking *What will we do?* or *What will we build?* the emphasis should be on *What will we learn?* "And then you work backwards to the simplest possible thing—the minimum viable product—that can get you the learning," he says.

Just this one change—before you get to any of the more complex Lean Startup methodology—can make a world of difference, Ries insists. For one thing, it can help unlock the creativity that's already there in your company. "Most companies are full of ideas, but they don't know how to go about

What is your tennis ball? (and other entrepreneurial questions)

Drew Houston, founder of the online storage service Dropbox, thinks all would-be entrepreneurs should try to answer the above question. "The most successful people are obsessed with solving an important problem, something that matters to them," according to Houston. "They remind me of a dog chasing a tennis ball." To enhance your prospects, "find your tennis ball—the thing that pulls you." PayPal cofounder Peter Thiel believes entrepreneurs can find ideas to pursue by asking themselves, *What is something I believe that nearly no one agrees with me on?* If self-examination doesn't work, try looking around: Brian Spaly, a serial entrepreneur in the apparel industry, advises, "Whenever you encounter a service or customer experience that frustrates you, ask, *Is this a problem I could solve?*" Lastly, don't just focus on the mercenary question *Will consumers pay for this?* The startup business coach Dave Kashen thinks the better question to ask about any new venture is, *Will this make people's lives meaningfully better?*

finding out if those ideas work," Ries says. "If you want to harvest all those ideas, allow employees to experiment more—so they can find out the answers to their questions themselves."

Peer Insight's Tim Ogilvie points out that it's also important for companies to give people a safe place to test ideas and run experiments. To that end, he says, companies need to be able to answer:

Where is our petri dish?

That question is really asking, *Where in the company is it safe to ask radical questions?* "As an established business," Ogilvie says, "you've got all these promises you're keeping to your current customers—you have to stay focused on that. But that may not have a future." So the question becomes "Where, within the company, can you explore heretical questions that could threaten the business as it is—without contaminating what you're doing now?"

Company leadership needs to "provide permission and protocols for experimentation," he says. That means providing the time and resources for people to explore new questions, as well as establishing methods: "How might we?" questioning sessions, ethnography, in-market experimentation. It can also mean cordoning off this area of the business—although a clear line of visibility should remain between the core business and the "petri dish" part of the company, so that each can influence the other.

Ogilvie says that yet another way to phrase this question is *Where is the place we can be a start-up again?* Surprisingly, he thinks it's a question that even start-ups should ask themselves. "Start-ups are so desperate not to be a start-up," says Ogilvie (himself a former start-up CEO). "They're so anxious to be postrevenue and postprofit that you can almost give up what's great about being a start-up too soon. They get built for execution, and once they're having success, they'll very quickly start thinking, 'We've got to stick to our knitting.'" All of which means they've outgrown their original petri dish—and might need a new one.

If we brainstorm in questions, will lightning strike?

In the business world these days, brainstorming has a mixed reputation. Increasingly, it's understood that people tend to do their best creative thinking—particularly in coming up with fresh insights and random associations by way of connective inquiry—in informal, relaxed settings, when they're not really trying.

A brainstorming session runs counter to that: Everyone is stuck in a room trying desperately to come up with original ideas. "There is too much pressure and too much influence from others in the group," according to Debra Kaye, author of the book *Red Thread Thinking*. "The free association done in brainstorming sessions is often shackled by peer pressure and as a result generates obvious responses."

But many businesses are reluctant to walk away from brainstorming because they recognize the critical importance of being able to tackle challenges as a group. Collaborative thinking in problem solving is essential because it brings together multiple viewpoints and diverse backgrounds. While it's understood that creativity sometimes requires solitude ("Be alone, that is when ideas are born," Nikola Tesla said), we also know that it flourishes when diverse ideas and thoughts are exchanged.

One solution to this conundrum may be to shift the nature of brainstorming so that it's about generating questions instead of ideas. Interesting findings about this are coming from a number of groups and individuals, working in both the education and business sectors.

The Right Question Institute—which specializes in teaching students to tackle problems by generating questions, not solutions—has found that groups of students (whether children or adults) seem to think more freely and creatively using the "question-storming" method, in which the focus is on generating questions. The RQI's Dan Rothstein believes that some of the peer pressure in conventional brainstorming is lessened in this format. Answers tend to be judged more harshly than questions.

In the business world, Hal Gregersen has been studying the effectiveness of question-storming at major corporations and has found it to be far more effective than conventional brainstorming. "Regular brainstorming for ideas often hits a wall because we only have so many ideas," Gregersen says. "Part of the reason we hit that wall is we're asking the wrong questions." When people in a group are struggling with an issue and find "they're getting nowhere, they're stuck," Gregersen says, "that's the perfect point to step back and do question-storming."

Gregersen will typically advise group members to try to generate at least fifty questions about the problem that's being "stormed." As those questions are being written down for everyone to see, "other team members are paying attention and thinking of a better question." It's usually easier to come up with questions than ideas; we don't have to divine a solution from the air or connect ideas in a fantastically original manner; we just have to come at the problem from a slightly different angle of inquiry.

After observing about a hundred Q-storm sessions around the world, Gregersen has noted some patterns. "At around twenty-five questions, the group may stall briefly and say, 'That's enough questions.' But if you push on beyond that point, some of the best questions come as you get to fifty or even seventy-five."

The RQI approach to question-storming focuses less on volume and moves more quickly to "improving" the questions generated by the group, by opening closed questions and closing open ones. The key is to converge around the best questions, as decided through group discussion. This gets to one of the big problems with brainstorming in general: Many ideas are tossed out, but the groups often don't know how to winnow down to the best ideas. It can be easier to winnow down questions because the best questions are magnetic—they intrigue people, make them want to work more on those. RQI recommends coming out of a session with three great questions that you want to explore further.

Question-storming can be more realistic and achievable than brainstorming. Instead of hoping that you'll emerge from a meeting with "the answer" (which almost never happens and thus leaves people feeling frustrated), the goal is to come out of it with a few promising and powerful questions—which is likely to provide a sense of direction and momentum.

As I WAS examining the ways some of today's cutting-edge companies are trying to reinvent brainstorming, an interesting trend surfaced: a specific form of questioning using three words—*How might we?* It's a simple way of ensuring that would-be innovators are asking the right questions and using the best wording. Proponents of this practice say it is surprisingly effective—and a testament to the importance of wording a question just right to spark creative thinking and freewheeling collaboration.

When people within companies try to innovate, they often talk about the challenges they're facing by using language that can inhibit creativity instead of encouraging it, says the business consultant Min Basadur, who has taught the *How might we?* (HMW) form of questioning to a wide range of companies over the past four decades. Basadur explains. "People may start out asking, 'How *can* we do this?' or 'How *should* we do that?' But as soon as you start using words like *can* and *should*, you're implying judgment: Can we really do it? And should we?" By substituting the word *might*, he says, "You're able to defer judgment, which helps people to create options more freely and opens up more possibilities."

Tim Brown, the chief executive of IDEO, says that when his firm takes on a design challenge of almost any type, it invariably starts by asking *How might we?*

What would Neil Patrick Harris do?

Andrew Rossi of the marketing firm M Booth has found that one of the best ways to stoke creativity during brainstorming sessions is to ask people in the group to think about the problem they're trying to solve from an unusual perspective. So, for example, if a company is introducing a new toothpaste, they might ask: *How would IKEA tackle a challenge like this?* Another approach is to add in an odd constraint, such as *What if your idea had to involve speed dating?* Rossi's group sometimes suggests adopting the perspective of a well-known artist or entertainer: *What would Jay-Z do in this situation? How would J. K. Rowling think about this? What might Neil Patrick Harris do?* (The latter has been described as "an actor, singer, dancer, producer, director, writer, child stardom survivor, evil genius, amateur puppeteer, and magic enthusiast"—so he might do just about anything.)

Brown observes that within the phrase, each of those three words plays a role in spurring creative problem solving: "The *how* part assumes there are solutions out there—it provides creative confidence. *Might* says we can put ideas out there that might work or might not—either way, it's okay. And the *we* part says we're going to do it together and build on each other's ideas."

Although the HMW has been used at IDEO for a number of years, its origins can be traced back fifty years to Sidney Parnes, a leading creativity expert at the time who headed up the Creative Problem Solving Institute in Buffalo, New York. Min Basadur studied at the CPSI during his tenure as a creative manager at Procter & Gamble in the early 1970s, and he adapted some of Parnes' brainstorming ideas to help P&G's marketers—who, at the time, were working themselves into a lather as they tried to compete with Colgate-Palmolive's popular new soap, Irish Spring, which featured a green stripe and an appealing "refreshment" promise.

By the time Basadur was asked to assist on the project, P&G had already tested a half dozen of its own copycat green-stripe bars, though none could best Irish Spring. Basadur figured the P&G team was asking the wrong question (*How can we make a better green-stripe bar?*) and soon had them asking a series of more ambitious HMW questions, culminating with *How might we create a more refreshing soap of our own?* That opened the creative floodgates, and over the next few hours, Basadur says, hundreds of ideas were generated for possible refreshment bars—with the team eventually converging around a theme of finding refreshment at the seacoast. Out of that came a coastal-blue and white-striped bar named (what else?) Coast, which became a highly successful brand.

As the Coast story suggests, there's more to HMW methodology than just using those three words. Basadur employed a larger process to guide people toward the *right* HMW questions. This included a number of Why questions (as in, *Why are we trying so hard to make another green-striped soap?*). He also urged the P&G team to step back from their obsession with a competitor's product and look at the situation from a consumer perspective. For the customer, it wasn't about green stripes—it was about feeling refreshed.

Basadur maintains that it's common for companies to expend efforts asking the wrong questions and trying to solve the wrong problems. "Most businesspeople have limited skills when it comes to 'problem-finding' or problem definition," he says. "It's not taught in MBA programs." To fill that void, Basadur opened a consultancy, Basadur Applied Creativity, which developed its own "Simplex" process of creative problem solving for business—with HMW questioning at the core of it.

Gradually, Basadur took the How might we? approach beyond P&G to other companies, including the tech firm Scient. One of his converts at Scient, the designer Charles Warren, then took the methodology with him as he moved to IDEO. IDEO's Brown confesses that when he was introduced to the notion of encouraging businesspeople to ask *How might we?*, "I was skeptical at first—it sounds a bit Californian." But before long, says Warren, IDEO was conducting companywide question-storming sessions with seven hundred people asking the question together.

When Charles Warren then moved from IDEO to Google, the infectious HMW approach found a new host. Warren led the user-experience design team that took on the challenge of creating Google+. "We were asking *How might we?* questions every day," he says. At Google, such questions can run the gamut from *How might we predict whether a flu outbreak is going to happen, based on search queries?* to *How might we help more people feel more comfortable sharing more of their lives in social media?* Most recently, HMW was carried from Google to Facebook by a member of the Google+ team.

HMW proponents say this form of questioning can be applied to almost any challenge—though it works best with ones that are ambitious yet also achievable. Brown says it doesn't work as well with problems that are too broad (*How might we solve world hunger?*) or too narrow (*How might we increase profits by 5 percent next quarter?*). Figuring out the right HMW questions to ask is a process, Brown says; "You need to find the sweet spot."

Will anyone follow a leader
who embraces uncertainty?

"The most important thing business leaders must do today is to be the 'chief question-asker' for their organization," says the consultant Dev Patnaik of Jump Associates. However, Patnaik adds a cautionary note: "The first thing most leaders need to realize is, they're really bad at asking questions."

That shouldn't be surprising. Patnaik notes that most business execs rose up through the ranks because "they were good at giving answers. But it means they've had little experience at formulating questions." The questions they are accustomed to asking are more practical and interrogative: *How much is this going to cost us? Who's responsible for this problem? How are the numbers looking?* (Or, to cite one of Patnaik's favorite dumb questions, *What's our version of the iPad?*)

That kind of practical, give-me-the-facts questioning has its place. Such questions can help in running a business, but not necessarily in leading it. Adam Bryant, who writes the *New York Times* Corner Office column, featuring weekly interviews with top CEOs, says the best leaders understand that asking open, exploratory questions can help them figure out what's coming and where new opportunities lie, so that they can lead their company in new directions. Ron Shaich of Panera observes, "When you're leading a team, a start-up, or a public company, your primary occupation must be to discover the future. A compelling and even subversive question is an effective tool for navigating uncharted terrain."

The problem with asking questions, for some business leaders, is that it exposes a lack of expertise and, in theory, makes them vulnerable. That many of today's most successful CEOs are questioners, as documented in the research of Hal Gregersen and Clay Christensen, would seem to disprove that theory. But the myth lingers that business leaders must be all-knowing, decisive, and in possession of infallible "gut instincts," all of which leaves little room for questioning.

Randy Komisar, a leading Silicon Valley venture capitalist, says the best business leaders and entrepreneurs have a different attitude toward "answers." "They understand that answers are relative. You can have an answer for right now, but it changes."

Because change is now a constant, the willingness to be comfortable with, and even to embrace, ambiguity is critical for today's leaders. The consultant Bryan Franklin has observed that effective leaders today may not appear to be entirely decisive because they are forced to reconcile conflicting forces and paradoxes in the current marketplace. Such leaders often find themselves "standing at the intersection between seemingly contradictory truths": How do you balance growth with social responsibility? How do you enrich your offering while streamlining production? And so forth.

In the midst of such complexity, leaders need extraordinary "sensemaking" capabilities, according to Deborah Ancona, the director of the MIT Leadership Center. Ancona defines this as "the ability to make sense of what's going on in a changing and complex environment." To do this, she maintains, leaders must be able to get beyond their own assumptions, take in vast amounts of new information, and figure out how to apply all of that to their business, sometimes doing that via experimentation. This adds up to a lot of Why, What If, and How questions.

Why can't everyone accept credit cards?

Jack Dorsey, one of the cofounders of Twitter, is a business leader who embraces the credo, "Question everything." Upon learning that a friend, glassworks designer Jim McKelvey, lost a $2,000 sale because he couldn't accept a potential customer's credit card, Dorsey wondered, *Why is it that only companies are able to accept credit cards?* Partnering with McKelvey, Dorsey envisioned an easy-to-use alternative to clunky, expensive card-reading equipment: *What if all you needed to swipe a credit card was a smart phone or tablet?* As to the "how" of making this feasible, Dorsey and the designers at his startup, Square, devised a small plastic plug (easily inserted into a smart phone jack) that serves as a card reader, and added a clean, intuitive user interface, accessible via a smart phone app. The elegant simplicity of Square (and that of Dorsey's earlier creation, Twitter) is a product of rigorous inquiry: Dorsey maintains that good design is about removing unnecessary features by continually asking, *Do we really need this?* and *What can we take away?*

THE LEADER NEEDN'T, indeed shouldn't, be asking these questions alone. "One of the most important things to know about becoming more of a questioning leader is that the questions don't all have to come from you," says Patnaik. If others are given permission and encouraged to question, they can contribute a range of perspectives and help raise the kinds of Why and What If questions that might never occur to the person at the top.

A great source of questioning input can and probably should come from outside the company—from those who have enough distance to question the company as a naïve outsider.

The late, legendary business guru Peter Drucker was known for coming into companies with an outsider's perspective, which enabled him to see problems and issues that insiders might have missed. Rick Wartzman, executive director of the Drucker Institute, says people often wonder how Drucker achieved his stature as "the man who invented management" and the go-to adviser for half a century for every company from GM to Procter & Gamble to Coca-Cola. The answer can be summed up in a word: questions.

Drucker "understood that his job wasn't to serve up answers," according to Wartzman. Drucker once remarked that his greatest strength was "to be ignorant and ask a few questions." Often those questions were deceptively simple, as in *Who is your customer? What business are you in?* The clients who hired Drucker may have started out expecting the great consultant to offer brilliant solutions to all their problems. But as he told one client, "The answers have to be yours."

Today, many consultants don't follow Drucker's model; they're more apt to adopt the role of "experts" whose job is to provide answers. (And as author Dan Ariely noted in *Harvard Business Review,* company leaders often prefer being supplied with answers over questions "because answers allow us to take action, while questions mean that we need to keep thinking.") But as Drucker knew, an outsider looking at your business will probably never understand it as well as you do. Hence, that outsider generally shouldn't be telling you what to do. He/she should be helping you to see things from a different angle, challenge your own assumptions, reframe old problems, and ask better questions—so that, in the end, you can figure out the solutions yourself.

WHILE THE LEADER can look outside for help with questioning, certain core leadership questions can only be answered by looking inward. When Jim Hackett, the CEO of Steelcase, first took the helm at that company, he struggled with what his role should be as a leader, wondering, *What does a CEO look like and feel like? What's the texture of what you're supposed to be?*

Hackett initially focused on some of the wrong questions; he was overly concerned with what others (in particular, the family that owned the company) wanted or expected from him. But gradually he concluded that his role as a leader was to "look at the chaos and provide a point of view about what needs to be done." Today, he maintains that one of the most important things a leader can do is project a clear and distinctive point of view that others can follow. But that clear vision is arrived at, and constantly modified and sharpened, through deep reflection and questioning.

Hackett told me he believes that deep thinking is a lost art in today's business environment. "There is an overcelebration of getting things done," he said. "For a long time, I have been asking myself this question:

"Where did the balance between thinking and doing get out of equilibrium?"

At Steelcase, Hackett has tried to emphasize—and even taught courses on—the importance of doing critical thinking and questioning before taking action. "We have to train ourselves to ask questions," he says. "We have to discipline ourselves to do it."

One of the critical things a questioning leader must do is find ways—as Hackett is doing at Steelcase—to spark and encourage questioning in others. There are various approaches to developing a culture that encourages questioning, as we'll see, but some of this rests on the individual leader and the way he/she interacts with employees. The most effective questioning leader won't just give answers to others (or demand answers from them via interrogation); the better approach is to use Socratic-style questioning to encourage deeper and more creative thinking by others.

Leaders must also know when to stop questioning. "You can question yourself right into inaction because there are so many different potential outcomes that you become concerned about how to move forward or even to move forward at all," says Casey Sheahan of Patagonia. "Questioning is critical, but at some point you have to take action when you think you've found the best path." How do you know when to stop inquiring and start doing? "I feel it mostly in my gut," Sheahan declares. "As a leader, at some point I get frustrated and say, 'Let's get going.'"

Should mission statements be mission questions?

The philosopher Bertrand Russell once said, "In all affairs it's a healthy thing now and then to hang a question mark on the things you take for granted." So let's apply this to the corporate mission statement—something that is often taken for granted, ignored, occasionally ridiculed. What if we were to take the typical mission statement and hang a question mark on the end of it?

First let's consider why a company might want to do this. It's assumed that a declarative "statement" makes a company seem confident, more sure of its mission, more determined. But mission statements tend to have a different effect. They often sound arrogant. They come across as not quite credible. They seem "corporate" and "official," which also means they're a bit stiff. Often they're banal pronouncements (*We save people money so they can live better.* —Walmart) or debatable assertions (*Yahoo! is the premier digital media company*) that don't offer much help in gauging whether a company is actually living up to a larger goal or purpose.

And sometimes they sound as if they're saying the mission has already been accomplished, and now the company is just in maintenance mode.

In these dynamic times, it seems appropriate to take that static statement and transform it into a more open-ended, fluid mission question that can still be ambitious (replacing, for example, *We make the world a better place through robotics!* with *How might we make the world a better place through robotics?*).

By articulating the company mission as a question, it tells the outside world, "This is what we're striving for—we know we're not there yet, but we're on the journey." It acknowledges room for possibility, change, and adaptability. "I'd rather have mission statements that start by asking *How might we?*" says the consultant Min Basadur. "You don't want the mission statement to make it sound like you're already there. If we say, 'How might we be recognized as the best car-parts manufacturer?' it says, 'We're always trying and we're willing to open our minds to new ways of accomplishing this.'"

Perhaps most important, a mission question invites participation and collaboration. Tim Brown, the chief executive at IDEO, points out that questions, by their very nature, challenge people and invite them to engage with an idea or an issue—and could therefore do likewise in engaging employees with a company mission. Indeed, thinking of a company mission as a shared endeavor—an ongoing attempt to answer a big, bold question through collaborative inquiry—seems vastly preferable to having to live up to a dictum handed down from on high.

What if a bookstore could be like summer camp?

It's no secret that local bookstores have faced a tough challenge in recent years. Independent booksellers such as Steve Bercu, of Austin, Texas-based BookPeople, find themselves asking fundamental questions such as *What can we offer that Amazon can't?* Here's one of Bercu's answers: a summer camp for kids. It started when a Book-People staffer wondered if the store could create a real-life version of Camp Half Blood, featured in the popular Percy Jackson series of young-adult books. Bercu knew nothing about starting or running a camp, so he experimented—finding a space in a local park, and offering a mix of outdoor activities with lots of book talk. The program now is so popular that local parents line up for hours to get their kids into the camp before it sells out. And the goodwill and local publicity generated have helped Bercu register best-ever book sales back at the store.

As to how it reflects on the company (which is what a lot of mission statements are about), which seems more impressive: a company that is striving to answer an ambitious question—or one that claims to have figured everything out and distilled it down to an official "statement"?

WHETHER OR NOT the mission statement is phrased as a question, it should be subject to constant questioning:

Does it still make sense today?

Are we, as a company, still living up to it (if we ever did)?

Is the mission growing and pulling us forward?

And lastly, *Are we all on this mission together?*

The first three of these are somewhat self-explanatory, but companies may need to think more about the last question. Mission statements are usually created by upper management (many of them read as if they were cobbled together by an executive committee). *But does a mission mean anything if the people throughout the company don't feel invested in it?* One way to help people feel more engaged with a company mission is to give them a role in shaping it or refreshing an existing one.

Keith Yamashita observes that some companies involve many people in the crafting of the mission, while others leave it to the leadership. "To me, there's no right or wrong way," he says. But he does note that being involved in the mission creation—"doing the introspection—gets people to more firmly and more deeply believe in what they are doing."

Yamashita points to the approach used by Starbucks in modernizing its mission a few years back. CEO Howard Schultz worked with his top leaders to rewrite every word of the mission. That team then convened the top three hundred leaders of the company to get them to commit to it; they in turn went to more than twelve thousand store managers, who spent four days in New Orleans committing to the mission. "This is a great example of mission-setting, starting with a few key leaders and ultimately rallying an entire workforce," Yamashita says.

A different approach by IBM under then-CEO Sam Palmisano sought even more direct input up front. Palmisano "hosted a worldwide online jam session—using technology to elicit the ideas, thinking, and stories from IBMers about what they most valued," Yamashita recalls. More than eighty thousand employees participated—and together, they wrote the company's values, which remain in place under current CEO Ginni Rometty.

Ron Shaich says that at Panera ideas about how to live up to the mission can come from anywhere. For example, the Panera Cares idea originated during a dinner conversation among Shaich and a group of franchisees—one of whom asked how the company might expand upon its efforts to serve the community. That got Shaich thinking about ways to elevate the company's existing bread-donation program to a higher level.

Whether mission questions come from throughout the ranks or are posed by leaders themselves, the point is to keep asking, *What are we doing? Why are we doing it? How might we do it better?* As Shaich says, "Figuring out what you want to accomplish is a continual search—and questions are the means to the search."

How might we create a culture of inquiry?

This is a critical question for business leaders to address, but first they might well ask, *Do we really* want *a culture of inquiry?*

"I think a lot of traditional companies may not want that," says Yamashita. "There are plenty of corporate cultures we encounter that shut down questioning." Why? Because as Dev Patnaik points out, there's a sense that if too much questioning is going on within a company, "it's distracting. Nature abhors a vacuum, and companies abhor ambiguity. They want to deal in answers. And even if they get to a point where they know they need more of a questioning culture, they're often unwilling to do what it takes to create that culture."

Inviting and encouraging more questioning creates some complications within a corporate culture. If employees in a company are given more leeway to question, it means policies may be challenged. Established methods and practices might suddenly be looked at in a new light: *Why are we doing it this way?* Not everyone wants to have to continually defend proven methods. To some leaders, as well as some midlevel managers, it can be frustrating to have to explain and rationalize.

Questioning within a business environment can also create a perceived threat to authority. Those with expertise may resent having their learned views questioned by nonexperts. Managers trying to keep things moving may feel they shouldn't have to answer a subordinate's questions. Questioning may be seen as slowing progress, particularly by those who believe that what the company needs most are "answers, not more questions."

Such concerns notwithstanding, for any company that needs to innovate or adapt to shifting market conditions, new competition, and other disruptive forces, a questioning culture is critical because it can help ensure that creativity and fresh, adaptive thinking flows throughout the organization. Having a leader serve as the "questioner in chief" is fine, but it's not enough. Today's companies are often tackling complex challenges that require collaborative, multidisciplinary problem solving. Creative thinking must come from all parts of the company (and from outside the company, too). When a business culture is inquisitive, the questioning, learning, and sharing of information becomes contagious—and gives people permission to explore new ideas across boundaries and silos.

If having a culture of inquiry is deemed appropriate, desirable, and perhaps even critical for a company, creating and nurturing it must start at the top—with company leadership that clearly demonstrates a willingness to ask, and tolerate, questions about anything from mission to strategy to policy. "As a business leader, if I'm trying to build a culture of inquiry, I have to start by asking a lot of provocative, disruptive questions myself," says INSEAD's Gregersen. "I have to walk the talk."

The company leadership must be willing to *answer* tough questions, as well as ask them—and ideally, those questions should be coming from all levels and departments. Google has maintained a wide-open (and sometimes chaotic) questioning forum through its weekly TGIF sessions, when all employees are invited to submit questions to the company's top executives, Larry Page and Sergey Brin. The questions are instantly voted up or down by others in the company; the highest-ranking—which are also often the toughest, most controversial ones—are then fielded on the spot by the bosses.

Charles Warren, a former top engineer at Google, told me, "It's very fulfilling to sit in those sessions and know that anybody in the company can ask *any* question, and nothing is off-limits." Warren said people running groups or projects (he was one of the leaders of Google+) also are questioned by employees throughout the company. The questioning culture at Google is not always polite. "Questions could get personal or become attacks," Warren noted; if you were developing a product some didn't like, you might be subjected to queries like *Why are you trying to ruin the company?*

But the overall message that comes through at Google is that anything the company does is subject to question from everyone—and that the questions will actually be heard. It's fine to tell employees they can ask whatever they wish—but if those queries end up in a question box no one ever opens, it can be counterproductive. Today, the updated version of the old question/suggestion box is the intra–social network used by many companies—and they are often "ablaze with questions," says Steelcase CEO Jim Hackett, whose company encourages any employee to ask anything of anyone else. The system pings Hackett or other executives every time a question is directed at them.

WHILE IT'S CRITICAL that companies show they are willing to tolerate and respond to questions, perhaps the bigger issue involves incentives: *How do you reward questioning?*

The Lean Startup's Eric Ries says that when a company is trying to build a culture of inquiry, "it's not about slogans or putting up posters on the wall, it's the systems and the incentives you create for people that promote the behavior. So if you don't like the level of questioning in your organization, and you're in senior management, look in the mirror." Ries points out that at most companies "the resources flow to the person with the most confident, best plan. Or the person with no failures on their record." The solution, Ries says, is that companies must direct more budgetary resources to those who are exploring unanswered questions, conducting promising experiments, and taking intelligent risks. It's a radical notion for most businesses, but "failed experiments" (which often pave the way for subsequent innovations) should be rewarded alongside proven successes, particularly if the experiment or the questioning provides valuable learning.

It's also critical for company leaders to be on the lookout for ways in which questioning gets punished—though the punishment may not be obvious or intentional. The operative question is *If an employee asks questions at our company, is he or she asking for trouble?*

The business writer Dale Dauten has described a common situation in which people who inquire about a problem at their workplace—say, something the company is not doing as well as it might—are then told, "You found the problem; now it's your job to fix it. In addition to your normal duties, of course." As Dauten notes, that is a surefire way to get people to stop finding problems and asking questions, because most are not seeking to add to their workload.

The better approach is to ask the problem-finders to what extent and how they would want to be involved in working on that problem. The understanding should be they won't have to go it alone; that they'll be given as much time and support as is feasible; and that, even if they never ultimately answer the question, they've earned credit just by asking it.

In general, people need time to be able to ask and to work on difficult questions. You can't "step back" if you're always rushing to get things done. Here, policies like Google's much-celebrated "20 percent time," which stipulates that employees can devote one fifth of their time to independent projects—in effect, to work on their own questions—can really pay off. Several of Google's most important innovations—including Gmail and Google News—have sprung from people using their 20 percent time to tackle a What If question that wasn't part of their regular workload. (Recent reports suggest that as Google has grown, it has become increasingly difficult for employees with heavy workloads to use, or justify using, 20 percent time.) Other companies have implemented similar programs, including LinkedIn—whose designated "Hack Days" provide employees "an opportunity to spend a day and develop things that they're really passionate about," according to LinkedIn's Jeff Weiner—as well as 3M and W. L. Gore.

In Gore's case, the program stipulates that 10 percent of employee time should go toward independent projects, and it has inspired some big breakthroughs. The company, known for creating the popular waterproofing material Gore-Tex, produces a wide range of products, including Elixir, a well-known brand of guitar string. It was developed by a Gore engineer, Dave Myers, who normally worked on medical products. As a side project, Myers wanted to see if he could answer, *Why can't I get the gears on my mountain bike to shift more smoothly?* He eventually developed a new, plastic-coated bike-cable product that became a successful product for Gore.

Subsequently, in a nifty bit of connective inquiry, Myers wondered, *What if I put plastic coating on guitar strings?* The result (after a couple of difficult years of technical challenges at the How stage) was a breakthrough, bestselling product that proved more durable and less brittle than existing strings. But it might never have happened if Myers hadn't been afforded the time and opportunity to step back from his normal work routine so he that he could pursue an interesting question.

GORE HAS QUESTIONING embedded deeply in its culture. "We see it as critical to growth and expansion," company vice president Debra France remarked. "With a culture of questioning, there's always more possibility."

Regarded as one of the world's most innovative companies, Gore is also known for its distinctive corporate structure: It is one of the flattest, least hierarchical large companies in existence. Its founder, Bill Gore, understood that corporate bureaucracy and hierarchy do not foster questioning or any open communication within a company. Bill Gore once observed that at most companies the only place where people speak freely is in the car pool. So as he started his own company Gore was, in effect, trying to answer, *How do you make a company that's more like a car pool?*

The company was set up with no titles—ten thousand employees and not one manager. When people are first hired at Gore, they often start out wondering, *Who's my boss?* Eventually, they realize there is no boss. The corporate structure is built around what Gore calls the Lattice, an elaborate networking system within the company that connects every employee to every other employee. When a new hire joins the company, their first relationship is with a sponsor (or mentor), "who will lend their credibility and their lattice to the new person, until that person has built up their own lattice," France says.

One of the most important effects of this networked, nonhierarchical structure is that employees, from day one, are self-directed. Since no one tells you what to do, you must use your own powers of inquiry (and help from your sponsor) to figure things out for yourself.

Communication flows freely through the Gore network. Any questions or ideas can be shared with anyone else. "It's very personal," says France. "If you have feedback for someone, you give it to them direct."

Gore believes so strongly in the value of inquiry that it trains everyone in the company on how to ask good questions—providing specific instruction on asking questions that can be applied to testing new ideas, weighing the value of pursuing possible opportunities or innovations (*Is this opportunity real? Is there a customer who needs it?*), as well as using questioning to improve collaboration with other employees. Particular emphasis is placed on effective questioning for sponsors to better coach/mentor new employees.

Gore's corporate structure is unusual—and few companies could (or maybe even should) get rid of managers and layers. But even a more traditional corporate structure can foster an atmosphere conducive to questioning and a culture that, in Dev Patnaik's words, "embraces curiosity as a fundamental value."

Since curiosity and learning go hand in hand, one of the big questions some companies are now working on is *How do we transform a workplace into a learn-place?*

Here again, Google seems to be ahead of the pack. The company established Google University as a platform for bringing in guest lecturers, then went a step further in creating Googler to Googler, a program in which Google employees host in-house classes to teach other Google employees. Not surprisingly, there are courses on technical or business skills, but the curriculum also includes courses on public speaking and parenting. Former Google engineer Chade-Meng Tan even teaches a course on mindfulness (useful in helping one to step back and question).

To create a learning culture, Google uses the "company as university" metaphor. MIT Media Lab uses both the "laboratory" and "kindergarten" metaphors. Some companies try to create "salons" or "studios"; others position themselves as "idea villages" or "idea cities."

A learning company might also think of itself as an ongoing "idea conference," as in *What if we could create the experience of a TED conference, every day, within the company?* TED founder Richard Saul Wurman told me that one of the best ways to stimulate curiosity among any group of people is simply to expose them to as many original ideas and unusual viewpoints as possible. Thus a company might not only bring in guests but have employees themselves do TED-like presentations for the group—focusing on something interesting they've learned that others might not know.

Whatever the metaphor, the best corporate learning environments have some common elements. Bringing in outsiders to teach and inspire; encouraging insiders to teach each other; putting employees' work on the walls to share ideas, especially on work in progress—all invite questioning and feedback from others and encourage greater collaboration.

AMID ALL OF that teaching, some time should be dedicated to teaching the art of questioning. If a company is going to encourage questioning, it must teach people to do it well—or risk being besieged by nonproductive questions.

Steelcase's Hackett points out that because of the growing interest in sparking more inquiry within companies, the tendency is to encourage all questioning, including what Hackett describes as "precocious questioning"—which may be uninformed or off-topic.

What should be encouraged, Hackett says, are "good questions"—meaning questions rooted in deep critical thinking about the particular challenges and issues the company faces. To that end, Steelcase has endeavored to teach critical-thinking skills at the company via a course called Thinking 2.0. "It's advocating that people have to learn how to find the tensions in arguments, and how to build the scaffolding of questions around problems," Hackett says. The course presents challenging questions like *What would you do if you ran the U.S. Postal Service?* and then guides the employee-students in developing their own questions and strategies around that larger problem.

Hackett says that in creating a truly effective culture of inquiry, management and employees must meet at a midway point. Employees need to understand that "if you ask questions that aren't critically thoughtful, you may end up missing out on the opportunity that comes with the freedom to question." What management wants and will respond to are questions that are considered and relevant to real problems. "You can ask precocious questions, but you might be wasting time." Meanwhile, Hackett says, management must understand that "the scaffolding around problems is made up of *a lot* of questions, so don't get perturbed by the number of them or try to limit them."

For innovative questioning to gain traction, there has to be a willingness throughout the company to build on ideas, to keep the tone of questioning generally positive (à la appreciative inquiry), and to use language that is open and inclusive (*How might we?*). Responding to exploratory questions with highly practical ones (*How much will it cost? Who's going to do all this new work? What happens if the idea fails?*) can have an important place in the discussion, but not necessarily at the early stages. Part of building a culture of inquiry is teaching people to defer judgment while exploring new ideas and big questions. This is necessary because many of us are conditioned to react to questions by trying to answer them too quickly or by countering them "devil's advocate" style. The more hardheaded within the group may need to be shown that innovative questioning works best when it starts with the impractical and works toward the practical. The "dreamers" should be given their moment to ask big, ambitious, impractical questions; the pragmatic "implementers" (to use Min Basadur's term) will likely hold sway during the down-to-earth How stages of developing an idea and trying to make it real.

IDEO's Tim Brown stresses that, for the most part, learning the art of questioning doesn't happen in company classrooms or conference rooms: "It's more about going out into the world and getting better at observing and listening." Contextual inquiry may be the most important questioning skill employees can pick up, but it's developed mostly through on-the-ground experience. Company leaders and managers may be able to provide some basic tips on what to look for, but the most important thing they can offer employees is the freedom to venture outside the bubble and do their own investigation.

ONE OF THE best ways to grow and maintain a culture of inquiry is to continually add new people who are naturally inquisitive. Ask the average company leaders or managers whether they're interested in hiring people who are good questioners and they'll likely say yes without hesitation. Yet, when they interview prospective employees, they often make judgments based purely on the answers given—following the "answers only" model of our test-based education system, which does a poor job of assessing one's ability to question, create, and innovate. All of which raises this question:

What if a job interview tested one's ability to ask questions, as well as answer them?

The logical way to achieve that would be to ask interviewees to generate questions. While job interviews often end with the interviewee being asked, *Do you have any questions?*, that's treated more as a rote throwaway line, and if anything it invites only closed, practical questions (*When would I start? How much travel will there be?*) as opposed to thoughtful, creative questions.

As an alternative approach, tell every person coming in for an interview to bring a few questions with them. Make it clear those questions should be ambitious and open-ended—Why, What If, and How questions are recommended. These should also be relevant to your company or industry. The questions might inquire about ways the company or its offerings could be expanded or improved; a customer or societal challenge that could be tackled by the company; an untapped opportunity to be explored. The questions this person brings will reveal a lot about him or her. Are the questions audacious and imaginative, or more modest and practical? Do the questions indicate that the candidate did some research before forming them (if so, good sign: it indicates the candidate knows how to do contextual inquiry).

To test whether the person can question on the fly, you might ask, during the interview, that the candidate build upon one or more of the prepared questions with additional questions (using the Right Question Institute practice of follow-up questioning to improve and advance existing questions). For example, if she has suggested a What If scenario, ask her to now challenge her own assumptions with Why questions, or get her to take her idea to a more practical level by generating How questions. This will show if a person knows how to "think in questions." If the candidate has come up with at least one interesting question and then improved on that question during the interview, that person is clearly a gifted questioner and is likely a welcome addition to a company's culture of inquiry.

CHAPTER 5

Questioning for Life

Why should we "live the questions"?

Why are you climbing the mountain?

Why are you evading inquiry?

Before we "lean in," what if we stepped back?

What if we start with what we already have?

What if you made one small change?

What if you could not fail?

How might we pry off the lid and stir the paint?

How will you find your beautiful question?

Why should we "live the questions"?

When Jacqueline Novogratz was about to graduate college in the early 1980s, the school's job-placement office informed her that the Chase Manhattan Bank was interested in interviewing her for a job. Novogratz had no particular desire to go into banking; she'd planned to take a brief postcollege break to tend bar and "figure out how I would change the world." But she dutifully went to the interview and, to her surprise, was offered the job. She took it, in part, because it promised an opportunity to travel around the world, working in a group that reviewed the bank's loans in overseas markets.

Novogratz liked the job well enough, but something bothered her: In developing countries where Chase was doing business, Novogratz encountered people with bright ideas and entrepreneurial dreams who didn't qualify for loans because they were not seen as creditworthy. Yet, it seemed to Novogratz, these were the very people who, given a chance, might be able to build the sustainable local businesses these countries desperately needed. Hence, Novogratz's question: *Why weren't loans going to the entrepreneurs who could, potentially, solve some of these countries' most pressing needs and biggest problems?*

Chase would never take on such high-risk loans, but Novogratz began to look around to see what others, outside the mainstream banking world, were doing along these lines. She learned, for example, that Grameen Bank in Bangladesh, led by an economist named Muhammad Yunus, had had considerable success in providing microloans to poor women in that country (who, it turned out, were reliable in paying back what they borrowed). During her research, Novogratz also learned of a small microfinance group that had been started by several women in New York with the aim of providing loans to women entrepreneurs around the world. Novogratz approached the group, mostly out of curiosity, but also to see if there might be a place there for her. There was: She was offered a job.

Now Novogratz had to ask herself some tough questions: *Did she want to leave a secure, well-paid job in banking for a risky one in the nonprofit sector? What was most important to her at this point in her life?* And, not least among her concerns: *What would her family think if she walked away from a promising business career?*

That last question weighed heavily on Novogratz because she came from a hardworking family of modest means; her family had been proud and excited when she'd landed her Chase Manhattan job. As she wrote years later in her autobiography, "I tried to imagine myself telling my uncles that I was leaving a well-paying job on Wall Street to work for a nonprofit women's organization that would send me overseas. They would think I'd lost my mind. Why would I give up my chance at making it?"

But she also had "this feeling that if I listened hard to the deepest part of myself, there was a person in there who wanted to be adventurous. And I knew if I didn't jump right then, I might never jump." She took the nonprofit job and soon was on her way to Africa. Having answered the question about what she wanted to do with her life, she would spend the next decade working on that other question—about finding a way to get loans to entrepreneurs.

NOVOGRATZ DID NOT have an easy time of it, especially in her early days in Africa. Reflecting on it, she admits she was, like a lot of young social activists who set out to help people in other parts of the world, naïve about the complexity of the problems she was confronting and sometimes oblivious of cultural nuances. But she told me her greatest asset in overcoming that was her inquisitive nature; when she found she didn't understand something, or that she'd gotten it wrong, she asked a lot of Why questions. Then, eventually, she had a big What If moment.

Novogratz knew of the growing interest in investing in the developing world, as well as the rising spirit of social entrepreneurship, which aimed to bring innovative approaches to global problems. She felt the best way to tap into both of those new phenomena as well as traditional philanthropy was to try a hybrid approach that combined venture-capital investing with philanthropy: The idea was to create a venture fund that would back entrepreneurs trying to start new businesses, create jobs, and solve everyday problems in the developing world. Early on, Novogratz thought of her idea in these terms: *What if we could invest as a means and not as an end?*

The investors would have every right to expect a return but also had to accept that those returns would be plowed back into the start-ups, to keep them going and growing—it was "patient capital," to use Novogratz's term. There was no way of knowing whether it would pay off in the long run, but Novogratz attracted enough interest in the concept to launch the nonprofit Acumen Fund in 2001.

Novogratz's team then set out looking for funding opportunities and found them in the form of people pursuing their own beautiful questions: *What if we could help parched small farms around the world to double their yield? Why can't we use solar power to create low-cost lights for the poor? Why doesn't India have its own 911-type ambulance system? What if we could limit the spread of malaria in Africa—and create jobs in the process?*

With Acumen's funding, entrepreneurs could tackle the How of answering these various questions and challenges. Some of the answers that emerged: a team of entrepreneurs with an idea for cheap solar lights has now brought light to twenty million people in the developing world (including eight million kids in school); a product designer has sold 275,000 irrigation-drip systems to small farmers in dry regions in Africa; a man with a plan for ambulance service in India now heads the largest ambulance company in Asia; and an African maker of simple bed nets (to protect from mosquitoes and malaria) has produced sixteen million nets and seven thousand jobs. Some of the projects have also turned out to be good investments: Acumen's $2 million stake in solar lights is now worth twice that, though the returns are being put back into the company, in hopes of bringing light to one hundred million in the next couple of years.

Convincing investors to fund these high-risk, slow-yield ventures was only part of the challenge for Acumen. In many cases, the ambitious-but-inexperienced entrepreneurs receiving the funds needed guidance, expert advice, moral support—and sometimes a second round of funding—as they took their Why and What If questions through the difficult How stage of bringing these innovations to market.

Novogratz observes that when you're trying to do something that's never before been done—and especially when you're trying to do it in developing markets, where resources may be scarce and infrastructure lacking—the key is to learn and adapt as you go. You have to ask a lot of questions, about what's feasible and what isn't, about what people actually want and need (as opposed to what one might think they *should* want and need).

Outside aid groups, though well-meaning, often don't do this kind of up-close inquiry; they tend to try to impose solutions from an outsider perspective. When you do that, Novogratz said, you end up foisting things on people that they aren't sure they want. Take the malaria bed nets: Novogratz figured people would want them for health reasons, "but what many people actually cared about was that they could sleep better without bugs, and also that the nets looked nice. Health concerns were way down the list." Having learned that, Acumen and the net maker were able to market the product more effectively.

"You just don't know about people and what drives them," said Novogratz, "until you spend time sitting on the floor, listening to someone tell you their story."

DURING A RECENT college commencement speech Novogratz gave in Pennsylvania, she focused a good part of her talk on urging the graduating students to embrace uncertainty and follow their own spirit of inquisitiveness. Quoting the famous line from the poet Rilke, she told the students to "live the questions."

I asked Novogratz about the speech and the questioning theme. "It's been a hallmark of my life to run up against walls and realize there are no easy, clear answers," she said. "And it took me time to learn that the best I could do was get smarter at asking better questions. So I wanted them to learn that sooner, rather than later."

Novogratz referred to the students as "kids who are on a track"—much as she was at that point in her life. "They're trying to do all the things they think they're supposed to—going to the right school, working two years at an investment bank, and so forth. And sometimes these college kids ask me, 'Okay, now what should I do next?' And I say, 'Do what your heart tells you to do'— and I get a blank stare."

With that in mind, Novogratz was hoping her message might

shift the thinking in some of the students—away from predetermined paths with designated next steps, to something a bit more open, unpredictable, and uncertain. "In a rapidly changing world, there really isn't a step-by-step map for them anyway," she said. "The best you can hope to have is a good compass to guide you. The ones who understand that—and can embrace that—are going to have the greatest adventures."

Why are you climbing the mountain?

Novogratz's advice applies not just to graduating college students but to "track kids" of all ages—which is to say, everyone who's following a path or climbing a ladder without necessarily knowing why; or those among us trying to do everything—attend every conference, take every call, answer every message, read every tweet, seize every opportunity—not so much because we want to, but because we feel we must, just to keep up.

People have been feeling "swamped" for some time, but in the past year or two it seems to have reached a tipping point: A mid-2013 *Huffington Post* conference urged people to slow down and check their ambitions lest they burn out ("The more, more, more approach can't last," the conference organizers declared); magazines ran cover stories about the importance of "unplugging" from social media and our various networked devices; interest surged in meditation and "mindfulness" as a means of coping with a frenetic world in which people seemed to be stressed-out, overworked, and inundated with information.

An interesting description of this current condition was recently offered up by the Oxford University psychology professor Mark Williams, who observed that when people are "always rushing around, going from one task to another without actually realizing what they're doing," the brain is on high alert—"it's almost as if they were . . . escaping from a predator."

But who or what is this predator, and why is it chasing us? The assumption might be that people are rushing around and frantically "doing" as part of a larger plan or purpose. But is that plan or purpose clear? Jeff Weiner, the chief executive of LinkedIn, observed that he often asks prospective employees this reasonable and fairly straightforward question: *Looking back on your career, twenty or thirty years from now, what do you want to say you've accomplished?*

"You'd be amazed how many people I meet who don't have the answer to the question," Weiner said.

This is not just about career planning, but extends to basic questions about identity or life goals. The filmmaker Roko Belic told me that he meets many people in his travels, and one of his standard questions when getting to know someone is *What are you all about? What makes you tick?* "It's incredible how few people can answer that," Belic said. "I know people are complicated and all, but to me, that is a question that—if you can't answer it in some way, then you're not paying attention to some real basic things about what it means to be alive. To me it means they haven't asked themselves some fundamental questions."

What is your sentence?

This is a favorite question of the author Daniel Pink, though he acknowledges in his book *Drive* that it can be traced back to the journalist and pioneering congresswoman Clare Booth Luce. While visiting John F. Kennedy early in his presidency, Luce expressed concern that Kennedy might be in danger of trying to do too much, thereby losing focus. She told him "a great man is a sentence"—meaning that a leader with a clear and strong purpose could be summed up in a single line (e.g., "Abraham Lincoln preserved the union and freed the slaves"). Pink believes this concept can be useful to anyone, not just presidents. Your sentence might be, "He raised four kids who became happy, healthy adults," or "She invented a device that made people's lives easier." If your sentence is a goal not yet achieved, then you also must ask: *How might I live up to my own sentence?*

If it's true that people are too busy doing things to actually ask why they're doing them, that habit seems to be forming early. The high school teacher David McCullough, son of the Pulitzer-winning historian, was reacting to the overachieving culture of his students when he gave a graduation speech (which later went viral on the Internet) in which he advised them, "Climb the mountain not to plant your flag, but to embrace the challenge, enjoy the air, and behold the view. Climb it so you can see the world, not so the world can see you."

McCullough's advice about *how* to climb the mountain, and what to do while you're climbing, is sound—but not everyone wants to climb the same way. Maybe you're climbing because you actually *do* want to plant a flag. And maybe being seen at the top is more important to you than seeing. But one can't make those judgments without first asking basic questions such as *Why am I climbing this mountain in the first place?*

If you take the time to ask that question—and give it the consideration it clearly deserves, given its significance—you might conclude, as Jacqueline Novogratz did, that you're climbing the wrong mountain. Or you might find yourself asking other questions, such as:

What is waiting for me at the top?

What am I going to do once I get there?

Am I enjoying the climb itself? Should I slow down, speed up?

What am I leaving behind, down below?

THE MOUNTAIN-CLIMBING METAPHOR obviously applies well to career considerations, since advancing in a career is often about scaling the ranks and trying to get to a higher position. There's little inclination to step back and question the career climb itself; to the extent we do ask career-related questions, they're more likely to be practical ones aimed at figuring out ways to keep moving up. *How do I improve my standing in the company and enhance my job security? How can I angle for a promotion?* Nothing is wrong with angling for a promotion—as long as you ask the Whys and What Ifs before going straight to the How. Too often, people get promoted out of doing what they actually like to do or are good at doing.

The tendency to follow a predetermined path without sufficiently questioning whether it's the right path extends beyond career decisions. For instance, *Why do so many people long for a big house in the suburbs?* It's a great choice for some, but not all; and the only way to know is to periodically ask whether, for instance, you might want to live in a walkable downtown instead.

Family relationships and dynamics also tend to go unquestioned; likewise with friendships. All of these human bonds are subject to change, and wear and tear, over time. That we're not questioning them suggests we're not paying attention, not trying to find ways to strengthen or improve them—that we may be taking them for granted.

So why then, do we tend to avoid taking the time to ask important and fundamental questions about our lives? As we rush around, from task to task and from one distraction to the next, is it possible that "questioning" itself is the predator we're trying to escape?

Why are you evading inquiry?

Among the reasons people tend to avoid fundamental questioning of much of what they do in their lives (especially the important things), four stand out:

- Questioning is seen as counterproductive; it's the *answers* that most people are focused on finding, because the answers, it is believed, will provide ways to solve problems, move ahead, improve life.
- The right time for asking fundamental questions never seems to present itself; either it's too soon or too late.
- Knowing the right questions to ask is difficult (so better not to ask at all).
- Perhaps most significant: *What if we find we have no good answers to the important questions we raise?* Fearing that, many figure it's better not to invite that additional uncertainty and doubt into their lives.

Since most schools teach us to prize answers over questions, while also generally teaching that most problems have one "right" answer, small wonder that our habit is to think that the answers we need are out there—just waiting to be "found," stumbled upon, looked up, acquired, purchased, or handed to us.

Whole industries are dedicated to providing off-the-shelf "answers" to people in the form of self-help books, seminars, life coaching, and so forth. It's natural to want an "expert" to come along and tell us what to do. And sometimes that outside perspective can be helpful. But the best coaches, consultants, and therapists all emphasize there is no substitute for self-questioning—often the most important thing that an adviser can do is guide someone toward asking the right questions (as the business consultant Peter Drucker did when he coached the world's top business executives). Anyone in a coaching/advising role who offers generic answers should be eyed warily because nobody can provide answers that will fit *your* life, your particular problems or challenges.

Even wise and trusted friends can't provide the right answers for you. The start-up entrepreneur Kasper Hulthin discovered this when he was wrestling with tough questions about whether to take the plunge into a new business. "If you ask people for advice," Hulthin says, "they'll tell you what *they* would do." But his friends' situations and motivations were very different from his. In the end, Hulthin had to sit at the kitchen table, alone, and work through his own questions.

One of the volunteer researchers helping me on this book told me that part of the reason she had gotten involved in the "beautiful question" project was because she found that, as she was thinking about the next stage of her career, she was inundated with career-advice books full of "answers" that seemed to conflict with one another. "I'm finding that answers don't cut it," she wrote to me in an e-mail. "I need help with the process of figuring this out for myself."

That word *process* is key. You don't just "find" answers to complex life problems (or any type of complex problem, including business ones). You work your way, gradually, toward figuring out those answers, relying on questions each step of the way.

This illusion that an "answer" is out there if we can just find it extends to everything from the dream job to larger concepts such as "happiness" or "purpose." Gretchen Rubin of the Happiness Project says the classic misconception people have about happiness is that it is a state of being you suddenly find or "arrive" at. But as Rubin and other experts on this subject tend to concur, creating happiness is ongoing. You don't find it, you gradually figure it out for yourself—questioning and experimenting as you try to understand what makes you feel happy and how to bring more of that into your everyday life.

Much the same can be said about "meaning" and "purpose." The author and creativity coach Eric Maisel says that when people ask, *How can I find the meaning of life?*, they're asking "a completely useless question." That classic query is based on the flawed notion that "meaning" is an objective truth to be found out there somewhere. Better to think of it this way, Maisel says: We have to construct meaning in our lives, based on everyday choices—and every one of those choices is a question. *Why should I do X? Is it worth my time and effort to do Y?*

As you make those daily choices about what to spend your time on and which possibilities to pursue, the author and consultant John Hagel suggests you ask yourself this question: *When I look back in five years, which of these options will make the better story?* As Hagel points out, "No one ever regrets taking the path that leads to a better story."

LIFE COACH KELLY Carlin is always surprised when people she coaches come to her with a distinct sense that many of the choices in their lives were already determined; that they are on a given path or have developed a certain way of living and feel it is too late to alter that. "And then, when someone points out to them that you can, in fact, change a lot of these things, it's a revelation," Carlin says.

So many of the things supposedly "decided" years ago haven't been fully decided by us. As in the case of the young Jacqueline Novogratz, perhaps an opportunity drops into your lap and suddenly you're a banker though you never planned to be one.

Those important early decisions may be influenced by what family or friends advise, or even be based on something you read in a book or saw in a commercial that hit you at a particularly impressionable stage. In a discussion of how common it is for people to follow paths determined by others, the author Seth Godin recommends considering this question:

Is there something else you might want to want—besides what you've been told to want?

It's never too late to ask such questions—nor too soon. The Silicon Valley venture capitalist Randy Komisar talks about the "deferred-life plan"—wherein ambitious young entrepreneurs devote themselves entirely to making money in the present, so that at some later point they'll have the means to pursue what really matters to them (once they take the time to figure out what that is). The same attitude can be found anywhere people are focused on building financial security so they can be in a comfortable position when they get around to asking what they *really* want to do with their lives. This harkens back to "climbing the mountain"— with the assumption being that things will become much clearer once we've reached the top.

But what about all those many critical questions having to do with the climb itself? We ignore them at our own peril. Moreover, as Komisar notes, most of the best-laid deferred-life plans don't go as planned. The world changes, the big idea fizzles, a radical midcourse adjustment is needed. Sooner or later, like it or not, you'll be faced with challenging questions—so why not get in the habit of asking them sooner?

IF YOU FEAR not having answers to the questions you might ask yourself, remember that one of the hallmarks of innovative problem solvers is that they are willing to raise questions without having any idea of what the answer might be. Part of being able to tackle complex and difficult questions is accepting that there is nothing wrong with *not knowing*. People who are good at questioning are comfortable with uncertainty.

Many of us, however, are not comfortable with it. The author

Jonathan Fields, who has written extensively and eloquently about uncertainty, points out that it's common to think about the unknown and get an unsettling feeling in the stomach. A questioner must come to terms with that sensation the way an actor handles performance anxiety—by forging ahead despite the butterflies. Eventually, as one does this, they become a welcome signal that you're moving into interesting uncharted territory, and that you might be on your way to something exciting. Questioning is a classic case of *the more you do it, the easier it gets.* Innovators tend to get better, over time, at embracing the unknown and solving problems because they become confident, through experience, that they'll eventually find their way through the darkness and into the light. Developing this level of comfort with uncertainty is worthwhile because, as Fields points out, life is filled with it.

For those concerned about not knowing what questions to ask, the work of the Right Question Institute (as well as Hal Gregersen's question-storming exercises on page 154) shows that if you force yourself to sit with a problem or a topic and try to think of appropriate questions, you will almost certainly come up with many. The challenge, though, is not just to think of questions, but to

How many people does it take to change a light bulb for a senior citizen?

In her inquiry into how to improve quality of life for older people, the British social designer Hilary Cottam found a key determining factor was "being socially connected and not having to worry about minor things like changing light bulbs." In 2007, Cottam's design group spent a year doing contextual inquiry while immersed in the lives of elderly residents in a poor London suburb, then began testing their theories with the Southwark Circle, a neighborhood network that combines the functions of a concierge service, self-help group, cooperative, and social club (members pay a small fee, and may barter services as well). Creating "social circles" for seniors lessened the need for costly at-home visits by social workers—while also providing more of a sense of community. Interestingly, Cottam found the ideal social circle as you get older "should include six people from very different roles," including family, friendly professionals, same-age peers, and young people.

then think *about* those questions—culling the best ones, improving them, and figuring out how you might begin to act on them.

Questioning should be done as a matter of habit and process—otherwise, it's not likely to find a place in busy schedules. In applying a rigorous system of inquiry to everyday life, aforementioned tools and techniques such as contextual inquiry, connective inquiry, and experimentation all can be useful. But it all starts with slowing down, stepping back, and trying to shift perspective in order to see your own life—and the problems, opportunities, and challenges worth tackling—more clearly.

Before we "lean in," what if we stepped back?

For people geared to achieving success or just getting things done, the idea of slowing down or, worse still, stepping back, can seem counterintuitive—and seemingly at odds with cultural messages urging us "go for it" or "lean in" as we pursue challenges and embrace opportunity. But while the notions of "stepping back" and "leaning in" might seem contradictory, someone who pauses, at times, to question and consider can also fully engage, act boldly, and seize opportunities. Stepping back to question can actually help with leaning in by providing a clearer sense of direction and purpose.

Finding the time and space to question, in a cultural landscape that doesn't encourage it, is challenging. If questioning might be considered a form of slow thinking, we have to get away from the fast thinking that is required in everyday life—especially in the current fast-moving, info-overloaded environment.

In one of his lectures on creativity, the comedian John Cleese talked about the need to find one's own "tortoise enclosure"—that sheltered, quiet place where you can go for extended periods to escape from the distractions of the outside world so that you can think without interruption. Cleese discusses this as a means of enabling oneself to write or engage in other creative activities, but going to the tortoise enclosure can also enable deep questioning (which is a form of creative thinking).

In today's world, stepping back or retreating to one's creative shell may require unplugging from the Internet. While the Web is a great source for quick answers to practical questions, it's more apt to keep you skimming the surface and jumping from one idea to another, as opposed to focusing, without distraction, on one deep question. The Internet also bombards you with other people's thoughts, ideas, and expertise—which may leave little room for your own creative thinking. And it's a source of endless interruptions, with every e-mail or tweet providing an excuse to stop thinking.

One of the current proponents of "unplugging" is the filmmaker Tiffany Shlain. A very plugged-in person (she specializes in Web-based films and has a large presence in social media), Shlain drew attention when she wrote about adopting a "tech Shabbat," on Saturdays, so that she and her family could have more time for reflection and quiet pleasures.

"It's completely changed my life," Shlain told me, referring to the weekly disconnect. "I find I've saved certain thinking for that day—big-picture thinking. While I love the kinetic thinking that happens when you're on the Internet, I also really value having a thought and not being able to act on it. It's great to just let that thought marinate and grow on its own."

Shlain said one of the benefits is that she is almost forced to grapple with her own questions instead of automatically going online to seek out answers. "On Saturday, when I'm stopped from doing that, I get to just sit with a question in a different way than I normally would," she told me. (One of the big questions she's "sitting with" these days involves our "love/hate relationship with technology. We're so enamored of it that we're not asking questions like *What is all of this technology taking away from us?*".)

In the current environment, it may be necessary to develop a routine and a habit that allows for quiet detachment and provides an opportunity to think deeply. This may start with logistical questions such as:

Where is my tortoise enclosure?

When is my tech Shabbat?

Having the time and a place to question is only part of it; discipline is required to "sit with a question," to create mental space for it by pushing aside the mundane "small thoughts," as Eric Maisel calls them. Such thoughts "steal neurons" when we're trying to think deeply. Practical questions (*What should I have for lunch later on? What time do I need to pick up the kids?*) have no place inside the tortoise enclosure, where the focus should be on larger Why and What If questions. The author William Deresiewicz has written, "Thinking means concentrating on one thing long enough to develop an idea about it . . . It's only by concentrating, sticking to the question, being patient, letting all the parts of my brain come into play, that I arrive at an original idea."

What if we start with what we already have?

When innovators look at the world around them, they're often looking for what's missing. But while questioning your own life, it's also important to look, via "appreciative inquiry," not just for what's missing, but also for what's there.

The main premise of appreciative inquiry is that positive questions, focusing on strengths and assets, tend to yield more effective results than negative questions focusing on problems or deficits. Strength-based questioning focuses on what is working in our lives—so that we can build upon that and get more out of it. This is important because self-questioning can easily drift toward dissatisfaction, regret, feelings of helplessness: *Why don't I have more money, a better job, a bigger circle of friends?*—and so forth. What is missing or lacking can point to opportunities for progress and improvement, but such questions can also evoke negative feelings, and as appreciative inquiry guru David Cooperrider points out, people are more likely to take constructive action when they feel hopeful and recognize all they have going for them already.

Happiness researchers such as Tal Ben-Shahar, author of *Happier* and *Being Happy* and a professor at Harvard University, believe it's important to "cultivate the habit of gratitude." Simply by asking, at the end of each day, *What am I grateful for?* and writing down the answers in a "gratitude journal," people tend to be "happier, more optimistic, more successful, more likely to achieve their goals," according to Ben-Shahar.

Ben-Shahar's point was echoed by the filmmaker Roko Belic, who believes that "gratitude is a shortcut to happiness." Belic has spent years trekking around the world and trying to answer his own questions about why some people are happier than others and whether it's possible for someone to *become* happier. The answer to his questions can be found in his documentary film *Happy*, but one of the key findings is that people who value and appreciate the basics—family and friends, a sense of belonging to a community, the simple pleasure that comes with engaging in a hobby or learning something new—tend to be a lot happier.

Belic's questions about happiness had been percolating for some time prior to his making the film. His first Why moment came at age eighteen, when he traveled to Africa as part of a group raising funds for refugees of the Mozambique civil war. "These were people who had suffered tremendously," Belic said, "but when we got there, we didn't find people who were miserable or angry. We found people who were just beaming with life, ecstatic at the smallest and tiniest things: seeing a ballpoint pen, looking at a magic trick, seeing us run around carrying each other on our shoulders. They had a genuine spark of joy that seemed to be missing in a lot of my friends back home." So Belic's question at that time was:

Why is it that people who have so little and have suffered so much seem to be happier than other people who are more fortunate?

Years later, when Belic was working in Hollywood, a similar question was raised by a friend of Belic's, the Hollywood director Tom Shadyac. Shadyac had read an article about how Americans, despite being relatively prosperous, tended to be less happy than people in other, poorer countries. "Tom said to me, 'I know this personally because I've been surrounded by talented, good-looking, lucky, healthy movie stars who are not as happy as the gardeners who tend my garden.'" So the new version of Belic's question became:

If being a beautiful, talented, wealthy movie star doesn't make you happy, then what does?

He and Shadyac joined forces to try to find an answer by way of their film. The journey to make it took Belic all over the world, including impoverished locales in India, Africa, and China. Regardless of circumstance, Belic found that "community and connectedness" formed the common thread among the happiest people. "It does not mean that to be happy you have to be very social or outgoing or have a million friends," he said. But the happiest people he encountered —including some living extremely modestly—had a strong connection to those around them. "They laughed and really enjoyed being around the people they love."

This link between happiness and strong relationships is hardly a startling revelation. Yet, as Belic points out, "most of us spend more of our time working to make money—often to support a lifestyle that involves bigger houses or nice cars and clothes—than the time we spend with our friends." Belic believes "these simple questions, like, *What is important to you?* can lead you to realize that you might want to do some shifts that could actually increase your happiness just by having your lifestyle reflect your values a little bit more."

When Belic examined his own life, he realized that he, too, had failed to devote enough time to being with friends and doing simple things that he truly enjoyed doing. "I always thought that as I got older, I would see my friends more; we would play more; we would go on adventures even more. But by the time I was in my thirties, I was seeing my best friends maybe once or twice a year. I was trying to be a responsible adult and devote myself to my career. I'd accepted this idea that kids play and adults work. As part of that, I'd stopped surfing, which is something I used to love doing with friends." The lessons learned in the film prompted Belic to ask how he might strengthen human connections and enhance simple pleasures in his own life—and spurred him to resume surfing with a close friend.

Belic's self-questioning led to other changes, as well. For example, he began to ask, *Why don't I know more of my neighbors?* Belic knew, from his film research, that in the happiest communities, "everybody knows each other," yet in his West Coast neighborhood, people tended to stay in their comfortable houses and keep to themselves. Belic wondered, *How might I find that sense of community and connectedness I experienced in those small villages in Africa and India?* When he visited a friend at an upscale trailer park in Los Angeles—where front doors opened into shared areas and neighbors practically couldn't help engaging with one another—Belic promptly pulled up stakes and moved there.

To MAKE CHANGES in his own life, Belic asked, in effect, *What has worked for me before—and how can I bring more of that into my life now?* Appreciative inquiry is usually focused on building upon current strengths, but sometimes by looking into the past, you can glimpse what might improve your life in the present and future.

Gretchen Rubin of the Happiness Project and the life coach Eric Maisel each suggest that we ask ourselves some version of the question *What did I love doing as a child?*

"The things we loved at age six or eight are probably still the things we love," says Maisel. He suggests drawing up a list of favorite activities and interests from childhood—"and see what still resonates with you today. And then it's a process of updating those loves. You may have loved something that doesn't even exist now, or doesn't make sense in your life now—but you may be able to find a new version of that."

This needn't be limited to childhood. Belic looked back at his young-adult years to rediscover the importance of surfing with friends. He was inspired by an even more recent experience when he decided to try to re-create that sense of community he had experienced in his travels for the film.

Jacqueline Novogratz has her own spin on this concept, phrased in the question *What are you doing when you feel most beautiful?* In her travels for the Acumen Fund, she sometimes asks her question in unlikely settings: "I decided to try it out on women living in a slum in Bombay." At first, it didn't go over well: "One woman said, 'There's nothing in our lives that's beautiful.' But finally another woman, who worked as a gardener, said, 'Well, I can think of one time. All winter long I slog and slog, but when those flowers push through the ground, I feel beautiful.'"

Novogratz maintains, "It's important to think about that time and place and activity where you shine, where you feel most alive. I get all kinds of different answers—when I'm solving a problem, when I'm creating, when I'm connecting with someone, when I'm traveling." Whatever it is, Novogratz says, you need to identify it and appreciate it—and if possible, find a way to do more of it.

Sometimes we're not aware of the things we're meant to do, the things we're good at—which is another reason it's important to step back and look at one's activities and behaviors from a detached, inquisitive perspective. "Ask yourself, *What do I find myself doing?*" recommends Gretchen Rubin. "What you spend time doing can also tell you what you should do. Because sometimes the things we do without thinking really are things we naturally enjoy or are good at."

Author Carol Adrienne shares this question, which can be helpful in identifying one's natural interests: *When you're in a bookstore, what section are you drawn to?* The things we care about, that we love doing and do well, provide great starting points for questioning. We might, for example, ask the following:

> *Why do I seem to "shine" when doing certain things? (What is it about those activities/places that brings out the best in me?)*

> *What if I could find a way to incorporate these interests/ activities, or some aspect of them, into my life more? And maybe even into my work?*

> *How might I go about doing that?*

Actually doing something about the answers you come up with is harder—though approaching change as a series of modest experiments can help.

What if you made one small change?

The word *experiment* may conjure up images of lab coats and microscopes. Maybe it brings back uncomfortable memories of the dissection of frogs. But experimentation can be thought of as, simply, the ways you act upon questions. You wonder about something new or different; you try it out; you assess the results. That's an experiment.

The psychologist and computer scientist Roger Schank has written, "In school we learn that experimentation is boring, is something done by scientists and has nothing to do with our daily lives." But as Schank points out, we're often experimenting without necessarily thinking of it in those terms—"when we take a new job, or try a new tactic in a game we are playing"—and we should be doing it even more than that because "every aspect of life is an experiment that can be better understood if it is perceived in that way." If you randomly try things in life, it can lead to haphazard results; but if you bring thought to trying new approaches or experiences—if you take time to consider why they might be worth trying, and what might be the best way to test them out, and then assess whether the trial was a success and worth following up on—it's a more practical way to bring change into your life.

When I was thinking about this theme of experimenting in life as a way to act on questions, a friend referred me to the writer A.J. Jacobs. "He lives his whole life as one experiment after another," the friend told me. I was familiar with Jacobs's humorous first-person essays in *Esquire* magazine, but I didn't have a full appreciation of the "experimental" nature of his work.

Jacobs is an intensely curious man who often finds himself wondering why some people live their lives in a particular way. He then speculates, *What if I tried that myself?* Then he jumps right into the How stage, as he starts to live the experience. For example, Jacobs found himself wondering about people who say, "I follow everything in the Bible." "And my question was "Yeah, they say that, but *what if you really lived by everything in the Bible?*" So Jacobs did that, for a year (the experience was chronicled in his book *The Year of Living Biblically*). He grew a large, bushy beard, wore flowing robes, and prayed constantly. Following the Bible's message about being thankful, Jacobs expressed his thankfulness hundreds of times a day. "When I turned on the lamp," Jacobs told me, "I was thankful for the light coming on. When I pressed the elevator button, I was thankful that the elevator came, and then thankful it didn't plummet to the basement and break my collarbone. You realize, doing this, that there are hundreds of things that go right every day and yet we focus on the three or four that go wrong."

One of Jacobs's other experiments was reading all thirty-two volumes of the *Encyclopaedia Britannica* from cover to cover (because he wondered what it would be like to "know" everything in there); another came about when he noticed that "outsourcing" was all the rage in business and he wondered, *What if I outsourced my life?* He then hired a team of people in India to do everything from answering his e-mails to reading bedtime stories to his son— "they even argued with my wife for me," he says.

As a humorist, Jacobs gravitates toward extreme experiences that yield offbeat surprises. But he also conducts small, everyday experiments that offer interesting lessons on taking the first small steps toward change.

In one of Jacobs's more practical projects, which began as an *Esquire* article called "The Rationality Project," he set out to catalog everything he did during his days and ask himself why he made each decision, no matter how small. *Why did he use Crest toothpaste?* Thinking about it, he realized, "It was because I had some friends at camp when I was twelve years old who used to tell me it was a cool toothpaste. That's literally why I've used it for thirty years." Such was the case with many of his daily activities and choices: "You discover that we do so many things by rote."

Jacobs believes every now and then one should go through one's day, from waking up until bedtime, questioning and reexamining everything. "One of my thoughts is that all of this is like when you're skiing and the skis create ruts and it becomes easier to just follow those," he says. But if you keep changing things up, "it keeps you from staying in these ruts and allows you to see the world in different ways."

The small changes could be in the route you take to work. It could be something done around the house, such as the way you make the bed. Cooking is a great opportunity for experimentation; the chef Chris Young told me that he tries to remind people, "You have a wonderful lab in your home that's ideal for experimenting—it's called the kitchen." The small change could be in the way you dress, the way you fix your hair: *Why do it the same old way? What if you tried something different?* Jacobs told me about an Orthodox Jewish woman he interviewed who said that on the Shabbat she always tries to find small things she could do in a slightly different way—"so instead of putting her lipstick on clockwise, she would put it on counterclockwise. Just being more aware of what you're doing, more mindful—there's something wonderful about that." When you change one small thing and it works, it can help breed the confidence to change other things—including bigger ones.

Jacobs offers another tip on small changes: If necessary, fake it until you make it. Or, to put it another way, Jacobs quotes Habitat for Humanity founder Millard Fuller, who said, "It's easier to act your way into a new way of thinking than to think your way into a new way of acting."

Jacobs has found this to be true in his own small-change experiments: "If you just go ahead and do something differently, and you do it enough times, it will change your mind. If you force yourself to smile, you trick your brain and then you start to become happier." Jacobs has tried this "act as if" approach with everything from changing his posture to behaving as if he were more confident than he is. When he finds that he's doubting himself on a project, Jacobs asks, *What would an optimistic, confident person do?* That person would probably cast aside those doubts and forge ahead, so Jacobs tries to do likewise.

EXPERIMENTATION CAN AND should be applied to big shifts as well as small changes. Career change is a good example: According to

Herminia Ibarra, a professor of organizational behavior at INSEAD in Fontainebleau, France, and author of *Working Identity: Unconventional Strategies for Reinventing Your Career*, the best way to find a new career is to keep asking, and quickly acting upon, the question *What if I try this?*

This is somewhat counterintuitive, Ibarra points out; most people assume that you should devote extensive time, research, and planning to figuring out the perfect new career before taking any action. The typical career change, she notes, often involves poring over self-help books, talking to people who can offer advice, and waiting for the epiphany that shows you your "true self"—at which point you can strike out confidently in a new direction. That's all wrong, says Ibarra; "We need to act." Through her research, Ibarra learned that most real-life career transitions take about three years, and they rarely happen in a linear path. It's a series of trials and errors, and where we end up often surprises us. But the main thing is to get the testing and learning under way as soon as possible.

A key first step to a successful career change, according to Ibarra, is crafting experiments. She advises looking for temporary assignments, outside contracts, advisory work, and moonlighting to get experience or build skills in new industries; executive programs, sabbaticals, and extended vacations can be valuable in providing opportunities to experiment. She concludes, "We learn who we are—in practice, not in theory—by testing reality."

Eric Ries of the Lean Startup has led a rapidly growing movement encouraging companies to do exactly what Ibarra is talking about for individuals—i.e., to experiment as a business, try lots of new ideas to see what works, and introduce new products and services quickly in order to "test and learn."

Ries feels the Lean Startup approach and philosophy can be applied to one's life, as well. The basic principles hold up; if you're starting a new career or even just embarking on a creative project or some other type of initiative, you're in "start-up" mode—and the "lean" rules apply. Ask yourself a lot of What If questions to come up with new possibilities that you can try out; give form to those ideas quickly and put them out into the world; get feedback on what works and what doesn't. In a word, experiment.

What if you could not fail?

One of the hallmarks of a powerful question is that it gets passed around, and that has certainly been the case with the question above. It was popularized a couple of decades ago by the American pastor Robert Schuller. The full version of his question was *What would you attempt to do if you knew you could not fail?*

In the past few years, the question has had another surge in popularity that seems to have been jump-started by the former DARPA director Regina Dugan, who used it in a widely circulated TED speech. The question has also been picked up and championed by the influential Google X founder Sebastian Thrun, who has quoted it on Reddit and elsewhere.

But even though the question has some mileage on it—and even though some people believe it's a flawed question—it exemplifies a beautiful question in its ability to inspire and spark the imagination. And it's an appropriate follow-up to the "make one small change" recommendation. While that's about encouraging modest actions, this question is about giving yourself permission to think big.

What if a TV drama could inspire real-life change?

When the gritty television series *The Wire* ended in 2008, lead actress Sonja Sohn wasn't ready to say good-bye to urban Baltimore, where the show was set. Sohn's own hard-knock upbringing had given her empathy for the troubled lives depicted in *The Wire*; she wanted to help in some way. So she asked: *What if we took* The Wire *into schools, dissected how characters negotiated their environment—and got kids to talk about how they did the same in their lives? Could that help them step outside themselves and see how they were making decisions and what they might do differently?* Sohn founded the community-based nonprofit ReWired for Change in 2009, and was gratified to find that episodes of *The Wire* (along with other exercises and life skills lessons) did indeed prompt hard-case kids to open up about their lives, while teaching them critical thinking about morality, cause and effect, decisions, and consequences.

We've seen that companies sometimes use a hypothetical What If question to temporarily remove constraints that can inhibit ambitious thinking (*What if cost weren't an issue—how might we do things differently?*), and the same principle applies when people are pursuing new ideas or embarking on change in their lives. Often the biggest constraint is fear of failure.

When I asked Sebastian Thrun why the *What if you could not fail?* question resonated with him, he responded, "People mainly fail because they fear failure." A central tenet of Thrun's approach to bringing about radical change, whether that involves reinventing cars or college courses, is "the willingness to fail fast and celebrate failures." Thrun added, "Innovators have to be fearless."

That was the message Dugan conveyed in her TED speech featuring the could-not-fail question. "If you really ask yourself this question," she told the audience, "you can't help but feel uncomfortable," because it becomes clear that fear of failure "keeps us from attempting great things . . . and life gets dull. Amazing things stop happening." But if you can get past that fear, Dugan said, "Impossible things suddenly become possible."

The notion that we should embrace failure has been a popular credo in Silicon Valley, though more recently the "failure is good" message has gone mainstream, showing up in, for example, a 2013 commencement speech by Oprah Winfrey. In fact, the sudden ubiquity of this idea prompted a mini-backlash from a writer on the website Big Think, who used the term *failure fetish* to describe the trend. The writer pointed out that failure, despite all its current good press, is in reality often painful and sometimes devastating.

Nonetheless, many are pushing the "embrace failure" message. The writer Peter Sims pointed out that fear of failure has been drummed into us, starting early in life: "Your parents wanted you to achieve, achieve, achieve—in sports, the classroom, and scouting or work. Your teachers penalized you for having the 'wrong' answers," Sims wrote in *Harvard Business Review*. And if anything, it only got worse as you moved into the business world, where, Sims noted, "modern industrial management is still predicated largely on mitigating risks and preventing errors."

Meanwhile, in the more entrepreneurial and creative sectors, failure has come to be recognized and appreciated as an unavoidable—and often highly useful—step on the road to creativity and innovation. Mick Ebeling, the Eyewriter inventor, observes, "When we hit failure, I start to laugh. It's almost like checking off a box—great, we got that out of the way. Now we're that much closer."

Experienced creators have always known this. The poet John Keats wrote, "Failure is, in a sense, the highway to success, inasmuch as every discovery of what is false leads us to seek earnestly after what is true." Those not comfortable enough to laugh at failure might start by questioning its nature, and how we perceive it. *What does failure mean to me: Do I see it as an end state, or a temporary stage in a process? How do I distinguish between an acceptable failure and unacceptable one?* (Not all failures are equal—and not all help you to move forward; some can shut everything down.) *Can I use productive "small failures" as a means of avoiding devastating "big failures"?*

THE AUTHOR, BLOGGER, and serial entrepreneur Jonathan Fields has known his share of setbacks and more than his share of successes; along the way, Fields has developed some interesting ideas about the questions we should ask ourselves about the possibility of failure.

Fields doesn't particularly like the *What if you could not fail?* question. "It proposes a fantasy scenario," he told me. "I'm more interested in taking people through a series of questions that will actually empower you to take action in the face of the reality that you *might* fail."

Fields thinks that as we embark on a new endeavor, we should begin by confronting that possibility of failure via this question: *What if I fail—how will I recover?*

Often when we think about failure, Fields says, we do so in a vague, exaggerated way—we're afraid to even think about it clearly. He suggests that anyone undertaking something with an element of risk start by visualizing what would actually happen if it failed and what would be needed to pick up the pieces from that failure.

This tends to clarify that failure in any endeavor is rarely total. There is a way back from almost anything, and once you acknowledge that, you can proceed with more confidence. The psychologist and author Judith Beck told me she uses a similar question with patients—*If the worst happens, how could I cope?*—because, as she explained, "people's anxiety goes down once they realize they will live through their worst fear, and that they have internal and external resources that will help them get through it."

Another important question Fields thinks we should ask:

What if I do nothing?

This underscores that when we undertake an important change, it's often because we *need* to change—and if we don't go ahead with it, we're likely to be unhappy staying put. Whatever problem or restlessness already exists may get worse. "There is no sideways," Fields says; generally, in life, if you're not moving forward, you're moving back.

Lastly, Fields says, ask yourself:

What if I succeed?

"That's important because the way our brains are wired, we tend to automatically go toward the negative scenario," Fields says. "So in order to give your mind a chance to latch onto something positive, something that will actually fuel action rather than fuel paralysis, it's helpful to create some level of clarity around what success in this endeavor would look like."

In other words, give yourself a strong incentive to want to risk failure. The blogger Chris Guillebeau put yet another spin on the Schuller question. "Instead of thinking about what you would do if you knew you wouldn't fail," Guillebeau writes, "maybe a better question is . . . *What's truly worth doing, whether you fail or succeed?*"

How might we pry off the lid and stir the paint?

Considering Guillebeau's question of what's worth doing even at the risk of failure, the challenges that may be particularly worthy of that kind of investment are those that spark imagination, speak to the heart—and bring people closer together. The late Fran Peavey, a social activist, excelled at what she called "strategic questioning," which I would characterize as questioning with an open mind and a caring heart. Peavey's questioning left a mark in various far-flung corners of the world: in the slums of Bangkok, in war-torn Bosnia, in the water of India's Ganges River, and in her adopted hometown of Oakland, California.

Peavey (who died in 2010) was, to put it mildly, a character. An oversize, exuberant woman (a journalist who interviewed her wrote that when she laughed, "her flesh wobbles . . . her chest heaves, her ears bob"), she was a sometime absurdist comedian as well as a full-time activist. When she traveled, she brought with her a hand-held sign, which she'd hold up as she sat in train stations and other crowded gathering spots, reading AMERICAN WILLING TO LISTEN.

It was an odd come-on, but it worked—people would approach Peavey, sometimes warily, to find out what she was up to. Over a couple of decades, she conducted thousands of interviews this way. "I refined my interviewing technique," she told the *Melbourne Age*, "asking open-ended questions that would serve as springboards for opinions and stories—questions such as *How would you like things to be different in your life?*"

Peavey believed that by employing the right kinds of questions—open, curious, slightly provocative at times, but never judgmental—one could have a meaningful dialogue with people who are very different from you, culturally, politically, temperamentally. Such questions could slip under and around the barriers between people; they could help identify common ground and shared concerns. And eventually, if the questioning and the discussion went deep enough, they might begin to resolve conflicts and problems.

Peavey used her "strategic questioning" to work with people on all manner of problems. As one news report noted, she helped Thai prostitutes who were facing eviction from their neighborhood; worked on a program to feed the homeless in Osaka; got a botanic garden replanted in the Croatian city of Dubrovnik; and even helped California skateboarders who were being chased off their favorite skating places. One of her more interesting projects was a public awareness campaign about cleaning up the Ganges River. She used a series of questions to gain a better understanding of the issue, asking local residents questions such as:

How do you feel about the condition of the river?

How do you explain the condition of the river to your children?

Peavey said she chose her language carefully, trying not to use the word *pollution* (which might offend people who believed the river to be holy) and instead framing the questions and the discussion around "taking care of the river." She could tell that people were daunted by the enormity of the task—so she began to focus the questions on a more long-term, ongoing objective:

How are you preparing your children to clean up the river?

When Peavey asked that question, people were forced to admit they weren't doing anything in this regard. "Their love of the river, their love for their children, and the void in their answers to that question could not long exist in the same minds," Peavey wrote. "The dissonance was too great."

Parents responded by organizing a poster-painting contest for the children, around the theme of the health of the river. The plan was to hang the paintings in public venues so that "adults will see what the children see and be embarrassed." In the years that followed, the contest became a large annual event. But as Peavey writes, the idea didn't come from her—it came from the residents themselves—though it seems to have been sparked by Peavey's question.

To Peavey, a question could serve as the lever to pry open the stuck lid on a can of paint. "If we have a longer lever, or a more dynamic question," she wrote, it can also be used to "really stir things up." In this metaphor, what's being stirred are the ideas and potential answers that people already have in their heads; they just need a little mixing to help those thoughts come together. But Peavey's approach to questioning also aimed to break down the "separation" between people based on differing cultures or views—which seems highly relevant in these polarized times.

When people are looking at issues from very different perspectives, it becomes problematic if one side tries to impose an answer on the other. Conversation either becomes argument or shuts down altogether. Perhaps the only way to break the stalemate on even the most divisive questions is to put the declarative statements on hold and try working on the following:

If we don't agree on an answer yet, can we at least come to terms on a question?

Former-adman-turned-activist Jon Bond, along with his wife, Rebecca, recently formed an anti-gun-violence movement called Evolve in response to the 2012 school shooting in Newtown, Connecticut. The group is working to reframe the conversation around gun control to focus on the larger question *How can we save lives?*

"We found the common ground between gun owners and nonowners by using questions," Bond told me. Among the questions people could agree on:

Do you care about gun violence?

Are you for gun responsibility?

"These elicited unqualified yeses," Bond said, "whereas statements like 'Gun owners must be more responsible' elicited personalized, defensive answers." Bond considers questions to be

---

What would you do to reach yourself?

As a pastor of a bible church in a drug-riddled Philadelphia neighborhood known as the Badlands, Joel Van Dyke was determined to reach the youth of that community—but for years had no luck figuring out how to do so. Then, after stumbling upon the E. E. Cummings line about "beautiful questions," Van Dyke decided to use questioning as an outreach tool. Instead of trying to tell local youths that he knew what they needed, "I decided to ask, 'What would you do to reach yourself?'" Van Dyke's willingness to immerse himself in the community and ask that question led to a surprising conversation. Community youths (including gang leaders) told him they very much wanted a place to play handball, but had been locked out of the local facilities. "Throw a big handball tournament," they told Van Dyke, "and we'll bring all our friends." Van Dyke's church went on to sponsor four tournaments a year, which also provided a venue to share the ministry's message.

"the verbal equivalent of nonviolent conflict resolution." The only way to get any traction on polarizing issues is to attract people on both sides, "not bully them into submission." As he noted, questions—if worded sensitively—can show respect to both sides of an issue, invite participation, and open up conversation. Bond, the former advertiser, described it as "the art of 'pull' versus 'push.' It can't be done without questions."

As both Peavey and Bond have noted, those questions must be culturally aware, insightful, respectful, and inviting. This may require contextual inquiry on the part of those doing the questioning. The approach used by Peavey, as well as another expert boundary-crosser, Novogratz, shows that there's no substitute for journeying into the world of people who hold different views from yours, "sitting on the floor with them," and trying to see the various issues from that perspective.

Short of doing that, at the very least we should heed the advice of Facebook cofounder Chris Hughes, who, in a recent commencement speech, urged graduating students to "create some habit that makes it easier to get out of your bubble. Follow someone you disagree with on Twitter."

Hughes would no doubt agree that we should also question the views of those with whom we disagree—yet with an open, curious mind:

Why might they see the issue this way? Why do I see it differently? What assumptions are we each operating under?

In this vein, one other question comes highly recommended from Michael Corning, a top engineer at Microsoft, who said he has relied on this in both his work and his life:

What are the odds I'm wrong?

As Corning points out, just pausing every once in a while to ponder this question can provide a check on our natural tendency to be overly certain of our own views. Plus, Corning adds, it can help to avoid all manner of trouble around the home, such as lengthy arguments that begin with a false accusation about who moved the car keys.

THE EMPATHETIC QUESTIONING that can help in "reaching across the chasm" on divisive issues can also be useful in "reaching across the room" to better connect with those closest to you—a close friend, neighbor, co-worker, brother, sister-in-law, eldest son, whomever. Questioning can be applied in various ways to get a better understanding of relationship challenges and to begin testing out possible remedies. If we take that hypothetical question raised earlier—*Why is my father-in-law so difficult to get along with?*—it should be checked for faulty assumptions by "questioning the question" (Is it true? Is he really hard for everyone to get along with?). If he gets along just fine with some people, including, say, another son-in-law about your age, then the better Why question is *Why is it difficult for my father-in-law to get along with me?*

One might also inject a few other Whys into the mix, as part of contextual inquiry:

Why, exactly, do I feel as if we're not getting along?

Why do I want to try to change that?

Why does the relationship with the other son-in-law seem to work better (and can I learn anything from that)?

The answers to these early questions can feed the next set of hypothesis questions (*Considering we only see each other at chaotic family gatherings, what if we could arrange to meet in a more relaxed setting?*) and How strategies (*How might I lure him to such a meeting—perhaps by inviting him to watch the ball game on my new big-screen TV?*). Through inquiry, you can begin to dissect the nature of a relationship problem, see things from the other person's point of view, and use tactical questioning to delicately float possible ideas and solutions.

Finding common ground with anyone is the key to connecting. With your family as a whole, it may require asking questions together. Bruce Feiler, author of *The Secrets of Happy Families*, dramatically improved communication in his family just by making time for regular weekly meetings—during which the same three questions were considered each time by the group:

What went well in the family this past week?

What could we do better?

What things will we commit to working on in the coming week?

Updating an idea that originated with the author Stephen Covey, Feiler also suggests families create their own "mission statements," similar to those used by companies. The idea of having a shared sense of familial purpose is a good one—but perhaps a "mission question" might be more engaging than a "statement." A family mission question could be *How might we, as a family, better serve the community?* Or *How might we carry on the tradition of our forebears?*

Part of the rewarding experience is figuring out, together, what might be the most meaningful, enjoyable, and promising question to pursue as a group. When searching for such a question—whether as a group or as an individual—you don't want to make the choice lightly.

How will you find your beautiful question?

When Doug Rauch came to the end of a successful career as the president of the Trader Joe's supermarket chain in 2008, he could simply have retired and played golf. But like a lot of people, Rauch wasn't comfortable with the traditional concept of retirement. "I think most of us find purpose when we engage with something bigger than ourselves," Rauch said. "If you're lucky in life, maybe you get to move from one area of significance—your career—to another."

But how would he find that new "area of significance"? Rauch wasn't sure, but as he began his search, he heard about a Harvard fellowship program formed to encourage retired business executives to take on worthy causes and projects, on the assumption that savvy, capable retired people are looking for big questions to pursue. The Harvard program was set up to provide coaching and university resources to the enrolled retirees as they tried to identify specific challenges of interest, but each individual in the program, Rauch included, had to figure what issue he or she wanted to tackle.

"I started looking at lots of challenges but I kept coming back to the idea of 'go with what you know,'" Rauch recalls. "And what I know is food." Something else he knew: "There are fifty million Americans who are hungry."

As Rauch began to think about this problem, he cycled through various Whys, What Ifs, and Hows (he was no novice when it came to questioning—he had practiced and honed the art at Trader Joe's based on his belief that "questioning is the heart of innovation").

He started with *Why do we have a situation in this country wherein one in six people is hungry?*

Compounding the mystery were other questions Rauch began to explore as he did his contextual inquiry into the nature of the problem. As he observed that hunger and obesity sometimes exist together in this country, he found himself asking, *How can an obese person be hungry?* In working through that one, Rauch had to get past some basic assumptions, one being that hunger is a shortage of calories. The reality is, people of limited means may tend to fill up on empty calories because that's more affordable. "If all you have is three dollars, you can consume a lot more calories with chips and soda," he said. But from a nutritional standpoint, you're still starving.

The most maddening question sprang from the realization "that 40 percent of what we grow in this country is never consumed," Rauch said. "And of course this causes you to wonder, *Why does so much good food end up in landfills?*"

What came next was a nice little bit of connective inquiry on

Rauch's part: "You start to put the pieces together, then you think, *What if you could use one problem to solve the other?*"

Being a supermarket guy, he knew one place where there was plenty of food—on store shelves—which led to *How do we get that food from the supermarket to the food desert?*

Rauch eventually came up with a potential solution—create an operation that would buy unused food at deep discounts from the supermarkets and from other producers, repackage it as convenient and nutritious take-home meals, and offer it for pennies on the dollar in a large, indoor farmers' market in Boston.

By mid-2013, Rauch was well on the way to turning the idea into a reality. He had raised the funds needed to launch the enterprise and he had a space picked out, with plans to give it a neighborhood feel with murals and community art on the walls. Rauch wants the food market to capture some of the allure of Trader Joe's, the sense that you're getting quality food at a bargain price. *Why not give the food away?* Rauch worked through that question and decided it's not sustainable, businesswise, nor is it what people necessarily want. Many tend to eye food giveaways with suspicion; but all people like to think they're getting a deal. This realization sparked one of Rauch's hypothetical questions: *What if we offer a bargain instead of a handout?*

The ending of Rauch's story is still to be determined—he was in the midst of the always-difficult How stage as of this writing (*How do we do the launch? How do we get people in the door? How do we make the numbers add up?*). But his story offers a good example of how one can come at the challenge of finding a beautiful question to pursue.

Rauch was bold and ambitious in staking out his question—he took on one of the biggest, thorniest issues around. He did so at a stage of life when, according to conventional wisdom, we should be pulling back from the hard and the new, to settle into a life more comfortable and familiar. In seeking out his question, he looked to others (the Harvard fellowship program) for help and counsel. He also looked around to see what was most needed in the world. But he looked inside himself as well—to inquire about what he was good at and how he might apply those skills in a fresh and meaningful way.

FINDING THAT ONE big, beautiful question to pursue isn't easy. So—starting as always with Why—let's first consider why it makes sense to do so. We all have goals, plans, passions, interests, concerns; we have lots to do and to think about, so why add on a big, difficult unanswered question? Because a question can be propulsive. You may have lists of things to do, goals to achieve, as we all have, in a drawer somewhere; but if you have one compelling question, it's harder to set aside and ignore. To quote David Cooperrider, a powerful question never sleeps. It can get deep into your head, to the point that you may find yourself working on it both consciously and unconsciously.

Articulating a personal challenge in the form of a question has other benefits. It allows you to be bold and adventurous because anyone can question anything. You don't have to be a recognized expert; you just have to be willing to say, *I'm going to venture forth in the world with my question and see what I find.* As you do this, you're in a strong position to build ideas and attract support. Because, whereas people are more likely to ignore or challenge you when you come at them with answers, they almost can't resist advising or helping you to answer a great question. All of this helps to build momentum. Questions (the right ones, anyway) are good at generating momentum, which is why change-makers so often use them as a starting point.

Should we retire the concept of "retirement?"

The aging of the Baby Boomers raises the question, *Can we still afford to have so many people retire in their sixties?* Moreover, *Is retirement really the most satisfying, productive way to spend one's later years?* Marc Freedman, founder of Encore.org, looks at the growth of the over-sixty population and asks: *Why can't we turn this dependence into abundance?* Freedman thinks older workers have a wealth of experience and knowledge that could be used in "encore careers" with nonprofits, charities, and schools, all of which have a growing need for high-level skills. Freedman's Encore.org movement offers support, job leads, fellowships, handbooks, and classes, readying millions of longer-living boomers to be a vital workforce for change. He also believes we should encourage people of all ages to plan for the "encore" stage of life by setting up Individual Purpose Accounts (patterned after IRA's) to help cover the inevitable costs of transitioning and retooling.

You may wonder, *Why would I want to limit myself to one? And if I did, how would I figure out the right one for me?* It can be worthwhile to zero in on a particularly significant question (or, at most, a couple of them) so that you can focus on it long enough to make some progress with it. The innovators I studied are full of great ideas; each has a hundred things he/she would like to achieve. But they tend to devote themselves to one question at a time.

Google's Sebastian Thrun likens each of his projects to climbing a mountain. You must start by picking a mountain and be sure it's a mountain you like, "not just one you want to be on top of"—because, with any luck, "you're gonna be stuck with it for the next couple of years," Thrun says.

As to which question to choose, to some degree the question chooses you. It's the one that resonates with you for some reason only you understand. What will make it a beautiful question for you, and one worth staying with, is the passion you feel for it. Look for a question that is "ambitious yet actionable"—or, as the physicist Edward Witten puts it, a question that's hard enough to be interesting, but realistic enough that you have some hope of answering it. (Not that you have to find an answer to all beautiful questions; the string theorist Witten, for instance, has never fully answered his biggest questions about the nature of the universe, but he told me that the pursuit of those questions has led him to many other interesting discoveries along the way.)

As some of the stories in this book have shown, people find meaningful questions in many ways and in various places. You can happen upon a great question by an unfortunate accident, as Van Phillips did. Or, as with Edwin Land, the question may be handed to you as an unexpected gift from an inquisitive child. Or the question can spring from trying to come to terms with a mundane problem: paying the rent, getting out of bed in the morning. An interesting thing about beautiful questions is that you may not have to search very far for them. They're often right in front of you—in your local community, your company, or maybe in the palm of your hand. The trick is to be able to see them, which may require stepping back, shifting perspective, exercising your powers of vuja de.

You can also find beautiful questions outside of your familiar environs. Gary White's ongoing effort to answer big questions about water, via his nonprofit group Water.org, all started when, as a student from the Midwest, he took a trip to Guatemala and saw that people in the slums lacked clean water. "It struck me that here I was, just a short plane ride from the U.S., with all we have—and here were these kids walking through sewage to collect contaminated water that could kill them. So I just couldn't help asking, *Why do so many lack this really basic thing that the rest of us take for granted?*" Once that question formed in his head, White was hooked.

There's no shortage in today's world of wicked problems wrapped around beautiful questions—meaning that somewhere deep inside that thorny issue, embedded at the core, lies an undiscovered question of great value. If those questions can be brought to the surface, we may be able to see the essence of the problem more clearly.

Think of a complex social issue—questioners are likely hard at work reframing it. Health care, hunger, protecting the environment, providing better care for the aging—all of these issues and many more cry out for new and better approaches that may only come to light via better questioning. Then, too, there is education, which is at the center of the questioning conversation. Think of the fundamental questions that need asking, by teachers, students, by education innovators such as the Right Question Institute, but also by parents—because we know that parents who take the time and trouble to inquire, *How can I encourage questioning in my child?*, are more likely to raise inquisitive kids who grow up to be resourceful, problem-solving adults. That makes it a beautiful question worth pursuing.

ON THE OTHER hand, maybe your beautiful question will focus on creating a more fulfilled, more curious, more interesting *you*. When I asked Paul Bennett of IDEO to share his own, personal beautiful question, he responded, "The question I constantly ask myself is *How do I stay inspired?*"

Bennett feels it's part of his job to do so: "As creative chief of six hundred people, you need to keep them inspired, but I can only do that if I keep myself inspired." He has trained himself to constantly notice and appreciate the inspiration that's all around. "You can't do it all the time, but there are moments in my day when I'll say, 'Stop—take a snapshot of this moment with your mind, remember this.' I think you need to be a good self-censor of the madness in the crowd and be able to pause and see something in the midst of all that—something interesting, something that matters, that you can share with others." Bennett culls all of these bits and shares the best of them with the people at IDEO, or with a larger audience on his blog, The Curiosity Chronicles.

For many of us, the beautiful question that calls to us is some variation of what Bennett is talking about: *How do we continually find inspiration so that we can inspire others?*

That question must be asked and answered fresh, over and over. There is no definitive answer, at least not for the creative individual who wants to keep growing, improving, innovating. To say, *I've figured it out—this is what I do and how I do it*, is to play it safe and thereby risk everything.

Keep yourself away from the answers, but alive in the middle of the question—this is the warning scrawled on the wall in the room where the acclaimed Irish novelist Colum McCann does his writing. I asked McCann what he meant by that line, and he wrote back, "We must embrace the notion that answers are in fact quite boring. The Irish are especially good or infuriating in this respect. We answer questions with questions. But in my opinion that's a good place to be. A little perplexed by the perplexity of life."

It's interesting that the beautiful questions about work—*Why do the work we do? What if we could take it to a different place and another level? How, exactly, might we do that?*—persist even for many of those who've "made it." I was intrigued to see a 2012 *New York Times* interview with the film actor Jake Gyllenhaal in which he was asked about taking a detour from films to tackle a demanding role in a live-theater production. Gyllenhaal indicated that his previous run of star turns in big films—for all the success it had brought—had somehow failed to answer some deeper question for him. "I wasn't really listening to myself about the project I wanted to do," he said. "I had to figure out what kind of actor I wanted to be and feel confident going for that." (He also said that it was hard for young film actors to do this kind of introspection because "asking questions isn't always a welcome thing in Hollywood, where everyone seems like they know what they're doing.") The actor-turned-director Ben Affleck seems to have had a similar questioning moment as he was embarking on his award-winning film *Argo*. He'd already directed two films; he'd proven himself, up to a point. "After that," Affleck told an interviewer, "the question became 'Okay, you can do it. Now what do you want to say?'"

That, right there, is a beautiful question for the ages: *What do you want to say? Why does it need to be said? What if you could say it in a way that has never before been done? How might you do that?*

WHEN YOU FIND your beautiful question, stay with it. If it's a question worth pursuing, it will likely also be confounding, frustrating, exhausting. If you find yourself stuck, follow the advice of Acumen's Novogratz—"just try to get to the next question." Break your big question into smaller ones and work on those. Keep cycling through Whys, What Ifs, and Hows, subjecting everything—even your being stuck—to a fresh set of queries.

Don't be afraid to change your question—even to ratchet it down a notch. You may also wish to expand it, broaden it, or possibly add pieces onto it, turning it into a compound question (which can be a clunky yet beautiful thing). Be sure to take your question for walks, and to the museum. Create the time and space for inspiration, which, as Van Phillips observes, comes in unexpected waves. As an innovator, "you're like a surfer waiting patiently for that wave to come in," says Phillips (yes, he surfs, as well as runs, on that foot he made). You don't know when the wave will come in—when those unpredictable connections in the nether regions of the brain will happen—but you must prepare and be ready for it. If you haven't sufficiently thought about your question—if you haven't even asked it—the connections are unlikely to happen and the wave will never materialize.

You may discover, as many questioners do when they begin to burrow into a problem, that there is much more to know than you could have imagined at the outset. Don't be put off by learning how much you don't know. That darkness was always out there, surrounding you; you just had no idea how vast it was until you began probing with your question flashlight. Questioners learn to love that great unknown—it's the land of opportunity, in terms of creativity and innovation. The author Stuart Firestein thinks we should all learn to see it likewise and offers up this beautiful question: *What if we cultivated ignorance instead of fearing it?*

If we did that, we would need some cultivating tools—including one, in particular, that could help us dig, uncover, plant, tend, and grow.

What if it turned out that tool had been right there in our back pocket, ever since childhood?

Acknowledgments

I'd first like to thank the editor of this book, Bloomsbury's George Gibson. It seems to be increasingly rare these days (unfortunately) for book editors to really get involved in editing, beyond making a few general suggestions and flagging typos. George warned me at the outset that he is an "activist editor" and it's true. He went through every line of the manuscript, tightening, clarifying, questioning—and the book is much better for it. Thanks also to my agent Jim Levine, who believed in the "question" idea and offered valuable input as I was shaping the book proposal. Jim also connected me with George, so I'm grateful for that, too.

This book started as a website, AMoreBeautifulQuestion.com, and on that site I asked for volunteers to help me work on the book. To my delight, many people responded and offered their help as members of my research team, including Harvey Richards, Philip Howell, Justin Hamilton, Larry Rubin, Katie Orthwein, Lana Rimboym, Chuck Appleby, Dinesh Balasubramaniam, and Sid Ramnarace. I want to especially thank a handful of people from that group who really went the extra mile in terms of tracking down stories and sharing ideas: Nikhil Goyal, Dave Baldwin, Daisy Azer, Theresa Garcia, Bill Welter, Damon Taylor, and Dan McDougall.

With regard to tracking down "question stories," I got special help from the outstanding researcher Susan O'Brien.

I want to thank all the people who granted interviews. I've

been a magazine/newspaper journalist and I've been a book author and there is an important difference that manifests itself during the research process: When you're calling from the *New York Times* or *Wired* magazine, people tend to respond because they want the publicity. But when you call and say, "I'm writing a book"—well, then you are dependent on the kindness of strangers. There's not much in it for the interviewee; they have no idea if the book will ever get written or if anyone will read it once it comes out. So I think they do the interview primarily because they have a genuine interest in the idea you're pursuing, and they want to be of help.

With that in mind, I'm grateful to all who took the time to talk about questioning, including: Dr. Ken Heilman, Gretchen Rubin, Irene Au, John Bielenberg, Sebastian Thrun, Jack Andraka, Jonathan Fields, Chen Bo Zhong, Doug Rauch, Tiffany Shlain, David Cooperrider, John Seely Brown, Roko Belic, Chris Young, A. J. Jacobs, Stephen Tobolowsky, Water.org's Gary White, and the Acumen Fund's Jacqueline Novogratz.

Also Robert Burton, Srikanth Srinivas, Dominic Randolph, Josh Aronson, Stewart Mostofsky, Eric Maisel, Mick Ebeling, Michael Corning, Jon Bond, Steve Bercu, Edward Witten, Colum McCann, and Kelly Carlin.

At the MIT Media Lab, thank you to Tod Machover and Joichi Ito, as well as to the former director Frank Moss. From Harvard University, my thanks go to Tony Wagner, Paul Harris, Paul Bottino, and Clayton Christensen. Representing Yale, the brilliant writer William Deresiewicz was an immense help. Stanford University's Bob Sutton provided inspiration with his ideas about vuja de.

There were a number of companies that helped greatly, starting with IDEO: thank you Tim Brown, Paul Bennett, and Fred Dust. I am also indebted to David Sherwin at Frog Design, and to the former Frog creative director Luke Williams. Also W. L. Gore's Debra France, Airbnb's Joe Gebbia, Steelcase's Jim Hackett, Patagonia's Casey Sheahan, Panera's Ron Shaich, and IBM's Eric Brown.

Special thanks to the outstanding business consultants and

"master questioners" Keith Yamashita, Eric Ries, Dev Patnaik, Tim Ogilvie, Jack Bergstrand, and the Peter Drucker Institute.

I'm grateful to the following people for the significant time spent talking to me for this book: the inspirational Min Basadur, the remarkable Van Phillips, Charles Warren, David Kord Murray, Randy Komisar, Gauri Nanda, Deborah Meier, and Hal Gregersen.

And I want to mention a few people who shared their time and didn't get quoted: Geoff Deane of Intellectual Ventures, Naomi Simson, Dennis Bartels of the Exploratorium museum, and Oliver Burkeman.

I'd like to give special mention here to the Right Question Institute, and the two people who created it, Dan Rothstein and Luz Santana. I believe the work they're doing on behalf of teaching the art of questioning is unquestionably valuable.

And I should also acknowledge and thank some people who provided inspiration at the formative stages: the designer Bruce Mau, whose "Ask Stupid Questions" principle was a starting point for me; the designer Brian Collins, who first suggested that "stupid questions" can also (in some cases) be thought of as "beautiful questions"; and TED founder Richard Saul Wurman, who was the first "master questioner" I interviewed (and who, in the process, questioned most of my questions).

My thanks to *Fast Company* and *Harvard Business Review* for running some of my early posts/articles about questioning. I also want to cite several publications/websites that were extremely valuable in terms of providing some of my raw material: *Fast Company*, which does a such great, exhaustive job of covering innovation; Brain Pickings, Maria Popova's amazing site for anyone interested in creativity; *Wired* magazine; and, of course, the *New York Times*, where a number of the "question stories" in the book were first reported (and special thanks to the *Times*'s Adam Bryant, whose "Corner Office" column provided many great leads on CEOs who question).

Thank you to the "Marmaduke Writing Factory," a New York–based writers' collective of which I am a founding member. I appreciate the support of fellow writers Bob Sullivan, Deborah

Schupack, Kate Buford, Marilyn Johnson, Mary Murphy, and Irene Levine (thanks also to Irene's husband, Jerome, for snapping a great author photo). Thank you to John Krysko and Nancy Rosanoff, who own the beautiful restored mansion where we write. And I'm indebted in particular to two members of the writers' group, Joseph Wallace and Benjamin Cheever, who were there to offer advice or just to listen.

Thank you to the Berger family and to the Kelly family for their support and encouragement. And above all, thank you to Laura E. Kelly, my creative partner in work and in life. She was incredibly involved in this book at each step of the journey—helping to shape the idea as well as the writing, applying her sharp editing skills, and doing a marvelous job creating the AMBQ website. When the book was finished, she used her new media/marketing savvy to help me to launch it into the world. She did everything, it seems—and I didn't even have to ask.

Notes

Introduction: Why Questioning?

PAGE 1: **That changed during my work . . .** The articles appeared in *Wired*, *Harvard Business Review*, and *Fast Company*; the book was *Glimmer: How Design Can Transform Your Business, Your Life, and Maybe Even the World* (New York: Penguin Press, 2009).

PAGE 2: **a company that "runs on questions" . . .** This Eric Schmidt quote has appeared in many articles, including an interview of the business consultant/author Paul Sloane by Vern Burkhardt, *IdeaConnection* newsletter, July 25, 2009.

PAGE 3: **"Ask yourself an interesting enough question . . ."** Maria Popova, "Chuck Close on Creativity, Work Ethic, and Problem-Solving vs. Problem-Creating," BrainPickings, December 27, 2012, http://www.brainpickings.org/index.php/2012/12/27/chuck-close-on-creativity/. The Chuck Close quote originally appeared in the book *Inside the Painter's Studio*, by Joe Fig (Princeton, NJ: Princeton Architectural Press, 2009).

PAGE 3: **he reckoned that if he had an hour . . .** As I noted, this may or may not have been said by Einstein. It is widely attributed to him in various articles and posts on the Internet. However, my researcher Susan O'Brien was unable to trace the quote back to Einstein. She also noted that another version of this quote is floating around, in which Einstein says he'd spend the first fifty-five minutes making sure he was "solving the right problem." However, we do know, from many other things he said, that Einstein was a firm believer in the importance of questioning. "The important thing," he said, "is not to stop questioning." For more on this subject see my post on AMoreBeautifulQuestion. com "Einstein and Questioning: Exploring the Inquiring Mind

of One of Our Greatest Thinkers," http://amorebeautifulques
tion.com/einstein-questioning/.

PAGE 4:   **A recent study found the average . . .** *Telegraph* staff, "Mothers
Asked Nearly 300 Questions a Day, Study Finds," *Telegraph*, March
28, 2013, www.telegraph.co.uk/news/uknews/9959026/Mothers
-asked-nearly-300-questions-a-day-study-finds.html. (Though the
headline says "nearly 300 questions," when the study focused on
four-year-old girls, the number of questions rose to 390 per day.)

PAGE 5:   **The business-innovation guru Clayton Christensen . . .** From
my interview with Christensen, January 8, 2013.

PAGE 5:   **rather, it has "turbocharged" it . . .** From my interviews with
Gregersen, January and April of 2013. The research conducted by
Dyer, Gregersen, and Christensen was conducted over six years,
involving more than three thousand business executives. It showed
"questioning" to be one of five key characteristics (and in some ways
the most important) associated with being a successful, creative
business leader. The results appeared initially in the *Harvard
Business Review* in December 2009 and later in Dyer, Gregersen,
and Christensen's *The Innovator's DNA: Mastering the Five Skills of
Disruptive Innovators* (Cambridge, MA: Harvard Business Review
Press, 2011).

PAGE 6:   **The neurologist John Kounios observes . . .** From my interview
with Kounios, November 2012.

PAGE 7:   **"We've transitioned into always transitioning" . . .** The general
principle of constant transitioning was discussed in my interview
with Brown, March 4, 2013. However, this particular quote appeared
in Heather Chaplin's interview "John Seely Brown on Interest-
Driven Learning, Mentors and the Importance of Play," spotlight
.macfound.org, March 1, 2012.

PAGE 8:   **The esteemed physicist Edward Witten . . .** From one of several
e-mail exchanges I had with Witten in February 2013. He also said
something similar in the article "Physics' Sharpest Mind Since
Einstein," CNN, July 5, 2005.

PAGE 9:   **on Google, some of the most popular queries . . .** Quentin Hardy
and Matt Richtel, "Don't Ask? Internet Still Tells," *New York Times*,
November 21, 2012.

Chapter 1: The Power of Inquiry

PAGE 11:   **Back in 1976, long before there . . .** From my interviews with Van
Phillips, beginning in 2009, and most recently in December 2012.
I also quoted several lines from Phillips's speech at the 2011 Cusp

Conference in Chicago. Other source material included Martha Davidson, "Artificial Parts: Van Phillips," *Smithsonian*, March 9, 2005; and Carol Pogash, "A Personal Call to a Prosthetic Invention," *New York Times*, July 2, 2008.

PAGE 13:   **"stopped thinking because he 'knows'"** . . . I came across this quote in Maria Popova, "Frank Lloyd Wright's Thoughts on Learning," *Atlantic*, June 8, 2012; excerpted from Bruce Brooks Pfeiffer, *Frank Lloyd Wright on Architecture, Nature, and the Human Spirit: A Collection of Quotations* (Portland, OR: Pomegranate, 2011).

PAGE 14:   **Mark Noonan, who once, after suffering** . . . From my 2009 interview with Noonan, originally for the book *Glimmer*.

PAGE 14:   **"We think someone else—someone smarter . . ."** From Regina Dugan's March 2012 TED talk, "From Mach 20 Glider to Humming-bird Drone," http://www.ted.com/talks/regina_dugan_from_mach_20_glider_to_humming_bird_drone.html.

PAGE 15:   **"are the engines of intellect . . ."** David Hackett Fischer, *Historians' Fallacies: Toward a Logic of Historical Thought* (New York: Harper & Row, 1970). Thank you to Bill Welter for bringing this to my attention.

PAGE 15:   **"shine a light on where you need . . ."** I am greatly indebted to the cofounders of the Right Question Institute, Dan Rothstein and Luz Santana. Most of the quotes from them come from my interviews with them in February and March of 2013. I also drew information from Rothstein and Santana's book, *Make Just One Change: Teach Students to Ask Their Own Questions* (Cambridge, MA: Harvard Education Press, 2012).

PAGE 15:   **The late Frances Peavey, a quirky** . . . The quote is from Fran Peavey, *By Life's Grace: Musings on the Essence of Social Change* (New Society Publishers, 1994). I found this quote in an excerpt from Peavey's book that was reprinted in "Creating a Future We Can Live With" (IC#40), published in spring 1995 by Context Institute.

PAGE 15:   **Paul Harris, an education professor** . . . From my interview with Harris, November 2012; I also drew information from Harris's book *Trusting What You're Told: How Children Learn From Others* (Cambridge, MA: Belknap Press, 2012).

PAGE 16:   **"I know more about my ignorance . . ."** From my interviews with Wurman, April 2008 and fall of 2012. Wurman has a chapter devoted to questioning in his book *Information Anxiety 2* (Indianapolis: QUE, 2001).

PAGE 16:   **The author Stuart Firestein, in his** . . . Stuart Firestein, *Ignorance: How it Drives Science* (Oxford: Oxford University Press, 2012); the book came to my attention when it was featured on BrainPickings, April 2, 2012, in a post that also highlighted Firestein's line "enthralled with answers," http://www.brainpickings.org/index. php/2012/04/02/stuart-firestein-ignorance-science/.

PAGE 17:   ***Harvard Business Review* writer Polly LaBarre ...** Polly LaBarre, "The Question That Will Change Your Organization," *Harvard Business Review*, November 10, 2011.

PAGE 17:   **How might we prepare during peacetime to offer help in times of war? ...** Information from The International Federation of Red Cross and Red Crescent Societies website at http://www.ifrc.org/en/who-we-are/history.

PAGE 17:   **The neurologist and author Ken Heilman ...** From my interview with Heilman, November 2012. He expands on this in his book *Creativity and the Brain* (Psychology Press, 2005).

PAGE 18:   **"You don't have to hold a position ..."** LaBarre, "Question That Will Change."

PAGE 18:   **"blend of humility and confidence" ...** From Jeff Dyer, Hal Gregersen, and Clayton M. Christensen, *The Innovator's DNA: Mastering the Five Skills of Disruptive Innovators* (Cambridge, MA: Harvard Business Review Press, 2011).

PAGE 18:   **"In our culture, not to know ..."** Robinson's quote, from his "School of Life" talk, appeared in BrainPickings, April 17, 2012, in Maria Popova, "Sir Ken Robinson on How Finding Your Element Changes Everything," http://www.brainpickings.org/index. php/2012/04/17/sir-ken-robinson-school-of-life/.

PAGE 19:   **according to David Cooperrider ...** From my interview with David Cooperrider, December 2012. Cooperrider is the author of many articles and books on appreciative inquiry, including *Appreciative Inquiry: A Positive Revolution in Change*, coauthored with Diana Whitney (San Francisco: Berrett-Kohler, 2005).

PAGE 19:   **"to organize our thinking around ..."** This quote first appeared in Leon Nayfakh's excellent article "Are We Asking the Right Questions?," *Boston Globe*, May 20, 2012. However, the quote was originally attributed in that article to Dan Rothstein of RQI; Rothstein informed me that the line actually originated with his colleague at RQI, Steve Quatrano, and Quatrano confirmed that with me.

PAGE 19:   **Sebastian Thrun, the engineer/inventor ...** From my e-mail exchanges with Thrun, February 2013.

PAGE 20:   **Reed Hastings, was reacting to one ...** The Netflix story has appeared in various interviews with Hastings, including Matthew Honan, "Unlikely Places Where Wired Pioneers Had Their Eureka Moments," *Wired*, March 24, 2008.

PAGE 20:   **to Pixar (*Can animation be cuddly?*) ...** Anthony Lane, "The Fun Factory," *New Yorker*, May 16, 2011.

PAGE 21:   **New York Times recently characterized** . . . Shaila Dewan, "To
             Stay Relevant in a Career, Workers Train Nonstop," *New York
             Times*, September 21, 2012.

PAGE 21:   **Thomas Friedman has written extensively** . . . For example, see
             Thomas L. Friedman, "It's a 401(k) World," *New York Times*, April
             30, 2013.

PAGE 22:   **Joichi Ito, the director of the** . . . From my interview with Ito,
             April 2013.

PAGE 23:   **"Right now, knowledge is a commodity"** . . . From my interview
             with Tony Wagner, January 2013.

PAGE 23:   **"the value of explicit information is dropping"** . . . Tony
             Wagner, *Creating Innovators: The Making of Young People Who
             Will Change the World* (New York: Scribner, 2012). I also
             discussed this directly with Bottino in my interview with him,
             April 1, 2013.

PAGE 23:   **The glut of knowledge has another** . . . Firestein, *Ignorance*.

PAGE 25:   **What if we could paint over our mistakes?** . . . From the Her
             Story Network website http://www.herstorynetwork.com/?s=Bette+
             Nesmith; and Jessica Gross, "Liquid Paper," *New York Times
             Magazine*, June 7, 2013.

PAGE 26:   **The author Seth Godin is** . . . Godin quotes are from his free
             e-book *Stop Stealing Dreams*, self-published in 2012, http://www.
             sethgodin.com/sg/docs/stopstealingdreamsscreen.pdf.

PAGE 26:   **To navigate in today's info-swamp** . . . Botstein's quote appeared
             in Julie Flaherty, "What Should You Get out of College?," *New York
             Times*, August 4, 2002.

PAGE 26:   **"Computers are useless—they only give . . ."** According to the
             website Quote Investigator, a version of this quote appeared in
             William Fifield, "Pablo Picasso: A Composite Interview," *Paris
             Review*, Summer–Fall 1964.

PAGE 26:   **The potential is mind-boggling** . . . This is from my visit to IBM's
             research facility in Yorktown Heights, New York, where the original
             Watson system is housed. I interviewed several people from IBM
             during my visit, primarily the engineer Eric Brown.

PAGE 27:   **A reporter doing an interview concludes** . . . This story is well
             traveled and appeared recently in an interview of Tiffany Shlain by
             Patt Morrison in the *Los Angeles Times*, November 26, 2011.

PAGE 27:   **Why did my candy bar melt? (And will my popcorn pop?)** . . .
             Drawn from the website Massmoments.org, which drew from
             "Percy Spencer and His Itch to Know," by Don Murray in *Readers'
             Digest* (August 1958); "Raytheon: A History of Global Technology
             Leadership" (Early Days link); and "Who Invented Microwaves?"
             from Gallawa.com.

PAGE 27: **Sugata Mitra, made just this point . . .** Mitra's TED talk was
"Build a School in the Cloud," February 27, 2013, http://www.ted.
com/talks/sugata_mitra_build_a_school_in_the_cloud.html.
Also, see the article "Is Education Obsolete? Sugata Mitra at the
MIT Media Lab," posted on the blog MIT Center for Civic Media,
May 16, 2012; as this post shows, the idea of "knowing" being obso-
lete was suggested by MIT's Nicholas Negroponte, in a class
discussion following Mitra's lecture at MIT.

PAGE 30: **"when someone looks at the way things . . ."** David Pogue, "A
Simple Swipe on a Phone, and You're Paid," *New York Times*,
September 29, 2010.

PAGE 30: **Gretchen Rubin showed how simple . . .** From my interview with
Rubin, February 20, 2013.

PAGE 31: **the business consultant Min Basadur . . .** I am greatly to indebted
to Basadur for a series of interviews he did with me in 2012, both on
the phone and at Basadur Applied Creativity headquarters in
Burlington, Ontario. During my visit, Basadur and his team gave
me a crash course in the firm's question-based creativity training
methods.

PAGE 31: **Why aren't the players urinating more? . . .** Douglas Martin, "J.
Robert Cade, the Inventor of Gatorade, Dies at 80," *New York
Times*, November 28, 2007. Also adapted from the website http://
www.cademuseum.org/museum/history.

PAGE 32: **For example, current theories of "design thinking" . . .** For
more on design thinking, see my book *Glimmer* as well as Tim
Brown, *Change by Design* (New York: HarperBusiness, 2009).

PAGE 33: **"even when you don't know what . . ."** This was said to me by the
designer and design-thinking teacher Bruce Mau during my interviews with him in 2008 and 2009 for *Glimmer*.

PAGE 35: **What if a car windshield could blink? . . .** Bob Kearns bio info
comes from John Seabrook's "The Flash of Genius," *New Yorker*,
January 11, 1993; story of Mary Anderson comes from Catherine
Thimmesh, *Girls Think of Everything: Stories of Ingenious Inventions
by Women*, (New York: Houghton Mifflin, 2000).

Chapter 2: Why We Stop Questioning

PAGE 39: Louis C.K. can be seen performing "Why?" on YouTube at, among
other uploads, http://www.youtube.com/watch?v=BJlV49RDlLE.

PAGE 40: **research shows that a child asks about . . .** This research appears
in Harris's book *Trusting What You're Told* and in Nayfakh's *Boston
Globe* article "Are We Asking the Right Questions?"

PAGE 40: **some of the lab's work is featured . . .** Shlain's ten-minute film, *Brain Power: From Neurons to Networks*, can be seen at http://let-itripple.org/brain-power/.

PAGE 41: **As the children's neurologist Stewart Mostofsky . . .** From my interview with Mostofsky, January 17, 2013.

PAGE 41: **Why is the sky blue? . . .** Drawn from Nicholas Christakis's essay in John Brockman's book *This Explains Everything: Deep, Beautiful, and Elegant Theories of How the World Works* (New York: Harper Perennial, 2013).

PAGE 42: **The physicist Neil deGrasse Tyson talks . . .** From the YouTube clip "Kids Are Born Scientists," http://www.youtube.com/watch?v=2ACkc4POpaU.

PAGE 42: **A recent University of Michigan study . . .** "When Preschoolers Ask Questions, They Want Explanations," *Science Daily* press release, November 13, 2009.

PAGE 43: **they immediately begin to ask fewer . . .** Lory Hough, "Why Do Kids Believe in God but Not Harry Potter?" *Ed., the Magazine of the Harvard Graduate School of Education*, May 2012.

PAGE 43: **The child psychologist Alison Gopnik has . . .** Alison Gopnik, "New Research Shows That Teaching Kids More and More, at Ever-Younger Ages, May Backfire," *Slate*, March 16, 2011; Gopnik's quote about kids being the R&D division of the human species is from her appearance on ABC's *Nightline*, April 2, 2010; her views on similarities between children's learning and scientific learning appear in her paper "Scientific Thinking in Young Children," published at the University of California, Berkeley, and also appearing on the website of *Science*, September 28, 2012, http://www.sciencemag.org/content/337/6102/1623.abstract.

PAGE 44: **In 2010, Professor Kyung-Hee Kim . . .** Po Bronson and Ashley Merryman, "The Creativity Crisis," *Newsweek*, July 10, 2010. Also, Andrew Grant and Gaia Grant, "The 7 Biggest Creativity Killers," *Fast Company*, June 12, 2012.

PAGE 44: The chart on the decline of questioning as children age was provided by the Right Question Institute, based on data on question-asking gathered by the National Center for Education Statistics for the 2009 "Nation's Report Card," http://nces.ed.gov/nationsreport-card/pdf/main2009/2011455.pdf.

PAGE 45: **When the engagement level of students . . .** The Gallup Student Poll surveyed nearly a half million students in grades five through twelve from more than seventeen hundred public schools in 2012. More on the study can be found in the Gallup blog post "The School Cliff: Student Engagement Drops with Each School Year,"

January 7, 2013, http://thegallupblog.gallup.com/2013/01/the-school-cliff-student-engagement.html.

PAGE 45:   **The author Daniel Pink asked . . .** Daniel Pink, "Does the 'school cliff' matter more than the fiscal cliff?" Daniel H. Pink blog, January 7, 2013, http://www.danpink.com/2013/01/does-the-school-cliff-matter-more-than-the-fiscal-cliff/.

PAGE 46:   **"I have so many state standards . . ."** Amy Harmon, "May Be a Sputnik Moment, but Science Fairs Are Lagging," *New York Times,* February 5, 2011.

PAGE 46:   **Dominic Randolph . . . uses the corporate term . . .** From my interview with Randolph, December 2012.

PAGE 47:   **Susan Engel of Williams College did . . .** Susan Engel, "Children's Need to Know: Curiosity in Schools," *Harvard Educational Review,* Winter 2011.

PAGE 47:   **Why do we want kids to "sit still" in class? . . .** Susan Saulny, "Students Stand When Called Upon, and When Not," *New York Times,* February 24, 2009.

PAGE 48:   **"Our grandfathers and great grandfathers . . ."** Godin, *Stop Stealing Dreams.*

PAGE 48:   **"It seems the main rule that . . ."** Jamie Angell, "Explaining Groening—One on one with the sultan of fun," *Simpsons Illustrated* 1, no. 9 (Summer 1993).

PAGE 50:   **New York's Harlem neighborhood in . . .** I am greatly indebted to Deborah Meier for doing a series of interviews with me in late 2012 and early 2013. Material was also drawn from Meier's blog, Deborah Meier on Education, http://deborahmeier.com/.

PAGE 51:   **Meier opened the first of her schools . . .** In my description of Central Park East schools, I quoted and drew heavily from Seymour Fliegel's excellent article "Debbie Meier and the Dawn of Central Park East," *City Journal,* Winter 1994.

PAGE 52:   **"an astonishingly rich educational program" . . .** Ibid.

PAGE 53:   **But such schools still represent just . . .** From my interviews with Nikhil Goyal, April 2013; for more, see Goyal's book, *One Size Does Not Fit All: A Student's Assessment of School* (Bravura Books, 2012).

PAGE 54:   **alumni have become known as the Montessori Mafia . . .** Peter Sims, "The Montessori Mafia," *Wall Street Journal,* April 5, 2011.

PAGE 55:   **Marissa Mayer—now the head of Yahoo! . . .** Steven Levy, "Larry Page Wants to Return Google to Its Startup Roots," *Wired,* April 2011.

PAGE 55:   **Dan Meyer, a high school math teacher . . .** Meyer gave his talk, "Math Class Needs a Makeover," at TEDxNYED, March 2010.

PAGE 55:   **Why do movie tickets cost the same for hits or duds? . . .** Robert H. Frank, "How Can They Charge That? (and Other Questions)," *New York Times*, May 11, 2013.

PAGE 56:   **Dennie Palmer Wolf, a professor . . .** Dennie Palmer Wolf, "The Art of Questioning," *Academic Connections*, Winter 1987.

PAGE 57:   **What is a flame? . . .** Kenneth Change, "A Challenge to Make Science Crystal Clear," *New York Times*, March 5, 2012. Also from articles on the Center for Communicating Science website, http://www.centerforcommunicatingscience.org/the-flame-challenge-2/about-the-challenge/.

PAGE 58:   **Joshua Aronson of New York University . . .** From my interview with Aronson, November 2012.

PAGE 58:   **A recent study of fourth- and fifth-grade . . .** Jessica McCrory Calarco, "Middle-Class Children: Squeaky wheels in training," Indiana University study (press release posted on *Eurekalert!*), August 19, 2012.

PAGE 59:   **One of the "master questioners" I . . .** Jack Andraka interview, February 12, 2012.

PAGE 60:   **When the Boston high school teacher . . .** Dan Rothstein and Luz Santana, *Make Just One Change: Teach Students to Ask Their Own Questions* (Cambridge. MA: Harvard Education Press, 2012).

PAGE 62:   **Luz Santana knew from firsthand experience . . .** From my interview with Santana.

PAGE 64:   **They found that their questioning techniques . . .** These case studies are cited on the website of the Right Question Institute.

PAGE 65:   **"seems to unlock something for them" . . .** Rothstein and Santana, *Make Just One Change.*

PAGE 65:   **The social critic Neil Postman wondered . . .** Neil Postman, *Building a Bridge to the 18th Century: How the Past Can Improve Our Future* (New York: Knopf, 1999).

PAGE 67:   **William Deresiewicz, the acclaimed author . . .** From my interview with Deresiewicz, January 30, 2013.

PAGE 67:   **"He had a young person's ability . . ."** Deresiewicz's description of his college professor is from his essay "A Jane Austen Education," *Chronicle Review*, May 1, 2011, http://chronicle.com/article/A-Jane-Austen-Education/127269/.

PAGE 67:   **How might parents make their kids better questioners? . . .** Hal Gregersen's quote is from my interview with him; Isidor Isaac Rabi's quote has circulated widely, recently appearing on Signals vs. Noise, an online publication of 37signals.com http://37signals.com/svn/posts/3424-my-mother-made-me-a-scientist-without-ever; Clayton Christensen's quote is from my interview with him; David Kelley's quote from his interview with Charlie Rose on *60 Minutes*, airdate January 6, 2012.

PAGE 68: **Thrun and one of his partners . . .** From my interview with Au, as well as my e-mail exchanges with Thrun. I also drew on an article profiling Thrun, Tom Vanderbilt, "How Artificial Intelligence Can Change Higher Education," *Smithsonian* magazine, December 2012.

PAGE 69: **One college professor recently observed . . .** Thomas Friedman, "Revolution Hits the Universities," *New York Times*, January 26, 2013.

Chapter 3: The Why, What If, and How of Innovative Questioning

PAGE 72: **Edwin Land was a brilliant inventor . . .** In recounting the Polaroid story, I relied on a number of sources, starting with *Life* magazine's cover story, "A Genius and His Camera," October 27, 1972. In the article, Land explains, in his own words, how his daughter asked him why she couldn't see the photograph right away. A good roundup on the Polaroid story also appears in Harry McCracken, "Polaroid SX-70: The Art and Science of the Nearly Impossible," *Technologizer*, June 8, 2011, http://technologizer. com/2011/06/08/polaroid/. Another good source was "Polaroid Corporation," *International Directory of Company Histories*, vol. 93 (Detroit: St. James Press, 2008). I first learned about the Polaroid question story from Mike Brewster, "The Great Innovators: Instant Photos, Lasting Fame," *Business Week*, June 29, 2004. Several good books have been written about Land and Polaroid, including Victor K. McElheny, *Insisting on the Impossible: The Life of Edwin Land* (New York: Basic Books, 1999). But I am particularly indebted to the Christopher Bonanos book *Instant: The Story of Polaroid* (Princeton, NJ: Princeton Architectural Press, 2012). See also Bonanos, "The Man Who Inspired Jobs," *New York Times*, October 7, 2011. Bonanos is slightly skeptical about the veracity of the "daughter's question" story, whether Land embellished his own tale; nevertheless I choose to accept Land's story as truth—if not a literal one, then a larger one.

PAGE 73: **"it wouldn't do to have a tank . . ."** Bonanos, *Instant.*

PAGE 77: **While everyone else nodded . . .** From my interviews with George Lois in 2008 and 2009, for *Glimmer.*

PAGE 77: **"Why does it pay to swim with dolphins?" . . .** The story about Marc Benioff's question was told in Jeff Dyer, Hal Gregersen, and Clayton Christensen's *The Innovator's DNA: Mastering the Five Skills of Disruptive Innovators* (Cambridge: Harvard Business

Review Press, 2011). The quote about "turning the software industry on its head" is from Jon Swartz, "Salesforce CEO leads charge against software," *USA Today*, July 24, 2007.

PAGE 78:   **Robert Burton, a neurologist and . . .** From my interview with Burton, November 2012. Burton's theories about certainty also appear in his article "The Certainty Epidemic," *Salon*, February 29, 2008; as well as in Burton's book, *On Being Certain: Believing You Are Right Even When You're Not* (New York: St. Martin's Press, 2008).

PAGE 78:   **A nice description of this phenomenon . . .** Maura O'Neill, "Disruptive Innovation Often Comes from Unexpected Places," *Huffington Post*, January 25, 2013.

PAGE 81:   **the late cofounder of Apple, Steve Jobs . . .** Jobs's interest in *shoshin* and other Zen principles has been chronicled in a number of places, including Walter Isaacson's biography *Steve Jobs* (New York: Simon and Schuster, 2011); as well as Daniel Burke, "Steve Jobs' Private Spirituality Now an Open Book," *USA Today*, November 2, 2011; and my own article for *Fast Company*, "What Zen Taught Steve Jobs (and Silicon Valley) about Innovation," April 9, 2012, http://www.fastcodesign.com/1669387/what-zen-taught-silicon-valley-and-steve-jobs-about-innovation.

PAGE 81:   **a bit of ancient wisdom, brought to . . .** As explained to me by Randy Komisar, in my interviews with him in the spring and fall of 2012. For more on Shunryu Suzuki, see his book *Zen Mind, Beginner's Mind: Informal Talks on Zen Meditation and Practice* (Boston: Shambhala Publications, 2011).

PAGE 81:   **Les Kaye is a Zen abbot . . .** From my interview with Kaye, April 2012, for my *Fast Company* article "What Zen Taught Steve Jobs."

PAGE 82:   **Randy Komisar, a partner in the renowned . . .** From a series of interviews with Komisar in 2012 (for *Fast Company* and this book). For more from Komisar, see his book *The Monk and the Riddle* (Boston: Harvard Business School Press, 2001).

PAGE 83:   **"we are often looking at a problem . . ."** From my interview with Tod Machover on April 12, 2013.

PAGE 83:   **a study conducted by the researchers . . .** From my interview with Darya Zabelina, December 5, 2012.

PAGE 84:   ***vuja de*, to use a quirky term . . .** Bob Sutton wrote about *vuja de* in his book *Weird Ideas That Work: 11½ Practices for Promoting, Managing and Sustaining Innovation* (New York: Free Press, 2002). The concept was also discussed in "Anthropologists in Pursuit of Vuja De," *Fast Company*, October 17, 2005. Also, see the post on my website "The Power of Vuja De," A More Beautiful Question, September 16, 2012, http://amorebeautifulquestion.com/power-of-vuja-de/.

PAGE 84:   **"see what's always been there . . . "** Tom Kelley, *The Ten Faces of Innovation* (New York: Doubleday, 2005).

PAGE 84:   **the term was mentioned, albeit briefly . . .** George Carlin's vuja de bit can be seen on YouTube, http://www.youtube.com/watch?v=B7LBSDQ14eA.

PAGE 85:   **the comedian and radio host Kelly Carlin . . .** From my interview with Kelly Carlin, April 10, 2013.

PAGE 85:   **George Carlin once said that . . .** Stephen Sherrill, "Oh, Happy Day," *New York Times Magazine*, June 3, 2001.

PAGE 86:   **"they stopped looking too soon" . . .** Kelley, *Ten Faces of Innovation*.

PAGE 86:   **business professor Vijay Govindarajan and . . .** Vijay Govindarajan and Srikanth Srinivas, "What's the Connection Between Counting Squares and Innovation?," *Harvard Business Review*, April 1, 2013.

PAGE 87:   **"shifting our focus from objects or . . . "** Sutton, *Weird Ideas That Work*.

PAGE 87:   **Why can't computers do more than compute? . . .** Tim Berners-Lee details from Peter J. Denning, "Innovating the future: from ideas to adoption: futurists and innovators can teach each other lessons to help their ideas succeed" *The Futurist*, January–February 2012; Mary Bellis, "Tim Berners-Lee," About.com http://inventors.about.com/od/bstartinventors/p/TimBernersLee.htm; and Academy of Achievement website http://www.achievement.org/autodoc/page/ber1bio-1.

PAGE 88:   **"How were we going to pay" . . .** From my series of interviews with Joe Gebbia, April 2013.

PAGE 89:   **"No one would want to stay in . . ."** Barney Jopson, "Dotcom Prodigy Builds Business From Airbed," *Financial Times*, July 29, 2011.

PAGE 90:   **Consider, for example, that the average power . . .** Jessica Salter, "Airbnb: The Story behind the $1.3bn Room-letting Website," *Telegraph*, September 7, 2012.

PAGE 91:   **"it creates dissonance," notes Paul Bottino . . .** From my interview with Bottino.

PAGE 91:   **Why can't India have 911 emergency service? . . .** From my interview with Jacqueline Novogratz of the Acumen Fund; plus, Shaffi Mather's November 2009 TED Talk, "A New Way to Fight Corruption." http://www.ted.com/talks/shaffi_mather_a_new_way_to_fight_corruption.html

PAGE 93:   **The five whys methodology originated . . .** Taiichi Ohno, *Toyota Production System: Beyond Large-Scale Production* (Portland, OR: Productivity Press, 1988). Also, Eric Ries, *The Lean Startup* (New York: Crown Business, 2011).

PAGE 94:   **IDEO example of five whys . . .** From the company's "Method Cards," published by William Stout, November 2003.

PAGE 94:   **character actor and author Stephen Tobolowsky** . . . From my interview with Tobolowsky, February 17, 2013.

PAGE 95:   **Why isn't the water reaching the people who need it?** . . . From my interview with Gary White; also, Ellen McGirt, "Can This Man Save This Girl?" *Fast Company*, July/August 2011.

PAGE 96:   **"only to end up in 'incubator graveyards'"** . . . Madeline Drexler, "Looking Under the Hood and Seeing an Incubator," *New York Times*, December 16, 2008.

PAGE 97:   **In the business world, IDEO has** . . . From my interviews with IDEO executives, from 2008 through 2013, including Tim Brown, David Kelley, Jane Fulton Suri, Paul Bennett, Fred Dust, and others.

PAGE 98:   **One classic example involved a hospital** . . . From my interview with IDEO's Bennett, who also tells the hospital story in his July 2005 TED talk, "Design Is in the Details," http://www.ted.com/talks/paul_bennett_finds_design_in_the_details.html.

PAGE 98:   **The Acumen Fund's Jacqueline Novogratz** . . . From my interview with Novogratz at Acumen's New York office, March 14, 2013.

PAGE 99:   **Eric Maisel calls a "productive obsession"** . . . From my interview with Maisel, fall 2013. From more on productive obsession, see Vern Burkhardt's interview with Maisel, "Your Brain Will Thank You, Part 1," IdeaConnection blog, December 5, 2010.

PAGE 100:   **Before he changed the way many** . . . The Pandora section relied on several articles about the company, as well as speeches and online interviews with Tim Westergren, including Rob Walker, "The Song Decoders," *New York Times Magazine*, October 18, 2009; Bill Moggridge's interview with Westergren for Moggridge's book/DVD *Designing Media* (the interview was posted online February 3, 2011, on the Cooper-Hewitt Museum website, http://www.cooperhewitt.org/conversations/2011/02/02/designing-media-tim-westergren; Westergren's Chicago Ideas Week speech in October 2011, http://www.chicagoideas.com/videos/53; and Rocco Pendola, "A Conversation with Pandora's Tim Westergren," *The Street*, February 12, 2013.

PAGE 103:   **"In order for imagination to flourish . . ."** Douglas Thomas and John Seely Brown, "Cultivating the Imagination: Building Learning Environments for Innovation," *Teachers College Record*, February 17, 2011.

PAGE 103:   **What if we combine three snacks into one? (And then add a prize?)** . . . Gary Satanovsky, "Prizes Inserted into Cracker Jack Boxes," *Famous Daily*, February 19, 2012; Manny Fernadez, "Let Us Now Praise the Great Men of Junk Food," *New York Times*, August 7, 2010.

PAGE 104:   **to use a term that seems to have** . . . Thackara talks about "smart recombinations" in his book *In the Bubble* (Cambridge, MA: MIT Press, 2006).

PAGE 104: **"The creative act is no longer . . ."** Jason Tanz, "Remix Culture: Humanities," *Wired*, September 27, 2010.

PAGE 104: **The book's author, Seth Grahame-Smith . . .** Michael Cieply, "The Great Emancipator, Vampires on His Mind," *New York Times*, May 20, 2011.

PAGE 105: **David Kord Murray, a former rocket scientist . . .** From a series of interviews I did with Murray in spring 2013; I also relied on Vern Burkhardt's interview with Murray, "Search and Combine Ideas," *IdeaConnection*, November 7, 2010. Murray explores the "connections" idea at length in his book *Borrowing Brilliance: The Six Steps to Business Innovation by Building on the Ideas of Others* (New York: Gotham, 2010).

PAGE 106: **it's a form of divergent thinking . . .** From my interview with Heilman.

PAGE 106: **More obvious mental connections and associations . . .** From my interview with Kounios.

PAGE 107: **Chen-Bo Zhong, a professor at the . . .** From my interview with Zhong, November 2012; from more on his research, see Chen-Bo Zhong, "The Role of Unconscious Thought in the Creative Process," *Rotman* magazine, Winter 2010.

PAGE 107: **What if dots and dashes could sort the world? . . .** Margalit Fox, "N. Joseph Woodland, Inventor of the Bar Code, Dies at 91," *New York Times*, December 12, 2012.

PAGE 111: **Google's scientist-in-residence Ray Kurzweil . . .** Kurzweil told this to Thea Singer, "6 Beautiful Minds," *O, the Oprah Magazine*, June 2007, http://www.oprah.com/omagazine/Modern-Day-Geniuses-The-Worlds-Brightest-Minds.

PAGE 111: **Sam McNerney pulled together a number . . .** Sam McNerney, "Unconscious Creativity: Step Back to Step Forward," Big Think blog, May 24, 2012; also, Sam McNerney, "Relaxation & Creativity—the Science of 'Sleeping on It,'" Big Think blog, May 8, 2012; and Annie Murphy Paul, "Why Daydreaming Isn't a Waste of Time," Mind/Shift blog, from KQED Public Media for Northern California, June 1, 2012.

PAGE 112: **"Museums are the custodians of epiphanies" . . .** Hugh Hart, "Seven Pieces of 'Damn Good' Creative Advice from 60s Ad Man George Lois," *Fast Company*, March 23, 2012. This quote originated in Lois's book *Damn Good Advice (for People with Talent)* (New York: Phaidon Press, 2012).

PAGE 112: **This idea's roots can be found . . .** I have discussed thinking wrong in my interviews with Bielenberg (February 2013); Sagmeister (multiple interviews in 2008, for *Glimmer*); and with Luke Williams, formerly of Frog Design (spring 2012).

PAGE 113:   **you "jiggle the synapses" in the brain . . .** Barbara Strauch, "How to Train the Aging Brain," *New York Times*, January 3, 2010.

PAGE 113:   **John Bielenberg, a designer best known . . .** From my interview with Bielenberg.

PAGE 114:   I attended a workshop run by the creativity consultant Tom Monahan, who teaches an exercise he calls 180-degree thinking.

PAGE 114:   **Luke Williams, a former creative director . . .** From my spring 2012 interview with Williams; also from his book *Disrupt: Think the Unthinkable to Spark Transformation in Your Business* (FT Press, 2011).

PAGE 115:   **What if prisons had no walls? . . .** Graeme Wood, "Prison Without Walls," *Atlantic*, September 2010.

PAGE 115:   **She was having trouble getting out . . .** From a series of interviews I did with Nanda, starting in 2009 (for *Glimmer*) and concluding in spring 2013.

PAGE 117:   **Nanda's quirky project drew the attention . . .** *Gizmodo*, http://gizmodo.com/036052/clocky-rolling-alarm-clock, and *Engadget* both wrote about Nanda and the Clocky in 2005, when the product was still being developed.

PAGE 118:   **"The important thing about telling everyone . . ."** Sam Potts, "My Six Point Plan for Doing Projects," *GOOD.is*, June 3, 2013.

PAGE 118:   **"If you want everyone to have . . ."** Clive Thompson, "Think Visual: Why the best way to solve complicated problems might be to draw them," *Wired*, October 2010.

PAGE 119:   **"A prototype is a question, embodied" . . .** This line, along with lots of other interesting thoughts on prototyping, can be found on Rodriguez's bog *Metacool*, http://metacool.typepad.com/metacool/2009/04/4-prototype-as-if-you-are-right-listen-as-if-you-are-wrong.html.

PAGE 119:   **"enabling a class of ordinary people . . .** J. Paul Grayson's quote appeared in Ashlee Vance, "A Technology Sets Inventors Free to Dream," *New York Times*, September 14, 2010.

PAGE 119:   **"How might we roll it instead of lugging it?" . . .** Joe Sharkey, "Reinventing the Suitcase by Adding the Wheel," *New York Times*, October 4, 2010.

PAGE 119:   **As the writer Peter Sims noted in . . .** Peter Sims, "The Number One Enemy of Creativity: Fear of Failure," *Harvard Business Review*, October 5, 2012; see also, Peter Sims, "Daring to Stumble on the Road to Discovery," *New York Times*, August 7, 2011.

PAGE 122:   **At Facebook, founder Mark Zuckerberg has . . .** Zuckerberg published his manifesto "The Hacker Way" as part of his letter to investors during Facebook's IPO in early 2012. *Wired* reprinted t he complete letter, http://www.wired.com/business/2012/02/zuck-letter/.

PAGE 123:   **"the trick is to go from one failure . . ."** This quote is worded differently depending on where you find it. On the site Lifehack, it reads, "Success is the ability to go from one failure to another with no loss of enthusiasm," http://quotes.lifehack.org/winston-churchill/success-is-the-ability-to-go-from/.

PAGE 123:   **How do you make a hard-boiled egg's shell disappear? . . .** Amy Wallace, "You Bring an Idea and They'll Do the Rest," *New York Times*, June 12, 2011.

PAGE 124:   **Stanford University's Bob Sutton says that . . .** Robert I. Sutton, "Learning from Success and Failure," HBR.org, June 4, 2007.

PAGE 124:   **"If you keep making the same . . ."** Ibid.

PAGE 125:   **How do you fit a large golf course on a small island? . . .** Adapted from Steven Feinberg, "Seeing: How to create advantages through 'tactical shifting'," *Conference Board Review*, Winter 2011, and Bruce Anderson, "A Golf Ball that Won't Carry as Far Enabled Jack to Build a Minicourse," *Sports Illustrated*, July 23, 1984.

PAGE 127:   **"When we think of inventors" . . .** Nicole LaPorte, "Don't Know How? Find Someone Who Does," *New York Times*, November 27, 2011.

PAGE 127:   **"if we have people with diverse tools . . ."** Claudia Dreifus, "A Conversation with Scott E. Page: In Professor's Model, Diversity = Productivity," *New York Times*, January 8, 2008. See also Page's book *The Difference: How the Power of Diversity Creates Better Groups, Firms, Schools, and Societies* (Princeton, NJ: Princeton University Press, 2008).

PAGE 127:   **"we all have two amazing things . . ."** From my interview with Mick Ebeling, April 2013. I also drew from Ebeling's TED talk, "The Invention That Unlocked a Locked-In Artist," March 2011. The speech was featured in April 2013 on the *Huffington Post*, http://www.ted.com/talks/mick_ebeling_the_invention_that_unlocked_a_locked_in_artist.html.

PAGE 130:   **Tod Machover of MIT Media Lab . . .** From my interview with Machover.

PAGE 131:   **How might we cut the cord? . . .** Details about Ran Poliakine's question comes from Erica Swallow's "How Powermat Is Leading the Charge for Wireless Electricity," Mashable.com, October 20, 2011, http://mashable.com/2011/10/20/powermat-wireless-charging-tech/. Meredith Perry's details from Alyson Shontell's "Open Letter to Meredith Perry and uBeam," on Businessinsider.com, July 12,

2012, http://www.businessinsider.com/open-letter-to-meredith-perry-and-ubeam-2012-7#ixzz2dUyhhiEI.

PAGE 132: **As the author Clay Shirky has . . .** The appeal of collaborative endeavors is discussed at length in Shirky's book *Here Comes Everybody* (New York: Penguin Books, 2009).

Chapter 4: Questioning in Business

PAGE 135: **Christensen introduced the term disruptive innovation . . .** The section on Clayton Christensen is from my interview with Christensen, plus the following sources: Christensen's online interview on the HBR Channel's *The Idea*, posted on www.claytonchristensen.com; Brad Wieners, "Clay Christensen's Life Lessons," *Bloomberg BusinessWeek*, May 3, 2012; Lahrissa MacFarquhar, "When Giants Fail," *New Yorker*, May 14, 2012; and Christensen, *The Innovator's Dilemma* (Cambridge, MA: Harvard Business Review Press, 1997).

PAGE 138: **"we're coming off a twenty-five-year . . ."** From my interviews and e-mail follow-up with Keith Yamashita, January and February 2013.

PAGE 138: **Small wonder, then, that for top . . .** From my interview with Dev Patnaik, December 2012.

PAGE 139: **"The industrial economy was all about . . ."** From my interviews with Eric Ries, January and May 2013.

PAGE 139: **"The pressure on short-term results tends . . ."** From my interview with Wagner.

PAGE 140: **Yamashita uses a set of questions . . .** Yamashita's questions appeared in my post "The 5 Questions Every Company Should Ask Itself," *Fast Company*, February 4, 2013, http://www.fastcodesign.com/1671756/the-5-questions-every-company-should-ask-itself.

PAGE 141: **"There is great tension every day . . ."** From my interview with Casey Sheahan, February 12, 2013.

PAGE 142: **Nike provides an instructive example of . . .** The Nike+ story appears in, among other places, Mark McClusky, "The Nike Experiment: How the Shoe Giant Unleashed the Power of Personal Metrics," *Wired*, June 22, 2009.

PAGE 143: **Jobs initially berated Nike chief executive . . .** This anecdote appeared in Ellen McGirt's profile of Parker, "Artist. Athlete. CEO," *Fast Company*, September 2010.

PAGE 143: **Are we really who we say we are? . . .** Polly LaBarre, "Hit Man," *Fast Company*, August 31, 2002.

PAGE 144: ***Fast Company* pointed out that a . . .** Austin Carr, "Death to Core Competency," *Fast Company*, February 14, 2013.

PAGE 144: **Even newer companies must make these kinds of major shifts . . .** Sheryl Sandberg's question-driven initiative was described by Kurt Eichenwald, "Facebook Leans In," *Vanity Fair*, May 2013.

PAGE 145: **Early in its history, the microprocessor . . .** This famous story from Intel's early history appears in many articles and sites, but I came across it on the website for the Center for Applied Rationality, http://rationality.org/rationality/.

PAGE 146: **Jack Bergstrand of Brand Velocity thinks . . .** From my interview with Bergstrand, January 2013.

PAGE 147: **Vijay Govindarajan notes, hospitals in India . . .** Kaihan Krippendorff, "Hurricane Sandy, a Drenching Reminder That Tough Times Inspire Innovation," *Fast Company*, November 1, 2012.

PAGE 147: **What if we were to compete against ourselves? . . .** The story of the *Atlantic*'s reinvention comes from numerous sources, including Jeremy W. Peters, "Web Focus Helps Revitalize The Atlantic," *New York Times*, December 12, 2010; Lauren Indvik, "Inside 'The Atlantic': How One Magazine Got Profitable by Going 'Digital First,'" Mashable.com, December 19, 2011, http://mashable.com/2011/12/19/the-atlantic-digital-first/; and David Carr, "Covering the World of Business, Digital Only," *New York Times*, September 24, 2012.

PAGE 148: **"The modern worker is not the salary . . ."** From my interview with Tim Ogilvie, January 4, 2013.

PAGE 148: **Panera CEO Ron Shaich recalls that . . .** From my interview with Shaich, March 8, 2013.

PAGE 149: **How can we drive more ounces into more bodies, more often? . . .** Michael Moss, "The Extraordinary Science of Addictive Junk Food," *New York Times Magazine*, February 20, 2013 (adapted from Moss's book, "Salt Sugar Fat: How the Food Giants Hooked Us."); also, Douglas McGray, "How Carrots Became the New Junk Food," *Fast Company*, March 22, 2011.

PAGE 151: **"What is your tennis ball? (and other entrepreneurial questions)" . . .** Drew Houston's comments excerpted from his commencement speech at Massachusetts Institute of Technology, June 7, 2013; Brian Spaly quote from "How Entrepreneurs Come Up With Great Ideas," *Wall Street Journal Reports*, April 29, 2013; Peter Thiel question from Trevor Gilbert, "Peter Thiel's Pointed Questions to Ask Startups," PandoDaily, April 19, 2012, http://pandodaily.com/2012/04/19/peter-thiels-pointed-questions-to-ask-startups/; Dave Kashen, "The Values-Driven Startup," Gigaom.com, December 17, 2011, http://gigaom.com/2011/12/17/kashen-values-driven-startup/.

PAGE 151:   **Ries believes one of the most . . .** Ries's question also appeared in my previously cited *Fast Company* post "The 5 Questions Every Company Should Ask Itself." See also Ries's book *The Lean Startup: How Today's Entrepreneurs Use Continuous Innovation to Create Radically Successful Businesses* (New York: Crown Business, 2011).

PAGE 152:   **In the business world these days . . .** For example, see Cliff Kuang, "The Brainstorming Process Is BS, but Can We Rework It?," *Fast Company*, January 31, 2012, http://www.fastcodesign.com/1668930/the-brainstorming-process-is-bs-but-can-we-rework-it.

PAGE 153:   **"There is too much pressure and . . ."** Debra Kaye, "Why Innovation by Brainstorming Doesn't Work," *Fast Company*, February 28, 2013.

PAGE 153:   **Hal Gregersen has been studying the . . .** From my interview with Gregersen. He also discusses the effectiveness of Q-storming, including the "stalling at twenty-five questions" part, in the online video "Question Storming Versus Brainstorming," posted in Vimeo in September 2012, http://vimeo.com/48200106.

PAGE 155:   ***How might we?* It's a simple . . .** The *How might we?* story comes from my interviews in September 2012 with Min Basadur, Charles Warren, and Tim Brown, for my *Harvard Business Review* post "The Secret Phrase Top Innovators Use," September 17, 2012, http://blogs.hbr.org/cs/2012/09/the_secret_phrase_top_innovato.html. Hat tip to Charles Warren, who first talked about the Basadur/*How might we?* story in this video: http://vimeo.com/21316624.

PAGE 155:   **What would Neil Patrick Harris do? . . .** From my interview with Andrew Rossi of M Booth; the description of Neil Patrick Harris from Hillary Busis, "No big opening number at this year's Emmys—and more hints from Neil Patrick Harris," Entertainment Weekly's Inside TV blog, September 6, 2013, http://insidetv.ew.com/2013/09/06/neil-patrick-harris-emmys-interview/.

PAGE 156:   **Although the HMW has been used . . .** Prior to Basadur's use, the phrase *How might we?* was being used as part of the Creative Problem Solving Process, developed by Sid Parnes.

PAGE 158:   **Adam Bryant, who writes the New . . .** Adam Bryant, "Distilling the Wisdom of CEOs," *New York Times*, April 16, 2011. See also Bryant's book *The Corner Office: Indispensable and Unexpected Lessons from CEOs on How to Lead and Succeed* (New York: Times Books, 2011).

PAGE 158:   **Randy Komisar, a leading Silicon Valley . . .** From my interviews with Komisar, fall 2012.

PAGE 159:   **Bryan Franklin has observed that effective . . .** From Franklin's TEDxSinCity talk, "The Most Dangerous Question on Earth," uploaded May 27, 2011, http://www.youtube.com/watch?v=tClHDEoje6Y.

PAGE 159: **Why can't everyone accept credit cards?** . . . David Pogue, "Card
Reader on a Phone Pays Off," *New York Times*, September 30, 2010;
Issie Lapowsky, "The Man Who Made the Cash Register Obsolete,"
Inc. Magazine, May 2013; Dorsey's views on simplicity taken from
"6 Questions with Jack Dorsey," *Detroit Free Press*, September 16,
2012; also, Daniel Terdiman, "Square's Jack Dorsey to Tech
Founders: Question Everything," C/NET, September 10, 2012.

PAGE 159: **leaders need extraordinary "sensemaking" capabilities** . . .
Sangeeth Varghese, "The Four Capabilities Behind Great
Leadership," *Forbes*, September 7, 2010.

PAGE 160: **The late, legendary business guru Peter Drucker** . . . From my
conversation with Rick Wartzman, as well as from his post "How to
Consult Like Peter Drucker," *Forbes*, September 11, 2012.

PAGE 160: **And as author Dan Ariely noted** . . . Dan Ariely, "Why Businesses
Don't Experiment," *Harvard Business Review*, April 2010.

PAGE 161: **When Jim Hackett, the CEO of Steelcase** . . . From my interview
with Hackett, though I also relied on Hackett quotes in Adam
Bryant, "Leadership Never Looks Prepackaged," *New York Times*,
August 19, 2012.

PAGE 163: **"In all affairs it's a healthy thing . . ."** Bertrand Russell's quote appears in
many places, including "26 Fantastic Thoughts and Quotes by Bertrand
Russell," on the Vivsingh quotations site, http://www.vivsingh.com/4161/
great-minds-genius-people-quotes-quotations/26-fantastic-quotes-
thoughts-bertrand-russell.

PAGE 163: **Tim Brown, the chief executive at IDEO** . . . From my interview
with Brown, April 21, 2013.

PAGE 163: **What if a bookstore could be like summer camp?** . . . From my
interview with BookPeople's Steve Bercu; also, Yvonne Zipp "The
Novel Resurgence of Independent Bookstores," *Christian Science
Monitor*, March 17, 2013.

PAGE 164: **A different approach by IBM under** . . . As told to me by Keith
Yamashita, who has consulted for IBM.

PAGE 166: **Google has maintained a wide-open** . . . Google's TGIF sessions
are well-known, but an insider's description of them was provided
to me by former Google engineer Charles Warren.

PAGE 168: **The business writer Dale Dauten has** . . . Vern Burkhardt,
"Interview with Dale Dauten," *IdeaConnection*, March 21, 2011.

PAGE 168: **As Google has grown, it has become increasingly difficult** . . .
Christopher Mims, "Google's 20% time, which brought you Gmail
and AdSense, is now as good as dead," Atlantic.com's Quartz blog,
August 16, 2013. (An update to the post suggested that the program was
still alive, though not used as much as in the past, for various reasons.)

PAGE 169: **LinkedIn, whose designated "Hack Days"** . . . From Bob Jeffrey's interview with LinkedIn's Jeff Weiner, "Innovating From Within," posted on Jeffrey's Worldmakers blog, June 24, 2013.

PAGE 169: **In Gore's case, the program stipulates** . . . The section on W. L. Gore comes primarily from my interview with Gore's Debra France, February 2013; another great source of information on the company, including the story about guitar strings, was Alan Deutschman, "The Fabric of Creativity," *Fast Company*, December 1, 2004.

PAGE 171: **The company established Google University** . . . Sarah Kessler, "Here's a Google Perk Any Company Can Imitate: Employee-to-Employee Learning," *Fast Company*, March 26, 2013.

PAGE 173: **This is necessary because many of** . . . The problem with playing devil's advocate in brainstorming sessions is well described in Tom Kelley, *The Ten Faces of Innovation* (New York: Doubleday, 2005).

PAGE 173: **the pragmatic "implementers"** . . . From my interviews with Min Basadur and my visit to his company in December 2012. The term *implementers* is one of the four Basadur uses to categorize people in creative/brainstorming sessions: *generators, implementers, optimizers*, and *conceptualizers*.

Chapter 5: Questioning for Life

PAGE 175: **When Jacqueline Novogratz was about to** . . . From my interview with Novogratz at Acumen, March 14, 2013.

PAGE 178: **Some of the answers that emerged** . . . Acumen success stories as told to me by Novogratz, though they are described in more detail in her book *The Blue Sweater: Bridging the Gap Between Rich and Poor in an Interconnected World* (Rodale, 2009).

PAGE 179: **During a recent college commencement speech** . . . Novogratz at Gettysburg College, 2012, http://www.gettysburg.edu/commencement/2012/novogratz.dot. Hat tip to Maria Popova's BrainPickings site, which featured the speech in the post "Live the Questions: Jacqueline Novogratz's Advice to Graduates," May 29, 2012.

PAGE 180: **A mid-2013 *Huffington Post* conference urged** . . . Alina Tugend, "A Budding Movement to Redefine the Successful Life," *New York Times*, June 14, 2013.

PAGE 180: **Magazines ran cover stories about the importance of** . . . Among those was *Fast Company*, which featured the "#Unplug" theme as its cover story in July/August 2013.

PAGE 180: **Oxford University psychology professor Mark Williams** . . . Mark Williams, "Stress and Mindfulness: A Primer," Mindful.org, November 2, 2012.

PAGE 181: **Jeff Weiner, the chief executive of LinkedIn** . . . Adam Bryant,

"In Sports or Business, Always Prepare for the Next Play," *New York Times*, November 10, 2012.

PAGE 181: **The filmmaker Roko Belic told me . . .** I am greatly indebted to Roko Belic, whom I interviewed at length in February 2013. Belic's film *Happy* was released in 2011 by Wadi Rum Films and Shady Acres, www.TheHappyMovie.com.

PAGE 181: **The high school teacher David McCullough . . .** The speech, at Wellesley High School, was widely covered at the time; both text and video of the speech were posted June 5, 2012, on Wellesley High's blog, The Wellesley Report, http://theswellesleyreport .com/2012/06/wellesley-high-grads-told-youre-not-special/.

PAGE 181: **What is your sentence? . . .** Drawn from Daniel Pink's *Drive: The Surprising Truth About What Motivates Us* (New York: Riverhead Books, 2009).

PAGE 184: **The start-up entrepreneur Kasper Hulthin discovered . . .** Kasper Hulthin, "Why Every Entrepreneur Must Learn to Ask the Right Questions," *Under30CEO*, March 22, 2013.

PAGE 185: **The author and creativity coach Eric Maisel . . .** From my interview with Maisel.

PAGE 185: **John Hagel suggests you ask yourself . . .** From Hagel's September 2012 post "The Labor Day Manifesto of the Passionate Creative Worker," *Edge Perspectives*, http://edgeperspectives.typepad.com/ edge_perspectives/2012/09/the-labor-day-manifesto-of-the- passionate-creative-worker.html.

PAGE 185: **Life coach Kelly Carlin is always . . .** From my interview with Carlin, wherein we talked about her father, George, but also discussed her experiences as a life coach.

PAGE 186: *Is there something else you might . . .* Godin's question was posed in his October 2012 interview with Jonathan Fields for the Good Life Project, http://www.youtube.com/watch?v=kwANZNEOAoY.

PAGE 186: **Randy Komisar talks about the "deferred-life plan" . . .** From Komisar's book *The Monk and the Riddle*.

PAGE 187: **The author Jonathan Fields, who has . . .** From my interview with Fields, March 4, 2013. Fields explores this subject at length in his book *Uncertainty* (New York: Portfolio/Penguin, 2011).

PAGE 187: **How many people does it take to change a light bulb for a senior citizen? . . .** From my interviews with Hilary Cottam in 2009; plus, Alice Rawsthorn, "A New Design Concept: Creating Social Solutions for Old Age," *New York Times*, October 26, 2008; Jonathan Freedland, "The Perfect Gift? How About An End to Loneliness—and Not Just at Christmas," *Guardian*, December 22, 2009.

PAGE 188: **need to find one's own "tortoise enclosure" . . .** Cleese has discussed this in speeches on creativity, as noted in Chris Higgins,

"John Cleese: Create a Tortoise Enclosure for Your Mind," *Mental Floss*,November11,2009,http://mentalfloss.com/article/23240/john-cleese-create-tortoise-enclosure-your-mind.

PAGE 189: **One of the current proponents of "unplugging"** . . . From my March 2013 interview with Shlain. She also discusses this in her article "Tech's Best Feature: The off switch," *Harvard Business Review*, March 1, 2013.

PAGE 190: **"Thinking means concentrating on one thing . . ."** William Deresiewicz, "Solitude and Leadership," October 2009 graduation lecture, U.S. Military Academy at West Point, printed in *American Scholar*, Spring 2010.

PAGE 190: **Happiness researchers such as Tal Ben-Shahar** . . . From Tal Ben-Shar's video interview on Big Think, "Five Steps for Being Happier Today," November 17, 2010, http://bigthink.com/videos/five-steps-for-being-happier-today.

PAGE 193: **When he visited a friend at** . . . Belic's trailer park was featured in Vanessa Grigoriadis, "Bohemian Cove," *Vanity Fair*, March 2011.

PAGE 193: **Jacqueline Novogratz has her own spin** . . . From my interview with Novogratz; her question was also discussed in Adam Bryant, "When Humility and Audacity Go Hand in Hand," *New York Times*, September 29, 2012.

PAGE 193: **Author Carol Adrienne related to identifying** . . . From the interview of Adrienne by Nancy Rosanoff for the online talk show *Listening Place*, January 5, 2012, http://www.youtube.com/watch?v=flsxwnSilGI.

PAGE 195: **"In school we learn that experimentation . . ."** From Schank's essay "Experimentation," Edge, http://www.edge.org/q2011/q11_2.html#schank. He was one of a number of leading thinkers writing in response to a question posed in 2011 by Edge: "What scientific concept would improve everybody's cognitive toolkit?" The essays are compiled in John Brockman, *This Will Make You Smarter* (New York: HarperPerennial, 2012).

PAGE 195: **a friend referred me to the writer** . . . The friend was multimedia producer Gordon Platt.

PAGE 195: **Jacobs is an intensely curious man** . . . The section on A.J. Jacobs is based on my interview with him, February 6, 2013.

PAGE 196: **One of Jacobs's other experiments was** . . . Jacobs wrote about this in his book *The Know-It-All* (New York: Simon & Schuster, 2004). He also wrote *The Year of Living Biblically* (New York: Simon & Schuster, 2007); *My Life as an Experiment: One Man's Humble Quest to Improve Himself by Living as a Woman, Becoming George Washington, Telling No Lies, and Other Radical Tests* (New York: Simon & Schuster, 2010); and *Drop Dead Healthy: One Man's Humble Quest for Bodily Perfection* (New York: Simon & Schuster, 2012).

PAGE 196: ***Esquire* article called "The Rationality Project"** . . . A.J. Jacobs, "The Rationality Project: One Man's Quest to Ignore His Gut Instinct," *Esquire*, November 2008.

PAGE 197: **"you have a wonderful lab in . . ."** From my interview with Chris Young, February 6, 2013.

PAGE 197: **When you change one small thing** . . . I am indebted to a friend, the art director and illustrator Jaye Medalia, for sharing this observation (based on her own experiences) in conversation.

PAGE 197: **"It's easier to act your way . . ."** Fuller's quote appears in various places, including the post "Millard Fuller: A Home for Everyone," Mark of a Leader, http://www.themarkofaleader.com/library/stories/millard-fuller-a-home-for-everyone/.

PAGE 198: **Herminia Ibarra, a professor of organizational** . . . Herminia Ibarra, "Managing Yourself: How to Stay Stuck in the Wrong Career," *Harvard Business Review*, December 2002.

PAGE 199: **It was popularized a couple of decades** . . . The quote appears in Schuller's *Possibility Thinking: What Great Thing Would You Attempt . . . If You Knew You Could Not Fail?* (Nightingale Conant, 1989).

PAGE 199: **in a widely circulated TED speech** . . . This is the same TED speech by Dugan cited in chapter 1.

PAGE 199: **What if a TV drama could inspire real-life change?** . . . Phil Zabriski, "After 'The Wire' ended, actress Sonja Sohn couldn't leave Baltimore's troubled streets behind," *Washington Post*, January 27, 2012; and the RewiredforChange.org website.

PAGE 200: **"failure is good" message has gone mainstream** . . . Richard Pérez-Peña, "Commencement Speakers: In Looser Tone, a Call to Take Risks and Be Engaged," *New York Times*, June 16, 2013.

PAGE 200: **who used the term *failure fetish*** . . . Daniel Altman, "The Failure Fetish," Big Think, June 11, 2013

PAGE 200: **The writer Peter Sims pointed out** . . . Peter Sims, "The No. 1 Enemy of Creativity: Fear of Failure," *Harvard Business Review*, October 5, 2012.

PAGE 201: **"When we hit failure, I start . . ."** From my interview with Ebeling.

PAGE 201: **"Failure is, in a sense, the highway . . ."** Manoranjan Kumar, *Dictionary of Quotations* (APH Publishing, 2008).

PAGE 202: **author Judith Beck told me she** . . . From my e-mail exchanges with Judith Beck, April 2013.

PAGE 202: **The blogger Chris Guillebeau put yet** . . . From Guillebeau's post "What Would You Do If You Knew You Would Not Fail?" from his blog, The Art of Non-Conformity, October 21, 2010, http://chris-guillebeau.com/3x5/what-would-you-do-if-you-knew-you-would-not-fail/.

PAGE 203: **Fran Peavey, a social activist, excelled . . .** For the section on
Peavey, I relied on Peavey's book *By Life's Grace: Musings on the
Essence of Social Change*, excerpted in the Context Institute's
"Creating a Future We Can Live With"; David Leser, "Good Will
Hunting," *Melbourne Age*, May 30, 1998; and Sharon Ede's post
"Strategic Questioning: Asking Questions That Make a Difference,
Cruxcatalyst, May 21, 2012, http://www.cruxcatalyst.com/2012/05/21/
strategic-questioning/#sthash.PnMnHmlg.dpbs.

PAGE 203: **"her flesh wobbles . . . her chest heaves . . ."** From Leser's
Melbourne Post profile.

PAGE 203: **"I refined my interviewing technique . . ."** Ibid.

PAGE 204: **One of her more interesting projects . . .** Peavey's account of this
project is from her book *By Life's Grace.*

PAGE 205: **Former-adman-turned-activist Jon Bond . . .** From my e-mail
exchanges with Bond, April 2013. Bond's initiative was also covered
in Joe Nocera, "Changing Minds After Newtown," *New York
Times*, March 2, 2013.

PAGE 205: **What would you do to reach yourself? . . .** From the Calvin
Institute of Christian Worship's website article "Dare to Ask a
Beautiful Question," http://worship.calvin.edu/resources/resource-
library/dare-to-ask-a-beautiful-question/.

PAGE 206: **we should heed the advice of . . .** This is from Chris Hughes's 2013
commencement speech at Georgia State University, as featured in
Pérez-Peña, "Commencement Speakers."

PAGE 206: **one other question comes highly recommended . . .** From my
interview with Michael Corning, December 2012.

PAGE 207: ***Why is my father-in-law so difficult . . .*** Just want to make clear
that this is a hypothetical scenario—I have no problem getting
along with my father-in-law, who is a terrific guy and great questioner in his own right—and who provided a number of excellent
ideas and tips for the book.

PAGE 207: **Bruce Feiler, author of *The Secrets* . . .** From A.J. Jacobs interview
with Bruce Feiler, Amazon.com, February 2013; also from Bruce
Feiler, "The Stories That Bind Us," *New York Times*, March 15, 2013.

PAGE 208: **When Doug Rauch came to the end . . .** From my series of interviews with Rauch, spring 2013. The Harvard program Rauch
enrolled in is also covered in Glenn Ruffenach, "Tools to Help the
World," *Wall Street Journal*, May 30, 2012.

PAGE 211: **Should we retire the concept of "retirement?" . . .** Adapted from
Marc Freedman's "A New Vision for Retirement: Productive and
Meaningful," HBR.org blog, February 25, 2013, http://blogs.hbr.
org/2013/02/a-new-vision-for-retirement-pr/; and also from the
website www.encore.org.

PAGE 212: **Google's Sebastian Thrun likens each of . . .** From Thrun's 99U speech, "On the Universal Law of Innovation: Build It, Break It, Improve it," April 2013, http://99u.com/videos/15737/sebastian-thrun-on-the-universal-law-of-innovation-build-it-break-it-improve-it.

PAGE 213: **Gary White's ongoing effort to answer . . .** From my interview with White in New York City, February 11, 2013.

PAGE 214: **Bennett culls all of these bits . . .** Bennett's blog, The Curiosity Chronicles, can be found at http://curiositychronicles.tumblr.com/.

PAGE 214: *Keep yourself away from the answers . . .* The quote written on Colum McCann's wall was mentioned in a profile of McCann by Joel Lovell, "The World Still Spinning," *New York Times Magazine,* June 2, 2013. I wrote to McCann to ask him about it; his quotes are from our e-mail exchanges, June 20/21, 2013.

PAGE 214: *New York Times* **interview with the . . .** Patrick Healy, "Now, the Next Stage," *New York Times,* August 26, 2012.

PAGE 215: **The actor-turned-director Ben Affleck . . .** George Clooney, "George Clooney on Ben Affleck," *Entertainment Weekly,* December 7, 2012.

PAGE 216: *What if we cultivated ignorance instead . . .* From Firestein's book *Ignorance.*

Index of Questions

Index of Questioners

A Note on the Author

Warren Berger has studied hundreds of the world's leading innovators, entrepreneurs, and creative thinkers to learn how they ask questions, generate original ideas, and solve problems. His writing and research on questioning and innovation have appeared in *Fast Company, Harvard Business Review,* and *Wired.* He is the author of the internationally acclaimed book *Glimmer,* an in-depth analysis of creative thinking that was named one of *BusinessWeek's* Best Innovation and Design Books of the Year. Berger has appeared on NBC's *Today Show,* ABC's *World News,* CNN, and NPR's *All Things Considered.* He lives with his wife, Laura E. Kelly, in Westchester, New York. Visit his website at www.AMoreBeautifulQuestion.com.